THE BRUIN 100

BY
SCOTT HOWARD-COOPER
FOREWORD BY
KAREEM ABDUL-JABBAR

THE GREATEST GAMES IN THE HISTORY OF UCLA BASKETBALL

ADDAX
PUBLISHING
GROUP

Lenexa, Kansas

Bob Snodgrass
Publisher

Hans Tesselaar/J. Nelson Elliott
Editors

Michelle Zwickle-Washington
Managing Editor

Darcie Kidson
Publicity

Randy Breeden
Art Direction/Design

Dust jacket design by Jerry Hirt

Development Assistance: Sharon Snodgrass, Jeremy Styno, Gary Carson

Published by Addax Publishing Group Inc.
Copyright © 1999 by Scott Howard-Cooper

ISBN: 1-886110-56-5

Distributed to the trade by Andrews McMeel Publishing, 4520 Main Street, Kansas City, MO 64111

1 3 5 7 9 10 8 6 4 2

Printed in the United States of America

This book is not an official publication of, nor is it endorsed by UCLA.

Library of Congress Cataloging-in-Publication Data

Howard-Cooper, Scott, 1963-
        The Bruin 100 : the greatest games in the history of UCLA
basketball / by Scott Howard-Cooper.
        p. cm.
        ISBN 1-886110-56-5
        1. UCLA Bruins (Basketball team)—History. 2. University of
California, Los Angeles—Basketball—History. I. Title.
II. Title: Bruin one hundred.
GV885.43.U423H69 1999
796.323'63'0979464—dc21

                                                                        98-44823
                                                                        CIP

Dedication

To Mom

For always believing it was possible.

Table of Contents

Ed O'Bannon was a four-year letterman, three-year starter and Wooden Award winner in 1995.

Acknowledgments

I am a USC Trojan who has come to honor UCLA, which is either a straight line for someone else to attach the joke or a way of coming clean before someone outs me in the name of "No wonder he put a loss as No. 1." Truth be told, I have been fortunate to include Bruins among my closest friends and people I admire and respect.

Many of them are included among these pages, because this project was entirely a group effort. It could not have been started without Roland Lazenby, a friend and colleague who first suggested the idea, and could not have been completed without the work and patience of Bob Snodgrass, Gary Carson, Michelle Washington, Brad Breon and everyone at Addax Publishing Group.

The UCLA sports information department, especially director Marc Dellins and assistant Bill Bennett, were invaluable in answering any questions they could and allowing me to dig through their files. I am also grateful to Vic Kelley, the former director who must have had the foresight 30 years ago to see this book coming because his efforts to preserve the moments of past decades made for clip files that are better organized than many other college or pro teams could offer for even the most recent seasons. What resources UCLA did not have, the Paul Ziffren Sports Resource center at the Amateur Athletic Foundation often did.

Paul Feinberg was a worthy associate in helping with the research, just as he is a valued friend. Thanks also go to many others who have offered encouragement or shared their time or resources, most notably: Kareem Abdul-Jabbar, Larry Brown, Frank Burlison, Don Casey, Jerry Crowe, Pete Dalis, Bill Dwyre, Jim Harrick, Steve Hartman, Walt Hazzard, Rick Jaffe, David Kahn, Tim Kawakami, Irv Kaze, Steve Lavin, Jim Milhorn, Joe McDonnell, Skip Nicholson, Steve Salm, Louis P. Smithers, Michael Sondheimer, Johannes Tesselaar, Tom Timmermann, Pam Walker, Bill Walton, Jon Wilner and Coach John Wooden.

Because many of the quotes used in the following pages came from post-game interviews, it was impossible to attribute each one to a specific newspaper since the same comments may have run in several others. But credit is due to several publications: *Los Angeles Times, Los Angeles Herald-Examiner, Los Angeles Herald-Express, Los Angeles Daily News, Orange County Register, Long Beach Press-Telegram, Santa Monica Evening Outlook, The (Riverside) Press-Enterprise, Pasadena Star News, Daily Bruin, Oregonian, Louisville Courier Journal & Times, Kansas City Star, San Antonio Express-News, Tucson Star, The National, Chicago Tribune* and the book by David Smale, *Pauley Pavilion: College Basketball's Showplace*.

Reggie Miller was a sharp shooter, but the ability to go to the basket made him more difficult to defend and one of the greatest scorers in UCLA history.

Introduction

The only thing greater than the difficulty of choosing, and then ranking, 100 games from the 2,041 UCLA had played by the end of the 1997-98 season was the enjoyment of the process. Long hours were invested, interviews were conducted, books were scanned, newspapers were read – and rarely has so much work not seemed like work at all.

Many of the selections were obvious for inclusion – with those, the positioning was the tough part. Many were recommendations to the committee of one who went about deciding which games made the cut. The records section of the UCLA media guide offered other suggestions. And some were discovered simply by pouring through the archives and, for lack of a better word, stumbling across an unexpected, but very worthy, finalist.

The intent was not to make this a history book, but a memory book, hopefully bringing an equal impact to long-time fans who had watched a game and forgotten certain parts and to those who had come long after a particular entry and now enjoy living the moment. The only era missed is from the inaugural season of 1919-20 to the start of 1930 because documentation of games was not available for those years. We apologize in advance to participants and fans of that important, early period in UCLA basketball.

That missing generation cost us a chance to put a deserved spotlight on the greatness of Sam Balter and Jack Ketchum and others. But we hope this stands up as the most comprehensive look at UCLA basketball that could be expected.

Not all games were picked for aesthetic value. Indeed, some were picked for reasons that had nothing to do with the actual events in the game, but maybe because of surrounding events or because of what they came to mean in time. Still others may have gained a high ranking because the circumstances—Final Four, etc.—outweighed the lack of great basketball.

If picking the 100 was a challenge, ranking them was the real invitation to criticism. This was intentional, as opposed to putting them in chronological order. What's the point in a partial debate?

Numerous people were consulted in the process of turning the possibilities into a final list and then putting them in order of importance. There was no voting, but some were especially helpful just by giving their opinions about certain games, without intending it to be, or even knowing it would be, a vote either way. In the end, the final decisions rested with the author.

Foreword

By Kareem Abdul-Jabbar

While so many UCLA games stand out in my memory, I don't think that there is a single one that is more important or significant than another. And while three consecutive NCAA Championships from 1967-1969 is considerable, truly it was all the games, practices, classes, teammates and friends that comprise my UCLA experience.

I would have to say that of all of my memories of UCLA, my greatest is of my decision to attend the university in the first place. Of the many factors that influenced my choice of UCLA, the most significant was its tradition of excellence among black athletes. That, along with the particular genius of John Wooden, who had just guided UCLA to its second NCAA championship, convinced me that I could truly be successful at UCLA as a student-athlete.

As a young man, I had been aware of great Bruins such as Jackie Robinson and Ralph Bunche. I was even fortunate enough to have received letters from them, highly touting the virtues of both academics and athletics at UCLA (Years later I lost those treasured mementos in a house fire!). However, the singular event that had the most impact on my choice was an appearance by Rafer Johnson on the *Ed Sullivan Show*. Rafer, who had played

basketball under John Wooden, was on the Sullivan show for reasons completely separate and apart from his athletic prowess. Rafer was appearing, not as an athlete that day, but rather in his capacity as Student Body President. It was clear to me then that UCLA was a place where a young black man could succeed not only on the court, but off it as well. Rafer's ability to achieve on so many levels and be a quality role model and leader convinced me that UCLA's diverse tradition was a place where I could truly develop as a person. It has been a choice that I have never regretted. In addition to my basketball success, I found my way as a human being, making lifelong friends in the process. I hope that some of UCLA's great basketball moments, detailed here in this book, recall for you a sense of that tradition as well.

Enjoy!

Kareem

Kareem Abdul-Jabbar

The Bruin 100 Game 1

Houston 71, UCLA 69
January 20, 1968

The audacity of picking a loss as the greatest game in the history of a program that has won 70% of its games and more NCAA championships than anyone comes with the even-more-dramatic counter of history, this merely being the night that changed an entire sport. The Bruins would have to accept their role, even as they contend to this day that it wasn't even their most important game of the season.

John Wooden called it a "spectacle." No wonder. The UCLA coach had been reluctant to accept scheduling of the game out of concern that the predictable emphasis on the Lew Alcindor-Elvin Hayes matchup would detract from the team play, but conceded to the wishes of Athletic Director J.D. Morgan when told it would be worth $80,000 to the school. Then Wooden arrived to see how organizers had plopped a court in the middle of the dirt floor inside the Astrodome, and a crowd of 52,693 came to watch, even when a so-called front-row seat was still 100 feet from the action.

But the showdown—the No. 1 Bruins versus the No. 2 Cougars, big man versus big man—became the first regular-season college basketball game to be televised nationally, syndicated to 120 stations in 49 states; it was the first step in what today is common for viewership. It was the first dome game, eventually to become a regular occurrence, once the Superdome and Metrodome and

Kingdome and RCA Dome and the other massive structures were built and tabbed as Final Four sites.

"There were so many firsts involved, people cannot put it out of their minds," Don Chaney, a senior guard for Houston on the historic night, told the *Los Angeles Times* for a story to commemorate the 30th anniversary.

Among them that it was the first loss for UCLA after 47 consecutive wins. It's just that it wasn't a tough loss to accept, certainly nothing to match the hype and supposed magnitude and hardly in a way that would indicate a close loss, sealed when Hayes scored the last of his 39 points on two free throws with 28 seconds left. To the Bruins, they had fallen a mere two points short while Alcindor suffered through double vision in one eye and the worst game of his college career.

So serious was the scratched cornea that the junior center had been forced out of the previous two games and spent days confined to a dark room at the Jules Stein Eye Clinic at UCLA. Wooden gave him the option of skipping the game, but Alcindor, having also lost some conditioning because of the missed practices, wanted to play.

"I remember Elvin Hayes said he didn't think it was that big of a deal," Kareem Abdul-Jabbar says now. "But my vision was badly affected."

He missed 14 of 18 shots and scored 15 points. The Cougars would say victory would have come no matter what because Hayes was virtually unstoppable on offense and also blocked three of Alcindor's shots even though the two main attractions were not matched up. The Bruins would say they had a 69-69 tie without really having Alcindor.

Losing in the Game of the Century?

UCLA got over it, fast.

"People think it was a terrible loss," Wooden recalls a little more than 30 years later. "Not to me it wasn't. Not more than other losses. It's not like a conference loss or something to knock us out of a tournament."

Houston would get that chance a few months later, this time at the Los Angeles Sports Arena in the semifinals. But the Cougars would not get the victory—UCLA won, earning vindication and a spot in the championship game.

Lew Alcindor (33) contests a shot by Elvin Hayes.

John Wooden has a ball after his last game, the 1975 title win over Kentucky in San Diego.

The Bruin 100 Game 2

UCLA 92, Kentucky 85
March 31, 1975

One more for the road.

John Wooden's departure as coach came in the only manner befitting a man of his success and dignity, with a victory and a victory in an NCAA championship game at that, providing the rightful combination of going out on his own terms and going out on top. As if his Bruins would have allowed anything less.

"We wanted to win it bad," senior guard Pete Trgovich said. "For The Man.

"We're not a team that jumps and screams before games. But I could look at each of the guys tonight and just tell. We were all ready, in our own ways."

Added Andre McCarter, a junior guard and one of four Bruins to play all 40 minutes: "There was no way we were going to lose coach's last game.

"I never got tired. There was so much at stake tonight. I'm sure Coach Wooden is a large part of the reason. He told us his leaving should have nothing to do with the game, but... well... he's such a great person."

Wooden's retirement announcement two days earlier, after the semifinal victory over Louisville, stunned players into silence and, upon picking their jaws off the ground, reflection best described as reverential. Wooden didn't use his departure as motivation for his players, in fact going to great lengths to say it shouldn't have any such emotional impact, but it didn't make a difference. Motivation it was.

The Bruins responded with nothing less than an awesome performance at San Diego Arena. Wooden used only six players, and all six posted big numbers: David Meyers had 24 points and 11 rebounds,

All-America forward David Meyers (left) and guard Pete Trgovich were the only seniors on the 1974-75 team.

Game 2

Richard Washington 28 points and 12 rebounds, Trgovich contributed 16 points, McCarter 14 assists, and each went the entire way. Marques Johnson, the starter who did come out, returned to become a key down the stretch when Kentucky stayed as close as three points into the final minutes. The one reserve to play, Ralph Drollinger from the San Diego suburb of La Mesa, contributed 10 points and 13 rebounds.

The 1975 championship team.

The 10th championship was the greatest of them all because of the emotional impact. Wooden would later admit to the personal importance of leaving with a win—making him 620-147 in 27 seasons at UCLA —but he was typically understated on this day. A brief postgame speech to the team, saying how proud he was of them, and then the obligatory press conference.

"I'm sad I'm getting out," he said, "but I'm going out pretty happy too."

Which, after 27 years, after 10 titles in 12 years, after a record 88-game winning streak, was what it had come down to.

"I told John the first championship was for him and his players," Athletic Director J.D. Morgan said in the aftermath. "I told him the next eight were for the school, the players, himself and everyone else involved.

"But this one, the last one, was for John."

The Bruin 100 Game 3

UCLA 87, Memphis State 66
March 26, 1973

He was stuck in the spotlight. There was no way around it. Bill Walton was going to be the most-watched man in St. Louis during Final Four weekend, especially once UCLA advanced to the championship game for the seventh year in a row, whether he liked it or not.

And he definitely did not like it. He was at once the star of the Bruins and the sideshow of the college basketball world, the best player for both and a junior who just so happened to be considering a hardship jump to the NBA. Even the most innocent of decisions meant headlines and speculation. Walton moved from the team hotel to another place the day before the final, and there just had to be some reason for the switch other than that the beds in the original digs weren't big enough. Like maybe it was the start of the separation process from teammates.

Bothered by the scrutiny but undaunted on his turf, Walton took the court at St. Louis Arena the night after Operation Mints On The Pillow and turned in arguably the greatest championship-game performance in the history of his sport, before or after. The result was a seventh consecutive title for the Bruins and a ninth overall, not to mention a victory that made them the only team to ever go undefeated in back-to-back seasons.

He took 22 shots – and missed one.

He scored 44 points, a championship record.

He got 22 in the first half and then another 22 in the second, despite picking up a fourth foul with 9:27 remaining as UCLA protected an eight-point lead and then coming out with 2:51 left after twisting an ankle, by which time the advantage was all the way to 15.

He grabbed 13 rebounds.

It was a brilliant showing. All those closest to the moment—his coach, his teammates, the opposing coach—spoke in terms that confirmed its place in sports history, not just the sport's history. Walton must surely have been proud, so a reporter asked if this was his best game ever.

"I don't want to talk about it, man," came the surly response.

To be sure, the Walton of the early '70s is an amazing contrast to the cheerful, friendly conversationalist of today. But long after tossing out a series of clipped responses to the media, he was gone, heading out with his "financial advisor," noted Bruin booster Sam Gilbert, to meet with 76ers General Manager Don DeJardin amid reports that Philadelphia was offering a $2 million contract.

"He did so many things so well that we just couldn't stop

him," said Memphis State Coach Gene Bartow—who would succeed John Wooden after two more seasons. "He's super—the best collegiate player I've ever seen."

The lone miss came in the first half on a lob pass from Greg Lee, just as many of the 21 baskets came on the same tosses as Walton commanded the skies above the rim like an air traffic controller. They went to that connection with such regularity that Walton was called for offensive goaltending four times in this game alone.

No wonder Lee finished with 14 assists against just three turnovers, while Keith Wilkes contributed 16 points and seven rebounds to the Bruins' 75th consecutive win overall and the 36th in a row in tournament play.

The 1973 championship team.

"What we did was a team achievement," Wooden said, "built around the tremendous ability of Bill Walton."

They could keep building. Walton would come back for his senior year.

The Bruin 100 Game 4

UCLA 91, Michigan 80
March 20, 1965

John Wooden, who knows a thing or 5,000 about impressive performances by UCLA players, lists this as the most spectacular showing during his 27 seasons there, more than when Lew Alcindor scored 56 points in his varsity debut or 61 points later that season or when Bill Walton made 21 of 22 shots in a championship game.

"I think it was Gail Goodrich's scoring 42 points against a powerful Michigan team when he was the smallest player on the court," Wooden said.

Period.

It came as the exclamation point in Portland, Ore. to the Bruins' second consecutive NCAA title, even more noteworthy since it was a showdown between the top two teams in the nation. It also came as part of an amazing scoring run by the All-America senior guard, who had set what turned out to be a very temporary school record with 40 points three games earlier against Brigham Young in the West Regional and had scored 28 in the semi-final win over Wichita State despite coming out with 12:25 remaining because UCLA had such a comfortable lead.

This time, he was removed from his final game with 1:22 left to a loud ovation from the 13,204 at Memorial Coliseum, the largest crowd to ever have watched a college basketball game in Oregon. The only achievement Goodrich missed out on was falling just one point shy of the four-game tournament scoring mark, set by Clyde Lovelette of Kansas at 141. Still, he played the major role in UCLA getting the team scoring record with 400, easily surpassing the 359 it had established a year earlier in the run that ended with a victory over Duke and the program's first title.

Gail Goodrich shoots down Michigan in the 1965 championship game, scoring 42 points in one of the greatest performances in tournament history.

Game 4

Michigan arrived as the top-ranked team, the Bruins second, but an informal poll of coaches not involved overwhelmingly predicted UCLA would become only the fifth team to repeat as champion. The so-called favorites, however, were hardly as convinced at first as they prepared to play a team with so much more size and strength. A pulled leg muscle that hampered Keith Erickson, suffered in practice the day before the semifinals, only added to the uncertainty.

"I honestly wasn't sure when we went out there on the floor whether we could win," Goodrich said later that night. "But after three minutes, I knew we were going to take it.

"Sure, they were hitting beautifully there at the start. But I knew they couldn't keep that up and I could see that our press and speed were going to bother them."

Erickson lasted only five minutes before the injured left leg forced him out. But his replacement, Kenny Washington, supplied a huge boost of energy, and the Bruins had an 11-2 rally just after the switch with Washington contributing six of the points and a spectacular steal. The same player who had 26 points in the title game a year earlier had come through again in the biggest of moments, this time finishing with 17.

Goodrich made sure it never got too interesting again. He had one stretch in which he scored all 12 points for the Bruins, 10 coming on free throws as the Wolverines fouled down the stretch to stop the clock and get the ball back. In all, he was 18 of 20 from the line.

The 1965 championship team.

Back in Los Angeles, students flowed through Westwood in celebration. An estimated 500 of them—either more daring or, uh, less aware of what they were doing—sat down in the middle of Wilshire Boulevard, a main thouroughfare, for a few minutes, without injury. They soon returned to campus for the more-traditional of victory rituals, the bonfire.

No wonder their Bruins were such an obvious source of pride. Not only had UCLA just gone 28-2 and won a second championship in a row, but the combined 58-2 record in that time was the second-greatest two-year total in NCAA history, behind only the Bill Russell-led teams at the University of San Francisco in 1955-56. Little did they know the real fun was just beginning.

The Bruin 100 Game 5

UCLA 75, Missouri 74
March 19, 1995

Steve Lavin, being of sound mind and soul, and of infinite appreciation, pledges to give his future son the first or middle name of Tyus because of the single greatest play in UCLA basketball history.

Why? The situation: A 5-foot-10, 150-pound senior point guard with a tweaked ankle gets the ball with 4.8 seconds left in regulation. His team trails by a point in the second round of the NCAA tournament. The play: He negotiates nearly the entire floor, 85 feet, with deft ball handling. He squirts through the defense with flair and determination to hit a four-foot bank shot which alters the course of history for individuals and an entire program. That's why!

As great as the drive by Tyus Edney was at the time, it took on even greater meaning with more time. The Bruins wouldn't have beaten Missouri without it and then wouldn't have gone on to reach the Final Four for the first time since 1980 and then wouldn't have won the NCAA championship for the first time since 1975. He wouldn't have gone on to the NBA with his back pocket stuffed with the highlight reel of one of the great plays in any school's basketball history. And for the coaches, the impact there was just about across the board.

"When people talk about it being a game of inches or when you realize how a couple of seconds could so

dramatically change someone's life or career, that's a prime example," Lavin said.

"All of our lives were changed. We went on to win the championship, Mark Gottfried goes on to get the Murray State job, Lorenzo Romar goes on to get the Pepperdine job, which moves me up to the top assistant job."

Which, in turn, put him first in line for the real top job when Jim Harrick got fired. It has remained prominent in Lavin's mind that Edney was also a coach's dream—classy person, student, positive role model—but it's the part about another kind of coach's dream that likely gives the name Tyus true staying power in the Lavin lineage. In all Bruin history, for that matter.

Just to be in such a position, UCLA had to recover from an eight-point deficit at the break, the largest of the season at a halftime, and from nine points down with 16:02 left in the game, and maybe the season. Giving the comeback angle its ultimate test, a basket by Missouri's Julian Winfield with 4.8 seconds remaining put them behind, 74-73, prompting a Bruin timeout. Ed O'Bannon, again asserting himself as the team leader, spoke up in the huddle, insisting they were still going to win.

Good thing UCLA had prepared for such situations— one drill in practice called for players to go the length of the court in six seconds. Even with a fraction less to work with, even with the sore ankle that came from a slight sprain two days earlier in the first-round victory over Florida International that had at least loosened up as this game went along, Edney still felt confident he could at least get to the rim and get a shot off.

Cameron Dollar immediately picked up about 10 feet of floor with the pass to Edney that came without defensive pressure. Edney took off. He reached halfcourt and continued to speed to the basket, even with a behind-the-back dribble. He went past Jason Sutherland of the Tigers and continued down the right side of the lane. The work was only partly done because it would still take a pretty tough shot to get it past 6-9 Derek Grimm.

Edney would later note that Grimm, likely wanting to avoid the foul that would have given the Bruins the chance to win with free throws, did not contest the shot that hard. When the ball banked in, UCLA had a 27-2 mark, a trip to Oakland for the West regional semifinals and a 15-game winning streak, its longest since the record-setting 88 in a row. Pandemonium reigned.

"This is the biggest shot of my life," Edney said when he met the press soon after. "I was almost in awe."

He wasn't the only one.

Tyus Edney became a permanent part of UCLA lore with his end-to-end sprint that gave the Bruins the win over Missouri.

The Bruin 100

The Bruin 100 Game 6

North Carolina State 80, UCLA 77 (2 OT)
March 23, 1974

A little more than 24 years later, John Wooden is home in Encino, Calif., far from Greensboro, N.C., just not far removed.

"Of all the losses I ever had at UCLA," he says, "that was the most devastating."

Because he thought his Bruins were superior to North Carolina State—even with the presence of the magnificent David Thompson, the inside play of Tom Burleson and the spark from point guard Monte Towe—especially since they had already beat the Wolfpack by 18 points in St. Louis early in the regular season. Because it came in the NCAA semifinals and meant elimination one game away from the opportunity to win an eighth consecutive championship.

"Because I thought we were a better team than they were and we didn't play like the better team," Wooden said.

Fate this time had put the Bruins in Greensboro Coliseum to play the team from neighboring Raleigh because it was the Final Four—just as they had won the 1972 and '68 titles at the Los Angeles Sports Arena and would eventually claim the 1975 crown down the road in San Diego. This was not about any homecourt advantage, though, not nearly as much as UCLA's inability to hold a lead, a season-long problem regardless of geographic considerations.

The most painful of Bruin seasons—the defeat at Notre Dame that ended the 88-game winning streak, the trip to the Oregon schools that became known as the Lost Weekend because of the back-to-back setbacks—ended in the most painful of ways. They had an 11-point advantage midway through the second half and even a seven-point cushion in the second overtime and wasted both, done in by poor shot selection and critical turnovers as well as the play of Thompson, Burleson and Towe.

And when the end came, the first tournament loss since the spring of 1963, a run that included not making the postseason in '66, it came with a ferocity. That lead of seven points in the second overtime was still a formidable 75-69 with 3:11 remaining when North Carolina State went on an 11-0 run, taking the lead and taking over as King of the Hill, to be made official when it went on to beat Marquette in the final and finish 29-1. The only UCLA basket the rest of the way was an inconsequential 15-footer by Bill Walton with five seconds left.

"Beating the Bruins is what I've always dreamed of," Thompson said following his 28-point, 10-rebound performance.

In the UCLA locker room, Greg Lee berated the referees, the Bruins feeling like they had been victimized by the two-man crew from the Big 10. Walton, after making 13

Game 6

of 21 shots and getting 29 points and 13 rebounds, stayed in the shower for 40 minutes. David Meyers joined the chorus of those saying the better team had lost.

"Do you think North Carolina State is No. 1 now?" someone asked Wooden in the postgame press conference.

"Well, let's see now," the coach replied. "We beat them by 18 on a neutral court and they beat us by three back here. I'd like to play them in L.A. now."

Of course, the Bruins would have liked the opportunity to play anyone anywhere at that point, excluding Kansas in Greensboro in the consolation game that became a 78-61 victory. The championship run had ended.

The two UCLA-North Carolina State duels, and the individual matchup between big men Tom Burleson (left) and Bill Walton, were highlights of the 1973-74 season.

The Bruin 100

The Bruin 100 Game 7

Notre Dame 71, UCLA 70
January 19, 1974

The final 21 seconds:

Tommy Curtis missed.

Bill Walton missed.

David Meyers missed a tip.

Pete Trgovich missed another tip.

Meyers missed yet another tip.

John Shumate grabbed the defensive rebound for Notre Dame.

And then it was over, the game and The Streak. The flurry of the final moments to hold on still brought a sudden, startling conclusion, that the Bruins had lost for the first time since Jan. 23, 1971, for the first time after 88 victories, an NCAA record.

"This has got to be the greatest feeling I've had in my life," Shumate said.

He had 24 points and 11 rebounds. Gary Brokaw went for 25 points. As emotional a game as it is every time UCLA goes to South Bend, there was something special about the Irish in these final 3 1/2 minutes, when they used a 12-0 run for the win. Dwight Clay forever made himself part of college basketball history by hitting the fall-away jumper from the right corner with 29 seconds

remaining that ended the amazing run, prompting this headline the next day in the *Los Angeles Times*:

FEAT OF CLAY

Their last defeat had come against the same team and in the same town, but the Bruins hadn't just lost, they had blown a lead, an early 17-point cushion. And Walton hadn't just lost for the first time in 89 games, but for the first time in 140 games, a personal ride that had lasted all the way back to high school. So much for the impressive return, the 24 points on 12-of-14 shooting after the All-America center had missed the previous three contests with a bruised back. So much for UCLA shooting 70.3% in the first half and 51.8% in the game.

So much for The Streak.

"We didn't figure to lose there at the end," Coach John Wooden said afterwards. "Of course, if you don't play your own ballgame, you're going to lose. They kept coming at us, and they deserve a tremendous amount of credit for their play.

"If ending the streak is good for basketball, then having the streak was bad for basketball. I think the streak was one of the finest things for college basketball. If it hadn't been for the streak, this would have been just another game and it would not have generated the enthusiasm and interest that it did."

Recalling that moment, Wooden says now that "I don't think we were too depressed" in the locker room. The Bruins were down, though.

"Yes," the coach says, "but not because of the broken record. Because it was a loss."

It probably didn't help at the time to know that, in an unusual bit of scheduling, they would next play Santa Clara at home and then get Notre Dame again and the chance for revenge, only at Pauley Pavilion. Talk about your unique concepts. UCLA having to avenge a defeat.

Classic Wooden: focused, instructing in the huddle, rolled-up program in hand.

The Bruin 100 Game 8

UCLA 75, Louisville 74 (Overtime)
March 29, 1975

The history of college basketball and of all UCLA changed when Terry Howard missed two free throws with 20 seconds remaining in overtime when they could have given Louisville a three-point lead. Richard Washington instead hit a seven-foot jumper with :03 showing to give the Bruins the victory at San Diego in the semifinals of the NCAA tournament.

The path had been cleared for John Wooden to announce his resignation. No matter the stories that came out on this day, and the ones that followed as UCLA prepared to face and then beat Kentucky for the championship, he will swear in 1998 that he would have stayed had the Bruins lost to Louisville. Maybe even—he will go so far as to say probably even—for two more years.

"I have a hunch," Wooden says.

If there is contradiction, his wife Nell indicated at the time that the decision had been made as far back as December. The coach himself noted on this day that he purposely steered clear of telling his Bruins the news at halftime or before the game. There appears to be just as much certainty now about the events. He thought he would keep coaching. He had no plans to make the Kentucky game his last. Period.

"But after the game, everyone was shaking hands on the court, I walked over to visit with Denny [Crum, the Louisville coach], I walked back to go to our locker room and then go talk to the media," Wooden said. "And I found that for the first time in my career that I didn't want to do it. I said to myself it was time to get out."

Then he said the same thing to the players and his staff.

"And they were stunned. [Trainer] Ducky Drake almost fainted. My coaches didn't know. My wife didn't know. I didn't know until just before."

"I don't care what anybody says."

"He was holding back tears when he told us," junior center Ralph Drollinger said soon after the announcement. "He loves this team."

Of that there has never been any doubt, then or now. It would also be his last team.

"We were just getting ready to celebrate when *The Man* walked in and told us," sophomore forward Marques Johnson said. "The room went quiet. It was a dramatic moment. I felt like I was sitting in on a little bit of sports history."

Even surrounded by four Washington State defenders, Lew Alcindor was virtually unstoppable.

The Bruin 100

The Bruin 100 Game 9

UCLA 100, Washington State 78
February 25, 1967

Lew Alcindor was so good, he wore himself out. He doesn't think it happened any other time in four years at UCLA, including the one with the freshman team. No, he's sure of it.

"I got in the locker room and I almost couldn't stand," Kareem Abdul-Jabbar says now in recollection. "I was exhausted. I remember that. It was the only game where I felt I needed to sit down afterwards."

It could have been worse. He could have been playing for Washington State.

If it was hard work that day being Alcindor, imagine being 6-foot-9 Jim McKean or (gulp) 6-7 Randy Stoll, the two Cougars defenders who were sent out to defend him almost entirely man-to-man, without benefit of so much as a cigarette or blindfold, instead left only to wonder what their coach had against them. So UCLA's superstar center piled up 28 points on 13-of-20 shooting and 14 rebounds... by halftime.

By the time it had ended, Alcindor, superior against his counterparts in size at 7-1 and even more in ability, had 61 points, 26 baskets in 35 tries, nine free throws in 18 attempts, and 24 rebounds. Oh, and seven assists. He had the greatest offensive outing by a Bruin before or since.

Sixty-one points. There were 12 UCLA games that season when the entire opposing team didn't score that many. It broke the school record and Pauley Pavilion record, set the day when Alcindor had 56 in his varsity debut earlier that season.

As the end of the game approached, though, there was considerable doubt whether he was going to get any record. He had 53 points with about 2 1/2 minutes left, so the crowd picked up the cause, breaking into chants of "Give the ball to Lew." About 10 seconds later, he got a layup.

"It is conceivable that we could get it to him every time, and he could have scored a lot more," Coach John Wooden said. "But this, of course, wouldn't be good for the game or our team."

Not that Wooden went much for the sympathetic route anyway. Alcindor's final basket, with the Bruins routing the Cougars to improve to 23-0 and clinch a trip to the Far West regional in Corvallis, Ore., in a couple weeks?

At the buzzer.

"We really wanted this one," Alcindor said afterwards. "I guess I may have been more up for this game because this was for the conference championship."

More up at least for the moment. That worn-out feeling was right around the corner, for Alcindor and for Washington State.

The Bruin 100 Game 10

Princeton 43, UCLA 41
March 14, 1996

It was a setup, right? The undisciplined, leaderless Bruins against the methodical, schooled-to-precision Tigers in the first round of the NCAA tournament. Princeton with the added emotional incentive of knowing it was the final season for legendary Coach Pete Carril. Everyone knowing Carril would run backdoor plays and UCLA still helpless to stop them, predictability be damned.

"I would say we learned a great lesson, yes," Bruins Coach Jim Harrick recalls, as if the world didn't already know that.

Like maybe how it feels to be a deer staring into the headlights? They saw this very game, the exact final play that produced one of the great upsets in any school's history, coming from a hundred miles away and still couldn't get out of the way.

"You could say our luck ran out," Charles O'Bannon said.

You could say that, but you'd be wrong. Cameron Dollar had the chance to give UCLA a 43-41 lead with 1:02 remaining at the RCA Dome and missed both free throws. Kris Johnson had the chance to put the points up, but missed a drive.

It had no more to do with luck than any of the other times Princeton had threatened traditional powers in pre-

vious years, only to fall short. This time, it was trying to bag one of the biggest elephants, not merely the epitome of tournament success, but the defending national champions in the opening round. Maybe the Tigers would go backdoor?

Yeah, maybe. Gabe Lewullis got behind O'Bannon, Gabe Lewullis beat O'Bannon. Steve Goodrich delivered the pass and Lewullis made the layup with four seconds to go for the 43-41 lead.

UCLA got a look for a last-second tie that would have forced overtime, but Toby Bailey's open 15-footer missed. To focus too much on the final attempt, though, would be to forget, or ignore, that the Bruins blew a seven-point lead and failed to score for the final 6:13.

"What I dread most is dealing with people, all those who were jealous and upset and didn't get excited about us last year," O'Bannon said later. "Now they're going to be able to throw it back in our face. But I have a championship, which a lot of people never get in their college careers. And I still have one more year to go."

Which, it turned out, was more than could be said for Harrick. He was fired before the start of the next season, making what many thought would be the final game for Carril into the end of the line for the ultimate coaching roller-coaster ride.

The Bruin 100 Game 11

UCLA 98, Duke 83
March 21, 1964

Duke had size, strength, shooting ability and defense. UCLA had the Bruin Blitz. Or as Kansas State Coach Tex Winter, the semifinal victim, said: "It doesn't matter how tall you are against UCLA. Those boys simply go after the ball faster than anyone else. They don't even have to jump too high to get the job done."

So it came to be that the Bruins, their tallest starter just 6-5, finished undefeated on the scoreboard and on the boards, capping 30-0 seasons in both at Municipal Auditorium in Kansas City, Mo., to become the first team to go undefeated since North Carolina in 1957.

Beat them? No one could catch them.

"They sure convinced me," Jeff Mullins, Duke's All-America forward, said after scoring 22 points. "I didn't think they could do it with their size. They really hustle and go for the ball."

"Our club is hard to figure out," UCLA Coach John Wooden said. "I'll say this for the boys. They meet every challenge with courage."

The 16th season under Wooden had brought the first national championship and, though no one could have known it at the time, the start of tournament domination. It was a team gifted in most every area other than stature, with Gail Goodrich leading in scoring at 21.5 points a game, point guard Walt Hazzard being named Player of The Year and a

The 1964 championship team.

hellish zone press.

And the Blitz. It had propelled the Bruins from also-ran at the outset of the season to No. 1 in early January for the first time in school history, and in the end it delivered the title.

As in:

Duke leading 30-27 with 7:14 remaining in the first half.

Duke trailing 43-30 with 5:34 remaining in the first half.

There went that threat.

"Duke has plenty of speed," Hazzard said. "But they couldn't run with us."

Couldn't rebound with the Bruins, either.

UCLA claimed a 51-44 advantage on the boards, keeping the streak alive, as Doug McIntosh came off the bench to contibute 11. Another front-court reserve, Kenny Washington, also became one of the many heroes, getting 26 points and 12 rebounds.

Goodrich recovered from his tournament slump to lead the offense with 27 points, including 17 in the first half. Jack Hirsch was a spark in the 16-0 run that put the Bruins in control, not to mention on the path to scoring more points than anyone had before in a championship game. Only one team has done better since, when Nevada Las Vegas got 103, coincidentally also against Duke, in 1990.

The 1963-64 team celebrates in Kansas City, Mo., after the first UCLA championship.

The Bruin 100 Game 12

UCLA 101, Houston 69
March 22, 1968

The Game of the Century got an epilogue, and UCLA got revenge. The defeat to Elvin Hayes and the Cougars two months earlier at the Astrodome was replaced by the victory the Bruins would rather have, the one at the Los Angeles Sports Arena with a trip to the NCAA championship game on the line.

Just try proving that the same teams were involved both times. A close game in January—71-69—became the rout in the rematch that washed away Houston's 32-game winning streak and No. 1 ranking with such ease that Hayes couldn't even get a shot off the first seven minutes against the diamond-and-one defense that designated Lynn Shackelford as his shadow. Hayes managed just one basket the first half and finished with 10 points.

So dominating were the Bruins that they went on a 33-12 run to take a 53-31 lead to the break, then to a 90-51 cushion with about seven minutes left.

So intent were the Bruins, they wouldn't have settled for anything less.

"In terms of focus and commitment and every player playing to 100% of their ability, that was a game of monumental proportions to us," Kareem Abdul-Jabbar, then Lew Alcindor, says now. "We wanted to run them off the court. I use the analogy of wolves. We had that pack mentality. Everyone wanted to attack."

Players had been annoyed the way fans had jumped off the bandwagon after the Astrodome loss, which came with Alcindor playing with double vision in one eye because of a scratched cornea. No one had to tell them, therefore, that this overwhelming performance would prompt a mad rush back to their side, just in time for the final game of the season.

They knew it. And they loved it.

"Total satisfaction," Abdul-Jabbar says of the feeling in the locker room at the Sports Arena. "Smiling. Relaxed. Not like smiling and whooping it up. But we had shown the nation, all basketball fans, who is No. 1."

That would become official the next night with a victory over North Carolina for a second consecutive national championship and a fourth in five years. That's if the semifinal game didn't make the follow-up contest anticlimatic, this powerful showing by the second-ranked team that came with Lucius Allen, Mike Lynn and Alcindor scoring 19 points each.

Game 12

The Bruin 100 Game 13

UCLA 92, Purdue 72
March 22, 1969

Victory came with survival, Lew Alcindor having overcome the opponents and the circumstances.

"We've been under the greatest pressure any team in collegiate history has ever experienced," his coach, John Wooden, explained. "For Lewis, it has been continuous. I'm just amazed he has maintained his composure through it all.

"For a number of weeks, not a single day has gone by when I haven't had at least three long-distance calls from agents and lawyers. The mail is tremendous. They're all after him."

Not to mention all the defenses, which, come to think of it, were rarely able to apply the same pressure as those interested in representing Alcindor as he prepared to enter the pros. Purdue was no different. The dominating college run concluded with 15 baskets in 20 tries, 37 points, 20 rebounds and a third NCAA title in as many varsity seasons, a fitting farewell if there ever was one.

"As an adult now," Kareem Abdul-Jabbar says, "if I went through all that again I would have been more

The 1969 championship team.

emotional. Everybody expected us to win every time."

Maybe because they did?

The easy victory at Louisville, Ky., that came with 12 points and 12 rebounds from Curtis Rowe and a great defensive effort by Kenny Heitz was the 88th in the 90 games of the Alcindor era and reaffirmed the Bruins as a powerful team after they had barely beaten plucky Drake in the semifinals. This was more their trademark. Overwhelming an opponent.

When it was over—the game, the season, the college career—Alcindor wore a huge smile on his face and a net around his neck. He waved his left index finger to signify No. 1. He held up three fingers on the right hand, just in case anyone had forgotten the title count.

It was a party, all right. Alcindor's father, a New York transit policeman and one-time jazz trombonist, sat in with the UCLA band, and Wooden sat in on history, winning his fifth championship to surpass Kentucky legend Adolph Rupp. Whatever encouragement Purdue may have received from watching the Bruins so uncharacteristically struggle against Drake never had the chance to materialize as anything tangible.

The long-shot chance ended when the Purdue shots didn't go in. The Boilermakers were a dreadful 29.3% from the field, with Rick Mount, the Blond Bullet who had just hit North Carolina for 36 in the semifinals and was regarded by many at the time as the finest pure shooter ever, going 12 of 36. Herman Gilliam was two of 14, though he did have 11 rebounds. Bill Keller chipped in by making four of 17 attempts.

Heitz, a senior guard also playing his last college game, got the assignment to slow Mount. It appeared even more of an unenviable task after the Purdue star made his first two tries, a pair of 20 footers. But that was followed by 14 consecutive misses, and the rout.

Lew Alcindor reaches the end of his brilliant career with 37 points and 20 rebounds against Purdue in the 1969 championship game in Louisville, Ky.

The Bruin 100 Game 14

UCLA 68, Villanova 62
March 27, 1971

A toast! To Steve Patterson!

The day after going to dinner with his parents and including a little vin rose wine with the meal—"Maybe that's what did it," he said—Patterson came through with a performance that would prove to be vintage, offering a performance that would hold up through the years as worthy of prominent mention alongside those of the other centers who bookended him. He came right after Alcindor and right before Walton, but on this day just came through.

It hadn't always been that way, of course, this up-and-down senior season that offered constant reminders of the difficulties in being the guy who took Einstein's place in the lab. Patterson had averaged 12.4 points in the second of two years as the starter, then in the championship game at the Astrodome, with a crowd of 31,765 in attendance to mark what was then the largest turnout ever for a tournament contest, upheld the tradition of the position that had come before and the one that would follow.

Twenty-nine points, 13 baskets in 18 shots, eight rebounds, that's how high he held it. He scored seven of the first 11 UCLA points, with all three of the field goals coming from at least 15 feet out, then went to work inside.

In short, he kept the streak of consecutive titles alive because the two stars, Sidney Wicks and Curtis Rowe, were largely ineffective, contributing just seven and eight points, respectively. That was Wicks' low as a Bruins regular, but the hero from the victory over Cal State Long Beach just days earlier played

The 1971 championship team.

largely on guts because of a painful sprained big toe.

"He was the sword that chopped our heads off," Villanova forward Clarence Smith said. "If it wasn't for him, they'd have been in big trouble because Wicks and Rowe sure weren't doing it for them."

When the game ended, Patterson's parents came on the court and joyfully hugged their son, dancing in circles with Steve. He looked up at the scoreboard and saw his name in lights, a big "29" alongside.

The hero shook his head, as if in disbelief of the showing that would also vault him on to the all-tournament team.

"I might as well die tonight," he concluded. "I can never do something like this again. What a way to end five years of college ball."

With a fifth consecutive championship for the Bruins. They got this one after a rare scare, having to protect a three-point cushion after Howard Porter's baseline turn-around with 2:38 remaining and then again as late as 63-60 with 1:53 left. Villanova got no closer, but that in itself was an accomplishment; the six-point final margin was the first time in the title run that the win came by single digits.

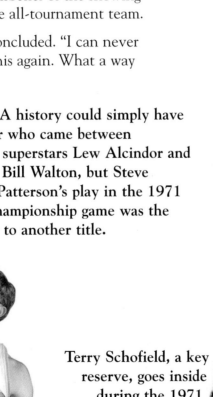

His place in UCLA history could simply have been as the center who came between superstars Lew Alcindor and Bill Walton, but Steve Patterson's play in the 1971 championship game was the key to another title.

Terry Schofield, a key reserve, goes inside during the 1971 championship game at the Astrodome.

Game 14

Dominant from the start, Lew Alcindor scored 56 points against USC in his varsity debut.

The Bruin 100

The Bruin 100 Game 15

UCLA 105, USC 90
December 3, 1966

Lew Alcindor made 23 of 32 field goals, 10 of 14 free throws, scored 56 points and grabbed 21 rebounds. As a 19-year-old sophomore. In his first varsity game ever.

"My shooting was only adequate," he said after.

Sure. Adequate.

"I could have done better," he added. "And my defense was poor. I need to work on it."

It's a wonder John Wooden didn't cut him on the spot. All Alcindor did in the season opener and his actual UCLA debut, discounting the freshman games the season before, was set the school scoring record (bettering the 42 by Gail Goodrich in the 1965 championship win over Michigan), the Pauley Pavilion scoring record (a mere 16 points better than Jerry Chambers of Utah got a year earlier), and even his personal scoring record (44 in high school and 48 during 1965-66).

Alcindor had proved, from the start, he would stand alone as the superior talent in college basketball. The home fans gave him a standing ovation—USC's Bill Hewitt also got one after scoring 39 points—when Wooden removed him with about three minutes left. His coach, normally low key and reserved, practically gushed.

"It was the most impressive performance by a sophomore I have ever seen," Wooden said.

"Naturally," the coach continued, "he was just awesome on offense. He even frightens me. If I had to predict before the game how many points he would have gotten, I would have said about 30 or 40."

Instead, Alcindor reached 44, establishing the school record, with 11 minutes still left. This came as Mike Warren, the only junior in a starting lineup filled with sophomores, was on his way to 17 points, and Lucius Allen to 14 points and nine rebounds, but that was like someone firing a hand gun at the enemy. Alcindor had the Howitzer.

USC Coach Bob Boyd, in his first game on the Trojan sidelines and the first of what would be many memorable meetings with UCLA, did his part. He used a man-to-man defense against Alcindor, apparently either disbelieving of all the buildup that had come with the arrival of college basketball's next superstar or just too stubborn.

He got his lesson. UCLA got its future.

"When Lew puts it all together," Wooden said, "we are really going to have something."

George Zidek was a hero at the 1995 Final Four, doing a good job against the opponent's major weapons, Bryant Reeves of Oklahoma State in the semifinals and then Corliss Williamson (34) of Arkansas in the championship game.

The Bruin 100 Game 16

UCLA 89, Arkansas 78
April 3, 1995

Jim Harrick can remember being alone in the locker room inside the Kingdome, moments before joining his team on the court for UCLA's first championship game in 15 years, and looking to the heavens and thinking one thing.

Why?

"Why would I go through 35 years of coaching and get to the stage I did, and then they take away one of my best players?"

Fate—a sprained right wrist suffered in the first half of the semifinal win over Oklahoma State— had cost the Bruins starting point guard Tyus Edney before the biggest contest of the season. Maybe of their lives. His great tournament run, the 76 points and 38 assists against just nine turnovers, had ended with a three-minute stint against Arkansas.

In the end, it only made the victory that much more impressive. Cameron Dollar stepped in, handled the Razorbacks' press and "40 Minutes of Hell" defense to finish with six points, eight assists and three turnovers. Ed O'Bannon, a star to the very end, had 30 points and 17 rebounds. Freshman Toby Bailey scored 26 points, increasing the expectations for the future that in some ways would haunt him the next three seasons. George Zidek, coming off a solid performance against Bryant Reeves and Oklahoma State, became the primary reason Arkansas' Corliss Williamson was held to 12 points. Harrick had his vindication from the seemingly constant stream of criticism.

The 11th NCAA title and the first in 20 years—with John Wooden on the sidelines for that one and in the stands for this one— came as the Bruins recorded a 19th consecutive victory. That gave them 31 for the season, a school record.

Jim Harrick coached the Bruins to the 1995 title and for eight seasons in all.

"That's a defining moment to me," Harrick says now.

Understandably so. The coach had taken his team to the Kingdome as a 15-minute detour during the regular-season trip to Seattle to play Washington, and now the Bruins were treating the massive arena, packed with 38,540 fans, as a homecourt advantage. They moved ahead with 10 seconds to go in the first half on J.R. Henderson's layup and never relinquished the lead against the defending national champions.

UCLA was up by as many as 12 points, at 65-53 with 11:20 remaining in the season. Arkansas

The 1995 championship team.

cut that to three with 5:22 left, but the Bruins surged again, using a 12-4 rally to clinch the win.

They were No. 1, again. And no one had to ask why.

Ed O'Bannon used Arkansas as the final step in his great season, and in the Bruins' championship run.

The Bruin 100 Game 17

Tulsa 112, UCLA 102
March 18, 1994

The day the Bruins learned the exact location of Tulsa: the second round.

Their lesson in geography—"To tell you the truth, I didn't even know Tulsa was in Oklahoma," junior Ed O'Bannon said a few days earlier, an educational shortcoming supported by similar claims from brother Charles and Tyus Edney among others—was second only to the lesson in humility. Figure next time they'll grab an atlas before speaking.

The Golden Hurricanes had runs of 10-0, 13-1, 10-0 and 8-0, and that was just in the first 20 minutes. The lead was 46-17 and then 63-38 at halftime. Or something like that—Ed O'Bannon said he lost track of the margin because "the numbers got so high."

That's what made it so staggering, unlike the shock of the two-point Princeton loss to come two years later in another first-round upset. The magnitude would be greater in 1996 because the Bruins were the defending champions, as opposed to a team already on a downward slide, but there was also no way to reason this day in Oklahoma City away. It wasn't just a loss.

"Tulsa was the low point because of the total embarrassment," says Steve Lavin, then an assistant coach. "We were belted off the floor so quickly."

Not to be forgotten was that UCLA had only itself to blame for the events, and not just the margin of defeat. It was the 7-6 record after the 14-0 start that meant entering the tournament as a fifth-seeded team in the region instead of a one, thereby having to play about 65 miles away from the opponent's home. ("The Bruins were concerned about playing the game in Tulsa's back yard, but they could have played in John Wooden's back yard and it wouldn't have made any difference," Thomas Bonk wrote in the *Los Angeles Times*). This was simply part of the greater meltdown, from No. 1 in the rankings at one point to No. 17, to bottoming out at season's end.

They trailed by 29 points in the first half, and then things got ugly. It ended the way it started, as a defensive disaster: the most points surrendered in school history in tournament play, the most ever in a regulation game no matter the time of the year, and the second worst all-time, behind only the 116 points Stanford got on Dec. 23, 1987. And it took the Cardinals double overtime to reach that.

"It wasn't a bad dream," Coach Jim Harrick said. "It was a nightmare."

The geographically challenged Ed O'Bannon provided the lone bright spot. He had 30 points, 18 rebounds, six assists and four blocks and led a furious comeback that cut the deficit to a workable 72-60 with 12 minutes left before the rally faded from exhaustion. More than that, though, amid the halftime explosion in which he threw a Gatorade tank and punched a chalkboard in an attempt to motivate teammates, it was the moment when he stepped forward to become the leader, a role in which he would blossom the next season.

Ed O'Bannon

The Bruin 100

The Bruin 100 Game 18

UCLA 80, Jacksonville 69
March 21, 1970

Lew Alcindor was a rookie with the Milwaukee Bucks, so the Bruins were vulnerable in the tournament, which, it turned out, was not to be confused with beatable. They were especially vulnerable in the title game because Jacksonville arrived in College Park, Md., not far from Washington, with a monumental front line of 7-foot-2 Artis Gilmore, 7-0 Pembrook Burrows and 6-10 Rod McIntyre.

UCLA countered with 6-9 Steve Patterson, 6-8 Sidney Wickes and 6-6 Curtis Rowe, and with its practices. Those from a year earlier, that is, when Wicks usually got the short straw and the assignment to play against Alcindor in practice. Gilmore was imposing, but not overwhelming for a defender who had dealt with far more.

Wicks didn't go it alone. In fact, Gilmore had scored 14 points in the first 15 minutes of the game at Cole Fieldhouse when Bruins Coach John Wooden altered his defense, having Wicks play behind the Jacksonville star as Patterson sagged down into the post to front Gilmore. That took care of that.

"The key to the game is when Sidney took care of Artis," said Rowe, a big factor himself with the team-high 19 points. "He ate him up."

The 1970 championship team.

Relatively speaking. Gilmore, so much bigger, ended with 19 points, but not being allowed to dunk the ball negated part of his major power advantage. Wicks blocked five of his shots, in addition to getting 17 points and 18 rebounds to lead the way to a fourth consecutive title, a sixth overall and the first after Alcindor.

"It was like playing last year against Lew," Wicks said. "But no matter what I did against Lew, he could score. Gilmore wasn't the same, but if he could have stuffed the ball there would have been no way I could have stopped him."

This came as John Vallely, the Bruins' only senior starter, scored 15 points and held another Jacksonville standout, Rex Morgan, to just eight. Batman and Robin, as the media had dubbed Gilmore and Morgan, had been foiled.

The best the Dolphins could do was a nine-point lead about midway through the first half, but that didn't even last to intermission. The Bruins were up five by then and never trailed again. They could handle life after Lew, all right, albeit partly because of life with Lew.

Sidney Wicks played a major role in three consecutive championships.

The Bruin 100

The Bruin 100 Game 19

UCLA 79, Dayton 64
March 25, 1967

The game was played in the city previously known as Louisville.

"This town is Lewisville now," declared the sign held by a UCLA booster.

It was a rapidly growing town, too. It was a third NCAA title for the Bruins with the win at Freedom Hall, and the first for a sophomore center named Lew Alcindor, to be followed by two more. The victory on this day, capping a run in which UCLA outscored four tournament opponents by a combined 95 points, made it only the fourth team to ever go undefeated en route to the title, joining its Westwood forefathers from 1963-64, North Carolina from 1956-57 and the University of San Francisco from 1955-56.

No opponent came closer than five points all

season, even as the 30-0 Bruins started junior point guard Mike Warren and four sophomores—Alcindor, defensive standout Kenny Heitz, scoring guard Lucius Allen and smooth-shooting forward Lynn Shackelford. There was no real threat this time either, not after unranked Dayton, having made it to this stage with a string of surprise victories in the tournament, missed its first seven shots and had another blocked by Alcindor and fell behind 20-4 with only 10:13 elapsed.

The 1967 championship team.

UCLA probably could have broken the NCAA record for biggest margin of victory in a championship game— Ohio State by 20 over California in 1960—but Coach John Wooden went to the bench. Alcindor and Warren came out with 5:17 remaining, after getting 20 points and 18 rebounds and 17 points and seven rebounds, respectively, with the lead at 70-46. A group of

Game 19

Dayton rooters marked the occasion by breaking into chant: "We're No. 2! We're No. 2!"

Thrilled just to be in the championship game, at least Flyers fans were willing to be realistic. The Bruins had dominated the day like they had the entire season, on one hand living up to the hype that came with the arrival of Alcindor while also battling against the opinion held by some that the sport's newest star wasn't as good as advertised. He really was as good, and so were they.

"I'm extremely proud of this team," Wooden said. "They stood up under tremendous pressure that started before we played our first game."

They kept standing, to the very end.

Lew Alcindor and John Wooden celebrate.

The Bruin 100

The Bruin 100 Game 20

UCLA 81, Florida State 76
March 25, 1972

Another year, another title. The sixth in a row came before 15,063 at the Los Angeles Sports Arena, where Florida State presented a challenge, just not as much as the challenge of living up to previous success.

At least no one had to worry about the victory party getting out of hand in the locker room. Bill Walton would have seen to that.

"I'm not that elated because we didn't play that well," the sophomore center said, the major component of the new class that also included Keith Wilkes and Greg Lee. "Florida State is an excellent team, but we didn't dominate the game like we know we can. If we had played our game the way we can, it would have been different. No excuses, but I don't like to back into things. I like to win convincingly."

That was after he piled up 24 points and 20 rebounds.

"I felt like we lost it," Walton added.

Maybe it was that the standards were so high, the Bruins having set an NCAA record that season by outscoring their opponents by 30.3 points a game. Or maybe it's like Henry Bibby said after scoring 18 points, adding to the 23 points and 10 rebounds by Wilkes, and winning his third consecutive championship:

"It gets to be old after a while."

He said it while offering a wry smile, so the senior point guard was as much sarcastic as serious. When it came right down to it, there was no consideration of a team vote to decline the trophy.

"We didn't play that well," Bibby said. "But I'm happy we won. We made mistakes we shouldn't have made, but any team would like to be in our position right now."

"I don't think we played as poorly as they [his players] do," Coach John Wooden countered. "Very few championship games we've been in—or I've seen—have been exceptionally well played. There's so much emotion involved, so much at stake."

Either way, this was not one of the Bruins' shining moments. When they trailed, 21-14, it marked their largest deficit of the season, the previous worst coming when Oregon jumped out to a 4-0 lead. Later, Walton got his fourth foul with about 11 minutes remaining and the Seminoles put together a 14-10 rally to get within seven points on three different occasions, the last at 79-72 with four minutes left.

But UCLA's ball-control offense drained most of that off the clock before the threat really turned white knuckle. Defense had also served the Bruins well, particularly the play of reserve guard Tommy Curtis and his efforts on Ron King after King was well en route to his game-high

27 points. That would have been the same Tommy Curtis who came from Tallahassee, was recruited by Florida State Coach Hugh Durham to stay at home and played pick-up games with many of the Seminoles in the summer.

"I don't think UCLA's players are any better than ours," King said, "but they got a hell of a coach. I don't know what that Coach Wooden does to them, but he does something. All those sophomores and they have so much confidence."

And so many expectations.

Henry Bibby celebrates the 1972 championship victory over Florida State.

The Bruin 100 Game 21

UCLA 78, North Carolina 55
March 23, 1968

Oh, yeah. The championship.

Still reveling in the semifinal win/revenge win over Houston the night before, and making little secret of appreciating that one more, the Bruins figured they might as well also pick up the crown as long as they happened to be in the neighborhood. So they stomped the Tar Heels at the Los Angeles Sports Arena in what marked the largest margin of victory in a title game.

"Friday night's game was the one that was really satisfying," Lew Alcindor said of the latest showdown with Houston. "They had a lot to say before the game. Yes, I guess you could say I definitely wanted to win that one more than any game since I've been at UCLA.

"Our win tonight might not have been as artistic as the one over Houston, but the result was equally rewarding."

The result, more specifically, was a second title for Alcindor, a fourth in five years for Coach John Wooden to tie him with Kentucky legend Adolph Rupp, and a 16-game winning streak to end the season after losing at the Astrodome. It came as Alcindor had 34 points on 15-of-21 shooting without benefit of the dunk, 16 rebounds and six blocks.

In its coverage the next day, the *Los Angeles Herald-Examiner* ran a headline that said North Carolina had been "Alcindorized" by the Bruins. That must have made his dominance official. He had become part of the language.

"Alcindor was even bigger and better than I thought he'd be," said Larry Miller, whose 14 points led the Tar Heels. "He's impossible

The 1968 championship team.

to stop on offense. We played good man-to-man defense, but there's just no way you're going to stop him. Take him away and they're on a level with anybody. With him, they're probably the greatest college team ever."

And maybe not even probably.

"They're the greatest team I've ever seen," North Carolina Coach Dean Smith said afterwards.

In the Bruins' mind, of course, they had merely finished the job, going from the major scare by Purdue in the season opener as the defending national champions to the loss to Houston in the so-called Game of the Century, to getting it all back. The weekend at the Sports Arena, merely a few miles east of campus, had brought the victory they had sought since losing to the Cougars, and the victory they had sought since the first day of practice.

All signs point to UCLA's continued standing atop the college basketball world in 1968. Just in case they don't, the right hand of Junior Lew Aleindor offers the reminder.

The Bruin 100 Game 22

Louisville 59, UCLA 54
March 24, 1980

On the other hand, the Bruins weren't supposed to be there in the first place.

The most unexpected of the 11 trips to the NCAA championship game came with the expected ending, or at least as predictable as anything could be in the charge from an 8-6 record about midway through the season to the final. It's just that the very end was such a shock.

UCLA led, 54-50, with 4:32 remaining in Indianapolis and appeared in position to add to that when Kiki Vandeweghe stole the ball and drove in for an apparent layup. A big man capable of handling the ball, a player who still stands as the fifth-best shooter in school history, Vandeweghe tried to avoid a defender and appeared to slightly lose his balance.

And then he missed.

Vandeweghe never should have become a permanent part of Bruin lore this way, not a player who that season was all-conference and scored 19.5 points a game without benefit of the three-point shot that certainly would have boosted the average. But scapegoat he became.

What came next didn't exactly help his cause. The opportunity for a

Rod Foster

six-point lead gone, the young Bruins promptly crumbled, never scoring again and getting outscored, 9-0, to end the game.

"We played a helluva game," Coach Larry Brown said. "We just didn't make our opportunities count. But we'll be back if I don't screw this bunch up."

He never really had the chance—Brown bolted after one more season. The Bruins didn't get back until 1995.

Getting there this time, of course, was the accomplishment. Louisville, meanwhile, came in with Coach Denny Crum, the former Bruin guard and assistant coach and the man many felt should have been on the other sideline that night, and Darrell Griffith. The Cardinals also came in with a 32-3 record.

Griffith, the national player of the year by some accounts and Dr. Dunkenstein by most all, finished with 23 points, right about his season-long average, and led all scorers. Darren Daye and Michael Holton drew the defensive assignment.

No Bruin scored more than the 16 of Rod Foster as UCLA suffered through a 36.5%-shooting night at Market Square Arena, the building where Brown would later coach the Indiana Pacers. Vandeweghe was second on the team with 14 points. Not 16.

Game 22

The Bruin 100 Game 23

UCLA 82, Notre Dame 63
January 27, 1973

The day UCLA finally ran down history, catching no less a difficult target than Bill Russell and K.C. Jones and the great University of San Francisco teams from the 1950s, began with the appropriate hype, beyond the buildup that came anyway with Bruins' visits to South Bend, Ind. The pep rally in another part of the massive Athletic and Convocation Center that started about 90 minutes before tipoff and lasted a half hour or so was merely the crescendo for the excitement level that had been rising for weeks.

"We could have sold 50,000 tickets for this one," said Roger Valdiserri, Notre Dame's sports information director.

The Irish had to settle for the capacity of 11,343, then had to accept a worse fate. Becoming the footnote to history.

When Bill Walton got 16 points and 15 rebounds, Keith Wilkes 20 points and nine rebounds and Greg Lee nine assists, the Bruins had their 61st consecutive victory and their record, replacing USF as owners of the longest winning streak in college basketball despite 20 turnovers. That it came at Notre Dame—sight of the last defeat, on March 23, 1971, as Austin Carr had 46 points—made the moment that much more special.

"They seemed to relish it," Coach John Wooden said of his players. "They wanted it. And they said they wanted to get it before a partisan crowd rather than at home."

Good thing, because that's what the Bruins got. By the time their lead had grown to 61-39, though, partisan had been replaced by words that offered far less dignity for the hosts, namely the fans at that point who started showering the court with coins and other small objects.

That wasn't the only hint of heated emotions, either. Wooden at one point had become so angered by John Shumate's aggressive defense on Walton that he walked down the sideline to Digger Phelps and shook his finger under the nose of the Notre Dame coach, as if a father scolding a child. Phelps appeared to take the incident in stride.

"He asked me if I had read his book," Phelps deadpanned when questioned by the media later.

Presumably, not the biography and instead Wooden's other tome. The record book.

"I'm very happy about it, but it doesn't compare with winning your first national championship," said Wooden, who regularly downplayed the Notre Dame rivalry in favor of putting all the emphasis on conference and tournament games. "It's the continuation thing that makes you proud. It's not something one team could do all by itself."

"Our goal this season wasn't to break the record, but we broke it and I'm proud we did it," Wilkes said. "It's hard to think about. I probably won't think about it 'til after I graduate."

There would still be plenty of time to build on it, after all. Another 51 weeks and 27 victories, to be exact, when the hype started anew and the Bruins stepped back into the lion's den.

Keith Wilkes and his signature jumper helped the Bruins beat Notre Dame and disappoint a jam-packed Athletic and Convocation Center.

Game 23

The Bruin 100 Game 24

UCLA 65, Indiana 62
March 29, 1985

Reclaiming at least part of its past, UCLA put together another in the long line of year-ending runs that carried through the postseason, this time a streak of eight consecutive victories that produced another championship. Make that a championship of another kind.

The other banner.

The NIT banner. Bumped from the spot that's normally reserved for them in the NCAA tournament, the Bruins at least salvaged what could have been a disaster of a season and discovered a positive out of what was once a 13-12 record. That it came against another prominent program and at Madison Square Garden, site of a loss to St. John's just before Christmas, made it all the sweeter.

"December 22nd," Coach Walt Hazzard quickly reminded in the postgame press conference, somewhere in between the snipes he delivered to the media he felt had unfairly criticized the Bruins. "We told you we were coming back. Here we are!"

Said Reggie Miller, the star forward who would later play some of his greatest games as a pro at Madison Square Garden: "We took a little bite out of the Apple Wednesday night [in the semifinal victory over Louisville]. We took the whole core tonight."

Except that they almost swallowed it whole and choked. What should have been a secure nine-point cushion with

1:47 remaining instead nearly became the final insult to the season, punctuated by an inability to get the ball in play after Indiana baskets. That usually routine function nearly resulted in defeat.

It happened the first time with 41 seconds left, when Miller was called for a five-second violation. Eight seconds later, the Bruins took a timeout to avoid another one. And still they couldn't get it right; they were forced to call a timeout again after Indiana's Steve Eyl hit a short jumper with seven seconds left to make it 64-62.

When play resumed, UCLA got the ball in and Brad Wright got fouled. He made the first free throw and missed the second, with the final second ticking off before the Hoosiers could launch a desperation shot. The Bruins had won for the 12th time in the last 13 games and had won an NIT title for the first time.

"I can remember coming to UCLA and seeing those banners hanging in Pauley Pavilion and wishing and saying 'Wow,' " said guard Nigel Miguel, who had 18 points and eight assists as he and Wright and Gary Maloncon played their final games as Bruins. "Now us three seniors can come into Pauley next year and say, 'I left this,' like coach always did with us."

The one Hazzard helped leave was for the NCAA championship in 1964, when he starred as a player, yet there was no doubt he appreciated this one as well. Like you couldn't tell it was the banner with an asterisk.

The Bruin 100 Game 25

UCLA 94, Notre Dame 75
January 26, 1974

The game that should not have brought any surprises, considering the teams had just played a week earlier, included the biggest one. A 17-year-old freshman named Marques Johnson was unexpectedly told minutes before tip-off that he would be moving into the opening lineup, then scored 16 points and provided additional muscle inside that Notre Dame could not counter.

It may have been part of a follow-up, payback at Pauley Pavilion in a schedule quirk after the Fighting Irish had won in South Bend the previous Saturday to end the Bruins' 88-game winning streak, but it was also a beginning. The first start for a forward who would go on to greatness, becoming the inaugural winner of the Wooden Award and having his uniform No. 54 retired.

"Johnson's starting was the key for them," Notre Dame Coach Digger Phelps said. "It gave them added strength on the boards. We're not a big team and with Johnson in there, it created some mismatches."

It wasn't just that either. Coach John Wooden also sent him in with the instructions to play tough defense on Adrian Dantley, and Dantley made just three of nine attempts. Johnson, meanwhile, was eight of 11, the perfect complement to Bill Walton, practically unstoppable en route to 32 points on 16-of-19 shooting.

"I didn't play very well in the first half," said Johnson, the first freshman starter at UCLA since Don Bragg and John Moore in 1952. "I guess I was just too tight. I found out I was going to start about five minutes before game time. I wasn't expecting it and I was really nervous.

"The coach didn't say anything to me at halftime, but I told myself to get out there and work the boards and take shots that really feel good. A healthy Bill Walton [he had recently missed three consecutive games with a bruised back] makes all the difference for our team. He was very high in practice and the way he worked was like a preview of tonight's game."

"Yes, I guess we played with a little more intensity than usual," senior forward Keith Wilkes said. "We were motivated."

Most everyone associated with UCLA was.

"To use a word, it was kind of mundane at home games, because you knew you were going to beat every opponent," said Michael Sondheimer, a student then and now an associate athletic director. "But because of what happened at Notre Dame, everybody was into it this time. It was like a national championship atmosphere. That's the best way to describe it. You didn't normally get that at a UCLA home game."

The level of emotion was understandable, what with the opponent and the timing of the revenge opportunity, so soon after the loss to Notre Dame that doubled as the first loss to anybody since midway through the 1970-71 season. The buildup was matched in intensity around campus, then inside Pauley Pavilion after tipoff. Walton dominated, Wilkes scored 20 points and a 17-year-old made a huge contribution.

Freshman Marques Johnson, an unexpected addition to the starting lineup, provided an inside presence that swatted away any hopes Notre Dame had of winning two in a row against UCLA.

The Bruin 100 Games 26-27

Oregon State 61, UCLA 57
February 15, 1974

It became known simply as the Lost Weekend.

Not as memorable but every bit as miserable as the defeat at Notre Dame a month earlier that ended the 88-game winning streak, the trip was nothing short of a fiasco. Twenty-four years later, Bill Walton still cringes at the memory of a team that went to Oregon with an 18-1 record and in control of the Pacific 8 Conference and was spit out like some Division II program.

"Maybe they just don't get up for games like they used to," Oregon's Greg Ballard said after the sweep had been completed.

Indeed, it was the way the Bruins lost.

Friday at Corvallis, they blew an eight-point lead from early in the second half and were outscored, 26-17, in the final 12:51 against a team that came in 9-10 and started three freshmen. Just a week earlier, UCLA beat the Beavers by five points at Pauley Pavilion.

"I guess you should be concerned when a team that's only 2-5 in our conference beats you," Coach John Wooden said, smiling wearily.

Saturday at Eugene, the Ducks, all of 11-9 when a national powerhouse came to McArthur Court, shot 61%, led by a sophomore named Bruce Coledren, who made 12 of 14 attempts. They stalled late in the game

Oregon 56, UCLA 51
February 16, 1974

and held UCLA without a point for almost 5 1/2 minutes, this team that a week earlier had lost in Los Angeles by 18 points.

Walton took only nine shots against Oregon State, finishing with 15 points, 14 rebounds and six turnovers. He had 11 points against Oregon while getting the double-team treatment from Ballard and Greg Willett.

Meet the unexpected co-leaders of the Pac 8.

"The worst thing a coach can do right now is panic," Wooden said after the Oregon game. "I'm not going to do that now, especially with a team that has an 18-3 record.

"I made some changes in our offense this past week to give us more movement. I thought it would make us sharper, but instead it had made us hesitant. Maybe, in retrospect, I've made a mistake by making this change."

The Bruins had lost two in a row for the first time since 1966—when it happened on the same swing. Walton couldn't even get away from the memories when he left school after this season. He went to play for the Portland Trail Blazers.

Games 26-27

The Bruin 100 Game 28

Oregon 65, UCLA 45
February 21, 1976

What had been nearly six years in the making took all of about 16 minutes to tear down, though there were numerous indications that the demolition actually came before tipoff and from within, an implosion of the grandest scale.

The defeat marked the end of the 98-game home winning streak, and the ease by which an opponent had won at Pauley Pavilion for the first time since March 6, 1970, made the moment that much more dramatic. But just in case that wasn't enough, Oregon players hoisted Greg Graham on their shoulders so he could cut down one of the nets, even if the action did not come with an explanation as to why a reserve guard with little impact on the outcome was chosen for such an honor.

It was Greg Ballard, the Ducks' star forward, who had 16 points and 10 rebounds. There was no singling out, though. Oregon, carrying strong memories of a 95-66 blowout loss on the same court the season before, joined its small contingent of fans in celebration, then moved the party to what quickly became a noisy locker room.

Said UCLA's rookie coach, Gene Bartow: "I had hoped to be here five years before the streak was broken. But it's history now. I just wish I wasn't on the bench when it happened."

As further testimony to the homecourt advantage that had just been trashed, the Ducks became only the second visiting school to ever win at Pauley, joining USC. The Trojans had done it twice, and then by one point in 1970 and by two points in '69. That made the Bruins 166-2 at Pauley by the time Oregon had arrived.

It wasn't long after that the outcome was decided. Giving the visitors a sense of being disrespected and themselves an even more obvious sense of being overconfident, the Bruins seemed far more concerned before tipoff with showing off than showing up, using the layup lines to showboat and see who could jump the highest for a dunk. The antics were so blatant that one of the referees came over and told them to tone it down a bit.

The Ducks shut them up for good once the game started, jumping to a 10-2 lead and then extending that to 28-6 with 15:40 gone. UCLA shot a brutal 22.2% in the first

half, never got closer than 14 points after the break, and finished at 31.7%. The top-scoring Bruins, Marques Johnson and Raymond Townsend, had 10 points.

"We weren't as serious as we should have been before the game," Johnson said. "... we were lackadaisical, showing off in the warmup. We showed no respect for this team, we took them too lightly. And they played a great game against us."

The loss cost UCLA a chance to virtually clinch a 10th consecutive conference title, instead cutting its lead over Oregon, Oregon State and Washington to one game with three to play. The Bruins then won their last three regular-season games, all on the road, but that could only recover some of what was lost on this day.

Marques Johnson was one of two Bruins to score in double figures as the Pauley Pavilion win streak ended against Oregon.

Game 28

The Bruin 100 Game 29

UCLA 60, Washington State 58
March 10, 1950

The moment came with perfect clarity, the vision of John Wooden's running game that embodied his earliest teams, the in-focus picture of a program taking off in only the second season with its new coach and destined for even greater times. All of which is significant because it was made possible by the nearsighted senior engineering major whose thick glasses were so prominent they became incorporated in his name.

Ralph "Bifocal" Joeckel had actually lost his spot in the opening lineup on this day because starter Jerry Norman returned after being sidelined with an appendicitis. The move came just as UCLA was set to open the best-of-three Pacific Coast Conference championship against the winner of the Northern Division, Washington State, a contrast between the fast breaking Bruins and the deliberate ball-control offense of the Cougars, between the up-and-coming coach of the Bruins and the Cougars' 21st-year coach, Jack Friel.

Washington State also had much better depth, likely one reason it was able to erase a nine-point deficit in the first half. The Cougars used five substitutes, Wooden just two all night, but Joeckel was one of them. In fact, the 21-year-old was in the game during the climactic final seconds, immediately moving from a supporting role as a reserve to the featured one when he grabbed the rebound after a miss by Cougars star Ed Gayda.

This being a team that drilled all season for the run, Joeckel took off. Still dribbling, he took a quick look at the time. Five seconds remained.

"I took a glance at the clock, saw it was getting late and let fly for the basket," he said.

Actually, the guy with bad vision released from a step behind midcourt and, as Jack Geyer wrote in his account for the *Los Angeles Times*, "let go with a shot that will be remembered as long as there's a UCLA." The ball arched to the basket, banked off the backboard and fell through the net with three seconds left.

"Just lucky," Joeckel said.

It became the critical moment of a critical time in team history—the shot that along with Norman scoring 12 of his game-high 18 points in the second half provided victory in the opener of the series and set the stage the next night for the Bruins to claim the PCC title for the first time with a 52-49 win over the Cougars. That was worth the first trip to the NCAA tournament for the emerging program.

"The most famous astigmatic in the history of UCLA," Melvin Durslag called Joeckel in the *Los Angeles Herald*.

Tiny Westwood gym, the Bruins' home, erupted. When the final buzzer sounded before the Cougars could get the

ball back in play, many of the approximately 2,600 fans in attendance spilled on the court and mobbed the players. They mobbed Joeckel so much, in fact, that two policemen finally jumped in to save him from harm.

The more-peaceful alternative was for supporters to hoist the hero on the shoulders and carry him to the dressing room. Had to be quite a view from up there.

The Bruins were flying high after winning the opening game of the best-of-three Pacific Coast Conference championship series against Washington State.

Game 29

The Bruin 100 Game 30

Stanford 109, UCLA 61
January 9, 1997

The Maples Massacre.

"They were sweet, we were nasty," Charles O'Bannon said.

"I've never been involved in anything like that," Toby Bailey added. "At any level of play, I don't remember anything like this."

No one would around UCLA, either. With good reason—it was the worst loss in school history.

It also came at about the worst time, with the controversial firing of Jim Harrick still fresh, Steve Lavin hoping to get the interim label removed from his job title as successor, and Stanford having recently received commitments from a pair of Los Angeles-area standouts, twin brothers Jason and Jarron Collins. And then this.

The 21st-ranked Cardinals jumped out to a 17-1 lead, and that was that. Stanford hit 10 three-pointers in the first half while building a 57-26 advantage and five more in the second half, shot 56.5% overall, won the battle of the boards by an overwhelming 45-26, and stayed in a zone almost the entire way while UCLA managed just 36.7%. Brevin Knight needed just 24 minutes to pile up 25 points on eight-of-11 shooting and Tim Young had 14 points and 10 rebounds in just 22 minutes.

The big, bold headline of the coverage in the *Los Angeles Times* simply said: 109-61

To this day, Lavin still mentions the game, or whatever passed for one, as a way of pointing out the way teams can bounce back and deal with adversity, aware in retrospect that the Bruins would beat Cal two days later and then gain revenge on Stanford when the teams met in Los Angeles later in the season and even win the Pacific 10 title. On that day, though, he simply had a brutal defeat on his hands.

"They played at a magic level," he said then amid the rubble. "It seemed like they could have drop-kicked the ball from halfcourt and it would have went in off the boards.

"It doesn't take a rocket scientist to figure out what happened tonight. Right from the start, they out-competed us in every way imaginable. They beat us to the punch on the boards, beat us down the court and played better defense."

That's all.

NCAA officials decided to count the statistics even though it came in a game when only one team showed. The only comfort for the Bruins was that it didn't happen at home, that they didn't get booed instead of essentially laughed at. But the location, Maples Pavilion on campus in Palo Alto, brought its own pain.

Lavin is from the Bay Area and this was his first trip home with the new gig, interim or otherwise, and he had family and friends among the 7,391. Two of his assistants, Jim Saia and Steve Spencer, also had roots there. At least misery had its company.

The Bruin 100 Game 31

Notre Dame 89, UCLA 82
January 23, 1971

The headlines the next day were predictable, yet still impossible for some to pass up:

BRUINS RUN OVER BY A CARR

Or something to that effect. Austin Carr, Notre Dame's star guard, had, after all, just hit UCLA for 46 points while making 17 of 30 shots, a showing made all the more impressive because it carried the Fighting Irish to victory in South Bend, Ind., while teammates combined for just 37.2% from the field. It was almost enough to single-handedly knock off the No. 1 team in the nation, the only other standout contribution coming from the 19 points and 14 rebounds by Collis Jones, especially since Carr scored 15 of his points in the critical final 6 1/2 minutes.

"There's no doubt that this is my biggest thrill in basketball," he said.

But the historical significance of the game could not be known on this Saturday afternoon as the Bruins dropped to 14-1. It would not be known for some time, in fact, until after they had recovered and beat Notre Dame the next week in Los Angeles and then beat everyone everywhere the next couple years.

This was the last loss before the record-setting 88-game winning streak.

This was the only loss in a stretch of 108 games.

As if Carr's dominance wasn't noteworthy enough. The senior came in averaging 37.2 points a game and had broken 40 on 16 previous occasions, so this sort of thing wasn't exactly unheard of for him. But by scoring 15 of his team's final 17 points, carrying the Irish on offense while most everyone else was unable to so much as hit a shot, meant the big finish was more than just a part of a 46-point explosion. It was the key to an upset victory.

Larry Hollyfield had the defensive assignment at that stage, the third Bruin, after Kenny Booker and Terry Schofield, to get worked over. Schofield did the best job, at the end of the first half, but then hurt his elbow; already dealing with a troublesome knee, he was pulled by John Wooden as the UCLA coach continued to put a far greater emphasis on having players ready for the conference schedule than available for what he considered mostly a media-generated rivalry.

His path now really cleared, Carr took off again in the second half. When Bruin star Sidney Wicks fouled out with 1:07 remaining trying to stop Carr on a drive, the crowd that had such an impact that UCLA players came to consider it another Notre Dame weapon went wild. And when the final horn sounded, the fans exploded even more, pouring from the stands to the court. They lifted Carr on to their shoulders, and he cut down one of the nets.

"I'm gonna hang this up in my room as a souvenir," he said.

The Bruins, of course, wouldn't need tangible reminders, stung by a great player while playing for the second time in 18 hours, having played Loyola of Chicago the night before and then bussing to South Bend. At least they seemed to respond to the loss.

Notre Dame's Austin Carr.

The Bruin 100

The Bruin 100 Game 32

UCLA Freshman 75, UCLA Varsity 60
November 27, 1965

It was impossible not to notice the symbolism: two new prominent parts of the campus skyline, two new much-publicized structures, being unveiled to the public for the first time on the same night. Pauley Pavilion and Lew Alcindor. The debut of the Bruins' building for the future and the Bruins' foundation of the future.

This was what you could call a proper coming-out party for both. If it appeared as a beautiful arena the first night out, it was still nothing compared to the performance of Alcindor, who arrived from New York City with so much hype and then exceeded even those expectations in his first official UCLA performance. Thirty-one points, 21 rebounds... and 18 years old.

Relegated to the freshman team because of NCAA regulations that prohibited first-year players from joining the varsity, he didn't offer a peek of the future so much as a picture window. Thus came the start of the new era, albeit one that would officially have to wait another year to begin, with an awesome showing in a rout of the two-time defending national champions that also offered impressive debuts by forward Lynn Shackelford and guard Lucius Allen.

To think it could have been a bigger blowout—the freshmen once led 62-44 before their coach, Gary Cunningham, cleared the bench in the final minutes.

They never panicked against the varsity's famed zone press that in previous years had flustered opponents with

far greater experience, usually opting simply to loft the ball to Alcindor, who then passed back to guards in position to then bring it up without much difficulty. Instead, with the inside presence, it was the newcomers who showed the best defense, forcing the varsity to settle for a lot of jumpers rather than deal with Alcindor and eventually finishing at just 35 percent from the field.

"We'll be all right eventually," Coach John Wooden said, "but we have a long way to go."

He meant the big club. The freshmen, not so long.

This wasn't a bad varsity team, either. It lacked the depth of the 1964-65 club that went 28-2 and beat Michigan for the title, but it still had talent, particularly Kenny Washington and Mike Warren, and would have looked better had a stomach ailment not sidelined Freddie Goss. The 65-66 returnees were held in such high regard that UCLA, despite the loss of Keith Erickson and All-America Gail Goodrich to graduation, was still the overwhelming preseason choice by the United Press International board of coaches to win the '66 national championship.

So the accomplishments of the freshman team on this night before 12,051 were significant, even when it turned out the varsity went just 18-8 and failed to make the tournament. Alcindor was dominant, Allen had 16 points, and Shackelford added 14 and noteworthy defense on Edgar Lacey. The rest of the country had been put on notice.

The Bruin 100 Game 33

UCLA 85, Arizona State 83
February 15, 1979

Shock.

"It was unbelievable that we lost after we had it won in the final seconds," Arizona State Coach Ned Wulk said.

Devastation.

"It is so disheartening because all week long we had told our youngsters that they had a chance to beat the No. 1 team in the nation," Wulk said.

Had the chance, nothing. The Sun Devils had done it. They had beat the No. 1 team in the nation, on its home court no less, needing only to burn the final 10 seconds off the clock while protecting a four-point lead. They even had, as it turned out, two more possessions.

So of course they couldn't have imagined the unimaginable. Defeat. UCLA scoring six points in the last nine seconds for a miracle comeback.

"This is one of the greatest victories I've ever experienced in coaching," Bruins boss Gary Cunningham said. "We did the impossible at the end."

No one would disagree with that. But they also had help, from a team that was to blame as much as it was victimized. Arizona State: unwitting accomplices in its own demise.

The Sun Devils had a 40-27 advantage at halftime as UCLA shot 28.9%, and were still up 83-79 after a three-point play by guard Blake Taylor with 24 seconds left.

Not only that, they were then able to whittle more time away before the Bruins scored. Just not enough time, starting the collapse.

0:09—Roy Hamilton hit two free throws for UCLA after being fouled by Kurt Numphius. It was 83-81, and Arizona State was still in relative control, needing only to get the ball back in and get the intentional foul or play a brief game of keep away.

Except that Kiki Vandeweghe stole the pass and was fouled by Lafayette Lever.

0:07—Vandeweghe hit two free throws. It was 83-83, and still the Sun Devils were in decent shape, having enough time at their disposal to run a quick play. At worst—the very worst—they'd get overtime and the opportunity to regroup. Taylor's missed 20-footer in the final moments set up that scenario.

Except that Tony Zeno recklessly went for the offensive rebound when he wouldn't have had time to put up a shot anyway and was called for going over the back of Brad Holland an instant before the buzzer sounded. So....

0:00—Holland hit two free throws. It was 85-83.

"I knew we'd come back," Holland insisted afterwards. "Coach Cunningham has put in our minds that you can't go crazy when you get behind. This is definitely one of our best spurts ever."

One of them?

The Bruin 100 Game 34

Ohio State 105, UCLA 84
December 28, 1961

One of the coaches at the Los Angeles Basketball Classic, an annual tournament that mixed teams from around the country in the field with the two local schools, was asked about USC's Chris Appel.

"Appel was the outstanding player of the tournament," the coach said.

How about Jerry Lucas? a reporter asked.

"I'm talking about the players who are human."

Lucas being more like superhuman. In the semifinals against UCLA, he bombed the Bruins like few others before or since, getting 30 points and 30 rebounds while going 11 of 13 from the field and eight of eight from the line.

"It was a treat to watch him work," Jack Disney wrote in the *Los Angeles Herald*.

"He's the best all-around college basketball player I've ever seen," Bruins Coach John Wooden said at the time.

Of course, that was before he saw Lew Alcindor or Bill Walton and others who had yet to play at UCLA. But if time had altered the rankings, it hadn't diminished in the least the opinion of Lucas on this night.

"It was a phenomenal performance," Wooden says now.

Help came from John Havlicek's 17 points and eight rebounds and 17 more points from guards Mel Nowell and Dick Reasbeck; some guy from the end of the bench named Bob Knight contributed one rebound, two fouls and a missed shot.

One night after killing the Bruins inside—the scores came on five tip-ins, five layups and one short jumper—the All-America center got most of his 38 points from the outside in the victory over USC for the championship of the Classic. In all, he combined for 68 points and 45 rebounds while making 27 of 39 shots in meetings with the Los Angeles schools on consecutive days.

UCLA managed to stay as close as 50-44 at halftime and then 65-62 after seven more minutes behind the hot shooting of Pete Blackman and Gary Cunningham, who would finish with 23 and 22 points, respectively. But Ohio State—NCAA champion in 1960 and runner-up the next two seasons—responded with a 13-2 run in the four minutes that followed.

The Bruin 100 Game 35

UCLA 89, Arizona 87
January 11, 1991

The Wildcats' home winning streak had carried them through 71 games, 39 minutes, 59 seconds, at which point it came to a screeching, though not entirely unexpected, halt. UCLA arrived a formidable foe, 9-0 and No. 12 in the country. UCLA had scorers like Don MacLean and Tracy Murray. It was not a surprise for Arizona to lose.

It was just a surprise for Arizona to lose on a shot by Darrick Martin.

When the 10-footer dropped through with one second remaining, the Bruins had become the first visiting team to win at McKale Center since Texas El Paso on March 13, 1987, nearly four years earlier, and Martin had another peak in his rocky season. After being in and out of the opening lineup, he started against the Wildcats, then finished the Wildcats.

"That shot was very special to me," Martin said. "It was like a relief. I've been through a lot this year."

Added MacLean, who had 38 points on 15-of-23 shooting and nine rebounds: "He's taken a few shots like that in the past three years that maybe weren't that good of shots, but I think it was great today what he did. He's been through a lot of adversity. Coach says the Lord works in mysterious ways. I think that's one of them."

If so, it wasn't the only spiritual intervention looming.

That leaning 12-footer Wayne Womack hit with 10 seconds left to tie the game at 87-all? "That was unbelieveable," Arizona guard Matt Othick said. "After he made that, I thought the McKale mystique was going to pull us through." He might not have been the only one, especially when a couple of the options UCLA Coach Jim Harrick put forth in the ensuing timeout didn't materialize.

Look to MacLean, who in one stretch of the second half had scored 12 consecutive points, or to Murray, Harrick told Martin. But don't force a pass and make a turnover. Do what you think is best.

So Martin did.

"I looked at both of those guys, but they were being denied," he said.

Instead, Martin drove left, around Othick and Damon Stoudamire. He got the shot away in time. Suddenly, it was so quiet in the arena, you could hear a streak break.

"It's great to let these Arizona fans see how it feels to leave losers," UCLA's Gerald Madkins said. "Maybe now people will realize we are for real and give us some credit for being a very good team."

The Wildcats already were.

"We dodged a bullet a few times," Othick said, "but this time it finally hit us."

The Bruin 100 Game 36

UCLA 99, Arizona State 79
January 28, 1956

The wrecking-crew of a game in Tempe, Ariz., was one of the many for Willie Naulls, and a one-of-a-kind game for UCLA. No one is school history had ever gotten 28 rebounds before, and the closest anyone has come since is 27, by Bill Walton.

Naulls also had 26 points, 18 of which came in the second half and actually became important in the eventual blowout victory when Arizona State made a brief rally, getting within 10 points with nine minutes to go before the fast-breaking Bruins pulled away for good. All part of a span in which his offensive success would culminate with the single-season scoring mark.

Naulls needed about another month to break Dick Ridgway's school record of 470 points set in 1950-51. This is the stretch that catapulted him to the top:

- Twenty-six points and 16 rebounds against Idaho at the Pan-Pacific Auditorium in Los Angeles.

- Twenty points and 19 rebounds in the same matchup and the same venue.

- Twenty-two points and 20 rebounds at Washington State.

- Twenty-four points and 16 rebounds, also in Pullman, Wash.

- Twenty-six points and 28 rebounds at Arizona State.

- Twenty-five points and 15 rebounds versus Washington at Pan-Pacific, highlighted by a tip-in at the buzzer of a miss by Morris Taft for the 61-60 victory. Teammates carried Naulls off the court, the second-most impressive performance of the day considering the 220 pounds on the 6-foot-5 frame of the one they affectionately called The Whale.

The Arizona State game symbolized the way he carried the Bruins during his senior season. Guard Carroll Adams made five of his first six shots, mostly from the perimeter, but had only two field goals the rest of the way, so Naulls took over. He went nine of 13 in the second half.

Willie Naulls, part of the tradition of star UCLA centers.

Game 36

The Bruin 100 Game 37

UCLA 43, Santa Barbara College 37
December 3, 1948

Game 1.

There could not, of course, have been any indication of the true significance of this game. That would be years—decades—in coming. For now, in the season opener, there was merely the Rookie of Westwood.

Like the story in one newspaper said that morning in previewing the game:

"Making his coaching debut at Westwood is Johnny Wooden. Now Mister Wooden is a firm believer in race-horse basketball and has been working the Uclans for such an attack for several weeks.

"He has a Bruin force that is admittedly not strong but it is unlikely that there is one in such physical condition. In all drills the ex-Indiana State mentor's command from start to finish has been hurry, hurry, hurry."

Indeed, the Bruins did not return a single starter from the team that went 12-13 the season before in the last of Wilbur Johns' nine campaigns, but Wooden did at least have eight lettermen back. He opened against the forerunner to what today is a sister school in the University of California chain, UC Santa Barbara, and versus a team coached by former UCLA football player Willie Wilton. Fittingly, he also opened with a victory. But uncharacteristically, there were some butterflies.

"To a certain extent," Wooden says now. "But, to be honest, my nature as a player and as a coach was to not have any."

Carl Kraushaar, UCLA's lanky center and a transfer from nearby Compton College, led all scorers "by accounting for 15 markers," one game report read. "George Stanich rang the bell for seven, while Santa Barbara's Gene Snyder hit the net for 11 points." Or as another account described it: "George Stanich, cavorting at guard, hit the basket for a couple of field goals and three gift tosses for seven digits to come out second best among the Bruins pointmakers."

So it went in the home gym—on the Westwood splinters, as they said. The first victory in what became a 22-7 season for the team that would exceed even Wooden's expectations and win the Southern Division championship of the Pacific Coast Conference. The first victory and the first game, period.

One down, 766 to go.

The Bruin 100 Game 38

Arizona State 78, UCLA 74 (Triple Overtime)
January 16, 1981

Along with the exhaustion and the disappointment—and of course the loss—came the appreciation.

"That was probably one of the greatest college games ever," Larry Brown, the Bruins' coach this night in Tempe, Ariz., says now.

No. 8 UCLA against No. 12 Arizona State. Three overtimes. The Bruins falling behind in the first half, recovering in the second and then playing the Sun Devils even until the final minutes. Johnny Nash playing 55 minutes for Arizona State and committing just two turnovers and nearly getting a time-aided triple-double with 13 points, 11 rebounds and nine assists. Teammate Alton Lister going 52 minutes and capitalizing on his height advantage over Kenny Fields to make 10 of 13 shots, score 22 points and grab 12 rebounds. Mike Sanders of UCLA playing 53 minutes and finishing with 19 points and eight rebounds.

The great plays. The most memorable came from the end of the second extra period, when Ralph Jackson, unable to add to the Bruins' two-point lead, missed the front end of a one-and-one with 16 seconds remaining and the Sun Devils got the rebound. Lafeyette Lever ended up with the ball, drove inside, forced the UCLA defense to adjust, and then kicked it out to Nash. The 16-footer that followed forced a third overtime.

"That was a spectacular play when we had to have it," Arizona State Coach Ned Wulk said. "Lever's done that before. He's just a tremendous ballhandler."

UCLA never led again. Paul Williams' jumper for the Sun Devils opened the scoring in the third overtime, the start of the 7-3 advantage in the finally-the-final period that sent them to victory. No Bruin at the time seemed to be thinking about this game's place among the great ones in history.

"I hurt and I know the kids hurt right now," Brown said afterwards. "It's tough when you've got kids who sucked it up so much against a great team and don't have anything positive to show for it."

Three overtimes, and still a third consecutive loss to Arizona State. The Bruins would win in the next meeting later the same season, but other disappointments would follow for the team that had reached the NCAA final in 1980 and was supposed to be better yet this time around. Instead, they went from beating the Sun Devils at Pauley Pavilion to losing three of the last seven games, capped by tournament elimination at the hands of Danny Ainge and BYU.

The Bruin 100 Game 39

UCLA 72, Ohio State 68
March 13, 1980

Four days earlier, Larry Brown had his assistant coaches, Larry Farmer and Kevin O'Connor, scout the start of the Ohio State-Arizona State second-round matchup in Tempe, Ariz., that followed the Bruins' upset of DePaul in Tempe in the same University Activites Center. Brown had to attend to his postgame duties, namely the obligatory press conference, before he could turn his attention to the next opponent. At one point in the first half, he looked up and saw the Buckeyes already leading by 25 or some other ridiculous amount.

Brown grabbed Farmer and O'Connor. No need to stick around.

"We ain't going to beat this team anyway," he said.

There was factual support for such a claim, not just Brown's legendary pessimism. UCLA, after all, was young and small, a bad combination as it prepared to face a front line with Herb Williams, the 6-foot-10, 242-pound Big 10 co-player of the year, and Clark Kellogg, along with arguably the best point guard in the nation, Kelvin Ransey. So of course the Bruins had no chance.

But this was the spring of 1980 and the most improbable of all UCLA tournaments, so of course the Bruins won. Displaying the same confidence and ability to overcome obstacles that had served them well against DePaul and would carry them all the way to the championship game, they pulled off another shocker.

"That was the most unexpected one," Brown says now, adding: "I thought we could beat DePaul because we had everything going for us. But Ohio State, I thought that would be a joke."

The days before had been peppered with rumors that he would be leaving UCLA for openings at Duke or North Carolina State or with the expansion Dallas Mavericks—"I hope to coach here a long time," he said, about a year before his last game with the Bruins—but stability came with tipoff on this Thursday night in Tucson. Ransey scored 29 points, but the Buckeyes were unable to use the size advantage to duplicate their dunkfest against Arizona State. Not only that, they couldn't even power their way to the basket to draw fouls.

Ohio State shot an incredible 10 free throws, making six, with the starting front court getting all of four tries in a combined 91 1/2 minutes, two by Williams in 40 minutes. It was the difference in the game. The Bruins won despite shooting 42.3% from the field and with five fewer attempts than the opponent because they went 28 of 35 from the line. They also had a 33-31 edge in rebounding.

Williams came in averaging 18 points a game and was held to 10, while being shut out for the final 19 1/2 minutes. James Wilkes gave away three inches and 35 pounds, but did the job, with regular weakside help. "I thought James did an excellent job on Ronnie Valentine of Old Dominion (in the first round) and I thought he did an excellent job on Mark Aguirre of DePaul (in the second), but this game was his greatest," Brown said afterwards.

Wilkes was a hero—again. Earlier in the day, he had saved a kid from drowning in the pool at the team hotel, jumping in for the rescue after the boy's parents apparently thought the youngster was playing. Wilkes' totals for the day: eight points, nine rebounds, four steals, one lifeguard mission. Mike Sanders and Rod Foster at least helped at night, scoring 19 points each, with Foster hitting two free throws with 19 seconds left to make it 70-66 and seal the victory.

The heroics of James Wilkes came earlier in the day, and then again to help UCLA upset Ohio State.

Game 39

The Bruin 100 Game 40

UCLA 72, USC 70
March 5, 1960

The ugliness seemingly emerged from nowhere, after 39 minutes 31 seconds at the Los Angeles Sports Arena as the Bruins held tightly to a 68-66 lead in the regular-season finale and their hopes of an at-large bid to the NCAA tournament.

Twenty-nine seconds remained when USC's Steve Kemp grabbed a loose ball as Bill Hicks of UCLA also tried to gain control. Kemp ripped the ball away, dumping Hicks. Hicks jumped right back up and lunged at Kemp. Hicks didn't throw any punches, but when Trojan John Rudometkin came to the aid of his teammate anyway and stepped in and shoved Hicks, the game was sent to a neutral corner. The brawl had been ignited.

It quickly turned into bedlam. Supporters left their seats to join in, pushing and shoving their way to surround the combatants, or at least the combatants who were supposed to be on the court. One fan, later identified as a member of the UCLA junior varsity football team, stormed from the stands to take on Rudometkin, only to first be popped in the face by Rudometkin.

Said prominent Los Angeles sportswriter Bud Furillo: "Rudometkin was rolling like Rocky Marciano at his best, taking on any and all comers, after popping Hicks first of all."

Rudometkin did emerge from the rumble with a puffy

face—one witness said a Bruins cheerleader smacked him from the blindside. Still other fans, in skirts or otherwise, took sneak punches at players and at each other. And when USC Coach Forrest Twogood and John Wooden moved in to try and separate the sides, Twogood accidentally butted his Bruins counterpart when whirling around in a pack, sending Wooden's glasses to the floor and leaving a bump on the side of his nose.

It was estimated that as many as 75 people were on the court as what had been a hotly contested cross-town rivalry, the UCLA domination still a few years away, simply became heated. Players from both teams landed punches before referees Al Lightner and Joe Frivaldsky, with help from the coaches and security, restored order and then handed out five ejections: Ken Stanley, Bob Hampton and Rudometkin of USC and Kent Miller and Hicks of UCLA. Three technical fouls were also called on each side.

UCLA went first, with sophomore Pete Blackman at the line. He made all three, worth a 71-66 lead.

USC turned to Jerry Pimm for the chance to counter. He made the first, missed the second and made the third.

It was 71-68, with a jump ball to follow as play resumed. The Trojans gained possession, and Kemp hit a 20-footer with 22 seconds left to cut the deficit to one. But they were also forced to stop the clock and hope for a miracle, so Kemp intentionally fouled Blackman with five seconds remaining. Blackman made one free throw, providing the final margin.

The Bruins finished 14-12 in the regular season, the only time they came close to being a .500 team under Wooden, but had also beaten USC in three of five meetings. No matter. The NCAA picked the Trojans for the tournament, the hardest punch of all to take.

The fight with USC involved players, coaches and fans and became one of the ugliest moments of the long rivalry.

Game 40

The Bruin 100 Game 41

UCLA 133, Louisiana State 84
December 23, 1969

The drooping socks. The floppy hair. The nickname. Pistol Pete.

The Maravichs had come to town, Press on the bench as the coach and son Pete on the court as the star, and 12,961 came to Pauley Pavilion to witness the merging of college basketball and showbiz. It's just that Pete didn't come as himself, beyond the signature appearance, a couple behind-the-back passes and dribbles and, as Dwight Chapin described it the next day in the *Los Angeles Times,* "a one-handed, under-handed, layin-in off an in-bounds pass while falling."

In reality, though, it was a disappointing showing, maybe even to the most faithful of Bruins fans, many of whom no doubt were hoping for a UCLA win and a dazzling display from Maravich. They packed the arena in what was a record home crowd at the time and got one, but not the other. Victory came with ease—133-84—but Maravich made just 14 of 42 shots and committed 18 turnovers.

Only in this way could 38 points be a letdown. He took just two shots the first six minutes. The first basket didn't come until more than nine minutes had expired. If it was frustrating for LSU, which committed 30 turnovers in all, it was also somewhat understandable.

"We've played four games in six nights, three of them on the road," Pete explained afterwards. "We started in Charlotte, North Carolina, then went to Corvallis, Ore., and then here. Tired? That's the understatement of the year."

Said Press Maravich, his father and coach: "We were awfully leg weary. We'd traveled all day to get here. You didn't see the real Pete out there tonight. He's a damned tired boy. Three games on the road—and 5,800 miles."

UCLA was aware of all this, of course, so John Wooden, himself battling a bad cold, went heavy with the defensive pressure. He put Henry Bibby, four inches shorter but also quicker, on Maravich with constant double-team help, usually from John Vallely, hoping to force Pete to give up the ball and then have to work extra hard to get it back.

Turnovers followed. Then, a rout.

"I think UCLA should join the NBA," Pete said later.

It was over by halftime, when the Bruins had a 69-40 lead. In the end, they had a 5-0 record, 23 points each from Curtis Rowe and Sidney Wicks, and 17 from Bibby.

Pete Maravich, floppy-socked and tired at the end of a long trip, struggled to keep up with the pace set by Henry Bibby and UCLA.

Game 41

The Bruin 100 Game 42

USC 80, UCLA 78 (4 OT)
February 28, 1985

Three hundred minutes later, the longest game either school had ever played was history. So, too, were the Bruins, their remaining hope for a bid to the NCAA tournament all but eliminated as soon as a reserve center named Charlie Simpson was left alone and allowed to make an uncontested layup with :02 remaining, their composure also quickly fading.

UCLA Coach Walt Hazzard said USC "lucked out," a comment for which he later apologized. What he didn't take back was the frustration of an outcome that dropped the Bruins into fifth place in the Pacific 10 Conference and had them staring at the real possibility of a sub-.500 finish for the first time since 1947-48.

"We've lost some tough games, and this is another one," Hazzard said. "Maybe I'll learn something as a coach from it. Right now, it doesn't taste good. I'm usually half-way congenial, but tonight I don't feel like it at all."

His Bruins were 13-12. Not just that, but they had just lost the season series to USC, in the same city but rarely in the same class, for the first time since 1961 and been swept by the Trojans for the first team since 1942 (4-0). All after blowing a great opportunity.

The teams had played a double-overtime game at the Sports Arena earlier in the season, and now they were deep into No. 4 at Pauley Pavilion, so deep that only 10 seconds remained. Dave Immel was at the line with the

chance to give UCLA a two-point lead. He would lead the Bruins in free-throw percentage a few seasons later, but on this night he missed both.

The Trojans got the defensive rebound and got the ball to guard Larry Friend, who pushed it ahead and then found Simpson alone underneath because of a blown defensive assignment. Friend delivered the pass and Simpson delivered the final blow, finally bringing conclusion to what had been an amazing night, with USC's Wayne Carlander getting 38 points and 13 rebounds while playing 59 minutes, the same amount as Reggie Miller and Nigel Miguel for the Bruins. It was the equivalent of nearly a full game and a half, and five others went at least 40 minutes.

Trojan fans danced around Pauley in celebration, some waving brooms. Coach Stan Morrison said it may have been the biggest victory for that program in 25 years.

"I've never been happier about a win," he added, "and I've never felt worse for a losing coach than I do right now."

What UCLA could not have imagined at the time was that one of the most painful of losses, even though it had committed just 10 turnovers in a four-overtime game, would also be the last loss of the season. The eight-game winning streak that followed and culminated with a victory in the NIT championship offered at least some redemption, for the season as a whole and for this night.

The Bruin 100 Game 43

UCLA 77, DePaul 71
March 9, 1980

Part of the improbable 1980 tournament run, one that would take UCLA from a fourth-place finish in the conference all the way to the championship game, included the rematch that really wasn't. The second round that also could also have been a first meeting.

DePaul had defeated the Bruins on Dec. 15 at Pauley Pavilion, just not these Bruins. Freshmen Rod Foster and Michael Holton and sophomore Mike Sanders weren't starting then, and Sanders had 15 points and 12 rebounds in the upset before 14,468 in Tempe, Ariz., that eliminated the top-ranked Blue Demons. Foster scored 18 points.

DePaul didn't play like before, either, maybe because of what had happened before. Its esteemed coach and soothsayer, Ray Meyer, later admitted the premonition of bad things to come and that he had told his wife before tipoff that "I don't want to watch this game." His players were overconfident, and it was obvious.

"They came out like if they just played an average game they were going to beat us," Kiki Vandeweghe said. "They weren't ready to play when they first came out."

"They were pretty cocky before the game and they might have overlooked us," forward James Wilkes added. "They just seemed to think by being there they were going to beat us."

And the Blue Demons still had the chance to do just that, to recover in time and escape to improve to 27-1 and end the Bruin run before it really started. The game was tied at 67 with 1:38 remaining, at which time the underdogs, having come in at just 18-9, scored 10 unanswered points to take control for good. Mark Aguirre, who began the day averaging 27 points a game, was held to 19 by a committee of Wilkes, Vandeweghe and Sanders.

"Ray Meyer has meant so much to the game and it means something special to me to be on the same court with him," UCLA Coach Larry Brown said. "I'm sorry that his season had to end this way."

He was sorry? Try being a Blue Demon.

"UCLA got lucky by getting its poor performance out of the way in the first-round victory in the tournament over Old Dominion," Joey Meyer, Ray's son and assistant coach, said in his diary for the *Chicago Tribune*. "They played badly then and won, and we couldn't get that lucky.

"I don't know what to say, except that we blew it."

"UCLA looked a little shaky, but we didn't take advantage of it," Ray Meyer said. "We thought we could just throw out our uniforms and UCLA would just fall down. But when we didn't do anything, it gave them confidence."

It also gave them another game, and then another after that, and so on. It gave them a major accomplishment, with more to come.

Game 43

Even with Bill Walton (32) in foul trouble, the Bruins still rose above
Tom Burleson and North Carolina State in St. Louis.

The Bruin 100

The Bruin 100 Game 44

UCLA 84, North Carolina State 66
December 15, 1973

No. 1 UCLA versus No. 2 North Carolina State.

"The game isn't particularly important to us," Bruins Coach John Wooden said.

He was serious.

"We'd rather have our players more ready for each conference game."

It was always like that with Wooden, not just this season or this night. But there was no debating the significance of the victory, beyond the $100,000 that lured the Bruins to St. Louis for the neutral-site contest, for the moment and for the rest of the season, considering what came later. The end of the record win streak about five weeks later at Notre Dame, for one thing, and eventually an anguishing loss to the same North Carolina State team in the semifinals. Maybe they should have savored this one more.

The Wolfpack's win streak ended at 29 games even though Bill Walton was slowed by foul trouble. In his place of prominence stepped Keith Wilkes, who had 27 points and 11 rebounds, to counter the 17 points and 13 rebounds from North Carolina State star David Thompson, while David Meyers added 15 points.

"Everybody thought it would be a big break for us when Walton got in early foul trouble," State Coach Norm

Sloan said. "However, you don't have a great basketball team like UCLA's if you are a one-man team. We made an awful lot of mistakes. Of course, UCLA had a lot to do with that. They did not wilt under pressure. They had been there before and they know what it is like."

Added Wilkes: "We came out expecting a tough game and it was. There are a lot of things we can do when Bill's in there that we can't do when he's not."

Indeed, Walton was in for the most crucial stretch, those five minutes midway through the second half when the Bruins went on a 19-2 charge to turn a 54-54 potential thriller into a blowout. In all, they out-rebounded the Wolfpack 22-11 after intermission.

"What an ass whuppin," UCLA guard Tommy Curtis said.

There was no way around that. A big payday for the Bruins all around.

"I'd like to be in the finals against them," Wolfpack guard Monte Towe said. "But after the jolt we've had we're going to have to take a look at ourselves, talk it out, pull back a little and pick up the pieces."

They looked, they talked, they pulled and they picked. And they didn't even have to wait until the finals to get another shot at UCLA.

The Bruin 100 Game 45

UCLA 71, Kansas 70
March 18, 1990

Kansas called one timeout. Then another, before play had even resumed.

"I wasn't really that calm," Tracy Murray said of the moment. "But when they called those two timeouts, I thought it was funny. You know, freeze the freshman."

Hilarious. The real punch line.

Murray, a freshman starting forward, a young player on a young team that made up in confidence what it lacked in experience, made one free throw with nine seconds left, then another to give UCLA the upset victory in Atlanta and a spot in the Sweet 16 for the first time since the run by the 1980 kiddie corps. The two shots that made the season a success, even when the loss to Duke in the East Regional followed.

"Hey, I don't even think of myself as a freshman," Murray said. "I've been playing for a long time, since I was two or three years old. I don't look at it as some freshman deal."

His coach, Jim Harrick, years later would still laugh at the notion that Murray might have been nervous standing there at the line. Murray's offensive abilities had never been in question, not by the end of the season in which he would post the second-highest scoring average

by a first-year player in school history, and neither had his confidence. Definitely not his confidence.

In that regard, at least, it wasn't some freshman deal. But it was in most other ways, those which deal in reality—a young player had ignored the dramatics of the moment to hit a pair of free throws in the second tournament game of his life to beat the No. 2 team in the nation, to beat a team that began this day 30-4, compared to UCLA's 21-10.

It came as the clincher to a day in which one sophomore starting guard, Darrick Martin, had 18 points and six assists and another sophomore starting guard, Gerald Madkins, hit his team's only three-pointer of the day to keep the Bruins close down the stretch. A senior, of all people, was also allowed to make a major contribution, Trevor Wilson getting 18 points and 12 rebounds and the layup that was worth a 69-68 lead with 40 seconds remaining.

Kevin Pritchard put Kansas back ahead when he made two free throws with 29 seconds left. When Murray, dependable but not outstanding from the line, countered that 20 seconds later, and when Wilson hounded Ricky Calloway of the Jayhawks down the sideline before Calloway missed a late 16-footer, youth had officially been served.

"That was a great, great basketball game," Harrick says now. "I don't know that our team played better all year."

"We did it for ourselves, but I guess it is an honor to be the first team in 10 years to do it," Don MacLean said of reaching the Sweet 16. "It's a steppingstone for us, and when I leave here I hope we'll be a perennial top 10 team."

As it turned out, this was likely, or at least arguably, the shining tournament moment for the core of the team. The next season brought first-round elimination by Penn State, and while the Bruins of 1992 got to the West Regional final, they also got sent home with a 27-point loss to Indiana.

Tracy Murray had the last-second heroics, but Darrick Martin had 18 points and six assists in the 1990 tournament.

The Bruin 100 Game 46

USC 46, UCLA 44
March 8, 1969

The night the other shoe dropped.

The opportunity USC had barely missed a day earlier and a few miles away at the Sports Arena, its home court, came, at last, in the regular-season finale and the second day of the back-to-back. What it lacked in potential history, as Trojan Coach Bob Boyd would quickly remind in exclamation, it made up for in vindication.

"They're damned lucky we didn't beat them twice!" Boyd shouted in the party that was the visitor's locker room at Pauley Pavilion, his tie already off and the blue shirt soaked in sweat.

UCLA needed two overtimes to escape in the previous meeting, a 61-55 decision that marked its 41st consecutive victory overall and a 25-0 start to the season, but there would be no avoiding defeat this time, just as there would be no undefeated season. It joined the historic Houston setback as only the second loss during the Lew Alcindor era, and it came as close to resounding fashion as possible for an eventual two-point setback, the Bruins having led only once in the last nine minutes.

Alcindor was held to just 10 points and, even more incredibly, four attempts and three makes, along with six rebounds. But he also tied the game at 44 with one free throw with 1:15 remaining, forcing the Trojans to make a shot on the ensuing possession instead of being able to simply run out as much of the clock as possible before UCLA was forced to foul.

As expected, USC showed extreme patience. With 19 seconds left, Boyd called timeout to set up the final assault. He called for a screen that would spring Ernie Powell.

Play resumed, the seconds drained away, and it was Don Crenshaw, in the midst of a game in which he would lead all scorers with 20 points, who had the key supporting role. Powell, the quiet senior forward, used the screen, went around Crenshaw about 20 feet out on the right side, came in a bit and pulled up for the 14-footer with six seconds left. Swish.

UCLA's desperate final bid ended when the 20-foot jumper by Sidney Wicks with about a second remaining bounced off the rim. USC fans stormed the court, punctuating the end of Bruin dominance on several fronts—gone was the 41-game winning streak, the 51-game winning streak at Pauley Pavilion, the 45-game conference winning streak, the 17-game winning streak in the cross-town series. All at once.

"I don't feel badly," UCLA Coach John Wooden said in

the aftermath. "The Trojans played their game. They did what they wanted to do, and they did it very well. We just weren't able to do much about it.

"Maybe this loss will help us, put us in good shape for the tournament. At least I sure hope so."

There went the chance for perfection. The Bruins would have to try to make up for it in the postseason. They would have to get their vindication.

Coach Wooden expresses his dismay to a referee.

Gene Bartow had the honor—and the impossible task—of succeeding
John Wooden.

The Bruin 100

The Bruin 100 Game 47

Indiana 84, UCLA 64
November 29, 1975

There was that exhibition contest eight days earlier against the Australian national team at Pauley Pavilion, but this was, officially, the first game of the post-John Wooden era. If you dared call it a game.

Gene Bartow's Bruin honeymoon lasted all of, oh, 20 minutes, if that long. By that point, his new team had been badly outplayed, but at least had the good fortune of trailing just 36-28 because the opponents shot only 34%.

When the Hoosiers also started doing that right early in the second half, the onslaught really began. A few Hoosier fans among the 19,115 in attendance at St. Louis Arena for the neutral-site game unfurled a banner that read "U'll C LA, Indiana No. 1" and several Hoosier players then pushed the lead all the way to 26 with 6 1/2 minutes remaining.

The game had its own importance to Indiana, which turned out to be a powerhouse-in-waiting on this Saturday relatively close to its Bloomington home but was also likely still thinking about the past. It was these Hoosiers, after all, who had claimed they, and not UCLA, would have won the national championship the season before if Scott May had not broken his arm. That would have made for a dramatic alteration of history, of course, because the Bruin title offered the storybook ending to Wooden's departure.

UCLA lost David Meyers and Pete Trgovich, most notably, from that team, but still had an impressive front line of juniors Richard Washington and Marques Johnson and freshman David Greenwood, so the Hoosiers were not about to miss the chance to make a point in the process of victory. Bobby Knight finally removed his starting lineup with 30 seconds left, the group that to that stage had gone with only one substitution. May had 33 points, Kent Benson 17 points and 14 rebounds.

As if replacing the legend wouldn't have been tough enough, fate had given Bartow an opener against a team that was driven because of the past while also motivated for the future, en route to becoming arguably the greatest squad of all-time with the 32-0 run to the title. It became the first season-opening loss for the Bruins since 1964.

"Indiana proved it deserves the No. 1 ranking they have," he said that night. "We are going to have a fine basketball team at UCLA, but now we are feeling our way around."

So began the new season and the new era.

"It was a good opener for college basketball," said the man suddenly on the hot seat more than ever, "but it was bad for Gene Bartow."

The Bruin 100 Game 48

UCLA 99, Louisville 86
February 28, 1987

The greatest scoring day for one of the greatest scorers in UCLA history came in the regular-season finale, the 27th game and 21st win for the Bruins as a prep for the inaugural Pacific 10 tournament and then the NCAAs.

"It's crunch time," the star of that day, and many others, said, "and crunch time is Miller time."

Reggie Miller time. He scored 42 points, tied for the seventh-best performance ever by a Bruin and tied for the third-best performer, alongside Gail Goodrich and trailing only Lew Alcindor and Bill Walton. It came as part of a complete barrage at Pauley Pavilion that also included seven rebounds and four steals in 35 minutes.

It also came with help—Dave Immel also got his career high, 23 points while making six of 10 three-pointers and also contributing seven assists. Miller was two of three from behind the arc, showing range, but his 15 baskets in 19 tries showed his offensive versatility, with scores coming from the perimeter, dunks and layups in transition, and off the give-and-go.

"They can shoot from anywhere," Louisville Coach Denny Crum, the former UCLA player and assistant coach, said of the Bruins in general and Miller and Immel in particular. "In fact, they did."

It became necessary, not merely optional, because the Cardinals were still within 49-42 approximately four minutes into the second half. But UCLA pushed the lead back to 61-47 behind the outside shooting of both, all the more apparent to Louisville because by day's end it had taken 31 fewer three-pointers for the season than Miller. Soon enough, the game was completely under control at 71-52, despite what would end up as a 19-point, 12-rebound, six-block counter by Pervis Ellison.

"We played 94 feet and a lot of people contributed," Bruins Coach Walt Hazzard said. "We had to make our three-point shots because Ellison was spiking anything from five feet. He shut the basket down like a goalie."

So the Bruins had 16 such attempts, with nine makes, while Louisville went four of six. Miller didn't match the output in that category, but he proved otherwise impossible to equal, getting 33 points in the second half alone one game after scoring 36 against USC and one game before hitting Arizona State for 39 points in the opener of the conference's postseason tournament.

The timing of his great stretch did not go unnoticed, and not merely that he was warming up for the NCAA tournament. It came not long after Jose Ortiz of Oregon State, and not Miller, had been named player of the year for District 8.

"His last two games have made a mockery out of picking the best player on the West Coast," Hazzard said after this showing. Just in case anyone around UCLA needed to be reminded.

Reggie Miller pulls an inside job to score two of his career-high 42 points against Louisville.

The Bruin 100 Game 49

Michigan 86, UCLA 84 (Overtime)
March 20, 1993

The Fab Five were sophomores and heading fast toward their junior season, what with Ed O'Bannon having scored 17 points in the first 10 minutes and the rest of the Bruins following that with a 12-0 run on Chris Webber, Juwan Howard, Jalen Rose, et al. The deficit reached 19. The only sign of the Wolverines was their hype.

What happened next culminated with a finish that was controversial for the moment in Tucson, Ariz., and a finish that carried over for two more years to Boise, Idaho.

The Michigan comeback began in the second half and quickly gained momentum, until it had built an eight-point lead with 3:48 left in regulation, a 27-point turnaround. Suddenly, it was left to UCLA to battle back, offering a response that resulted in a 77-77 tie, and then another opportunity that could have won the game.

Pressing after the two free throws by Tyus Edney that evened the score, the Bruins created a turnover when Shon Tarver knocked the ball loose. Edney gained control and took it inside, right at Howard.

"I went and got the ball and went right to the basket and saw Ed on my right and tried to get the ball to Ed," Edney said. "I could have taken the shot, but it would have been over a bigger player. I thought Ed had a better shot at the basket."

So Edney passed off, or at least tried to. Michigan's Jimmy King ruined the plan by coming from behind for the steal and the save, getting the Wolverines to overtime. Two years later, in a similar situation against Missouri in the 1995 tournament, Edney would finish the play himself and score, and then be reminded of the difference from his previous decision.

The extra period brought controversy. It also brought defeat for UCLA when Rose's shot came off the backboard and King put it in for the winning points. Confusion reigned as Bruins Coach Jim Harrick demanded to see a replay of the final sequence, wondering if Rose had gotten his try off in time to beat the shot clock and then whether it hit the rim to make King's follow legal.

About an hour after the game, Harrick got his second look, and the satisfaction of at least knowing his team hadn't been eliminated in the second round of the tournament on a bad decision. If that helped any.

"They made the right call," Harrick said of the referees. "Our players quit playing because they thought the shot clock went off. That's not an excuse, but I thought so, too."

The Bruins would get the chance for redemption on at least one of the plays a couple years later.

The Bruin 100 Game 50

UCLA 85, Michigan 82
March 15, 1998

The loss in the win would linger for a long time—freshman point guard Baron Davis landed awkwardly after a dunk and tore a ligament in his left knee, an injury that will also cost him at least a large portion of 1998-99. But the victory that came at the same time before 19,423 at the Georgia Dome offered both vindication and emotions of a different kind for the future of other first-year players.

Responding after the near-loss to Miami (Fla.) and what would have been another first-round disaster for the program that was only beginning to put some distance between itself and the memories of Princeton '96, Tulsa '94 and Penn State '91, UCLA played with what Coach Steve Lavin came to consider his team's best game of the season. So meaningful is it that he keeps the game ball in his office.

The Bruins earned the right to revel, or even stick it in the face of the numerous doubters who had appeared, noting that the team that had just struggled so much against Miami had no chance against a team with so much more size, that this would be the night the dismissal/voluntary departure because he had no choice of 6-foot-10 Jelani McCoy would ultimately doom the Bruins. Michigan's most prominent size, 300-pound Robert (Tractor) Traylor, went so far as to guarantee victory.

UCLA was already a sixth-seeded team playing the third-seeded club in the round of 32, and then lost Davis after 14 minutes. But the Bruins went ahead at 12-10 and led the rest of the way, holding off a series of threats by the Wolverines. It was left to Kris Johnson, in what became a final hurrah along with J.R. Henderson and Toby Bailey for the trio that had won an NCAA title as freshmen, to put Michigan away for good.

That's one of the reasons the game remains so close to Lavin, because it was a positive finish to the season, and the career, for Johnson after a suspension for violating team rules had stayed with the son of former Bruin star Marques Johnson in some form from Sept. 29 through Dec. 9. Actually, it stayed with the 6-4 swingman much longer, seeing as it was mentioned on a regular basis even after he had again become a member in good standing.

Lavin gave Johnson the chance to replace such talk, running plays for him on four consecutive possessions down the stretch because Johnson was the most dependable Bruin from the line and they were in the bonus. The payback came when he made eight in a row from the line in the final 37 seconds to clinch the victory.

"Maybe I would have been nervous in my freshman year, but I've been in that situation throughout my career," Johnson said after the upset. "I want to be there. I'm one of three seniors and that's why I wanted the pressure. We want to put the weight on our shoulders."

They all did, Johnson with the clutch shots, Henderson with defense inside against Traylor despite giving up about 70 pounds, Bailey with his perimeter game. And then there were the newcomers— seldom-used Travis Reed coming in to help out on Traylor, Earl Watson scoring 10 points, Rico Hines with his defense, and even Davis contributing seven points and a steal before the injury.

"You saw the freshmen come of age in that game," Lavin says in retrospect.

Coach Lavin sizes up the situation.

The Bruin 100

The Bruin 100 Game 51

UCLA 73, Houston 58
March 24, 1967

Commence rivalry.

"As far as I'm concerned, Jimmy Walker of Providence should be player of the year," Houston's Elvin Hayes said the day before the game in Louisville, Ky. "He's had three great seasons, and I just don't think Lew is a super player or anything like that."

Then the decent player, Lew Alcindor, got 19 points and 20 rebounds in victory in the semifinals of the NCAA tournament.

Hayes would not budge.

"He's not what they say he is," the Houston star said. "Neither on offense nor defense.

"It really irritates me, him getting all that publicity, because it's not really true."

And so it began, the stretch of three meetings in one year, all with major implications—this one for a trip to the championship, the mega-game at the Astrodome midway through the next season, and then in the semifinals again in March of 1968. If it's possible to have a great short-term rivalry, this was it, starting with pointed words.

There were the other kind of points as well. Alcindor, the sophomore center playing in the Final Four for the first time, got his. Lynn Shackelford had 22, along with eight rebounds, and Lucius Allen contributed 17 and nine rebounds.

Hayes, meanwhile, turned in a great performance, 25 points and 24 rebounds in 40 minutes. He didn't shoot well—12 makes in 31 attempts—but that just meant he played for the Cougars. They managed just 29.3% in a 28-point first half and finished at 34.7%.

The only Houston lead was at 17-16. The Bruins were up by nine at halftime and never in danger again, even as sophomore guard Allen, their second-leading scorer during the season, played with a sore left ankle, the result of an injury the day before in practice. The No. 1 team in the country, at 28-0 after knocking off No. 6 without much difficulty, would go on to beat Dayton the next day for a third championship in four years.

The domination of Alcindor and his Bruins, to continue the next two years, had officially started, even if few seemed willing to acknowledge as much. Dean Eagle, the sports editor of the *Louisville Times*, noted a dissent so obvious that "most coaches huddling in downtown hotel postmortems agreed with Hayes that Alcindor was a disappointment and didn't live up to his fabulous press clippings." Maybe that would change in time.

The Bruin 100 Game 52

UCLA 111, Dayton 100 (Triple Overtime)
March 14, 1974

Triple overtime? Not once before in 36 consecutive tournament wins, the streak that remained in the wake of the 88-gamer being broken by Notre Dame about two months earlier, had the Bruins so much as needed a single extra period. And then came this, the game that at the time tied an NCAA record for the longest postseason contest.

No wonder John Wooden was spotted consoling weeping Dayton song girls afterwards. Or was it the other way around? It was his team, after all, that arrived in Tucson, Ariz., for the first round of the West Regionals as the seven-time defending champion and then immediately fell on its own sword, wasting a 17-point first-half lead.

It had to happen in this season, of course. The loss at Notre Dame. The Lost Weekend at the Oregons. The 23-3 record during the regular season that marked their worst showing in eight years. The blown opportunity for an easy win in the tournament opener, or even a win in the first overtime, or the second overtime.

"Between each of the overtime periods, I told the players that we had been given a reprieve so we had better take advantage of it," Wooden said. "We finally did. I expected a tough game, but I didn't expect to have to win it in overtime."

The Bruins were fortunate to get that far—Donald Smith missed a 15-footer with four seconds left that could have won it for the Flyers in regulation. Meanwhile, UCLA starting guard Tommy Curtis had the flu and played just 10 minutes, and the two starting forwards, Keith Wilkes and David Meyers, both fouled out, though Meyers after contributing 28 points and 14 rebounds in 48 minutes.

Into Meyers' spot went Gary Franklin, a seldom-used senior. Franklin went 12 minutes in relief and turned in a huge defensive play in the third overtime, making a steal at mid-court and turning it into a layup for a 102-98 lead that finished Dayton for good. Finally.

"Gary's experienced and calm," Wooden said. "We felt he wouldn't make a critical mistake. He's a very sound player."

The lift from Franklin helped offset the 36 points and 13 rebounds the Flyers got from Mike Sylvester in 54 minutes and another 26 points from Smith. The unexpected contributor had helped the Bruins survive, at least for now.

The Bruin 100 Game 53

UCLA 64, USC 60
February 6, 1971

It was two games after Notre Dame had beaten the Bruins, what would become their last loss for about three years, so a USC fan had a sign at the Sports Arena that said, "Watch out, UCLA, we have two Austin Carrs."

It was the second week that the Trojans were atop the United Press International rankings, so a UCLA supporter countered with, "SC No. 1? They can't even count that high."

To be sure, this was not your average showdown, even as the emotional, and often heated, rivalry goes. UCLA chasing USC in the polls was not the norm since John Wooden had arrived, and certainly not once the 1960s and the Bruins' dynasty had arrived. No. 1 against No. 2 by some counts, and two of the three top teams by everyone's. Interest was so great this Saturday that KTTV, the Los Angeles television station among the 100 or so scheduled to carry the game, planned to show it live with the 8 p.m. tipoff and rebroadcast it at 10:30... and then again at 4:30 a.m. Sunday.

It was a game that lived up to the considerable hype. The Trojans, behind what would become 23 points from Dennis (Mo) Layton, built a 59-50 lead with 9:35 remaining, putting themselves in position to solidify the rankings. Or for a big letdown.

They scored just one point the rest of the way, a free throw by Dana Pagett with 5:19 to play. That came 11 seconds after Kenny Booker made a great steal and went in for a layup that gave UCLA the lead, part of its 14-1 run to end the game. It was also part of the emotional lift for Booker, the 6-foot-4 senior who had been hearing since early in the season how much the Bruins missed his predecessor, John Vallely.

Soon after Booker's basket, on a night when he would score 14 points, they stalled for about three minutes in an attempt to draw USC out of its zone defense. And then when the Trojans did get the ball back, they missed three shots on the same possession, 10 seconds of opportunities when a basket would have meant a 62-61 edge. Instead, Henry Bibby hit one free throw with 1:02 left to put UCLA up 62-60 and Sidney Wicks got the last of his game-high 24 points, which went with 14 rebounds, on two makes from the line with 20 seconds remaining to clinch the victory.

"We didn't lose our offense the last 9 1/2 minutes," Layton said. "We had no offense to lose. We got no rebounding and no spark. It was a little like our guys didn't even want the ball."

UCLA fans immediately went to the "We're No. 1!" chants. They were right. When the next polls came out,

UPI and the *Associated Press*, the Bruins were indeed No. 1, as if order had been restored, around the country and around the city.

Kenny Booker, a 6-4 senior, made the key defensive play and scored 14 points as UCLA beat rival USC in a Los Angeles showdown that had national implications.

The Bruin 100

The Bruin 100 Game 54

University of San Francisco 72, UCLA 61
March 16, 1956

The college basketball dynasty of the 1960s and early '70s was still forming when the Bruins tried to throw themselves in front of the late-'50s version in Corvallis, Ore., in a first-round tournament game, only to again become part of the very winning streak they would one day overtake.

This was consecutive victory No. 51 for USF, bound for 60 before the end finally came. The killer for UCLA, unlike the meeting in the ninth game of 1955-56, is that it came while the top-ranked Dons played without K.C. Jones, declared ineligible for the postseason by the NCAA. That left only one star, Bill Russell, for the Bruins to deal with.

Boy, they sure got off easy. Russell hit ninth-ranked UCLA for 21 points, and the damage surely would have been more severe if the Dons didn't have the game in control by the end of the first half, allowing him rest. It's like Jack Geyer wrote in the *Los Angeles Times:*

"The 6-foot-9 5/8-inch senior looked like a man among boys tonight.

"Bounding about the court with strides which would do credit to an antelope, Russell dominated the game as if he had invented it.

"On at least eight occasions, the big boy from the Bay City actually slammed what appeared to be certain UCLA baskets right down the shooters' throat.

And:

"Actually, the mere presence of Mr. Russell seemed to demoralize the Bruins right from the opening tip."

If not right then, then soon after. UCLA had one stretch in the first half of 11 minutes without a field goal and trailed by 20 before Jim Halster's basket cut the deficit to 39-21 at the break. The accomplishment from there was for the Bruins to rally to get as close as 57-48 with about five minutes to play, despite Willie Naulls having four fouls. But USF responded with a quick 6-0 burst to put the game away before things could get real interesting.

Gene Brown, the 6-3 sophomore who replaced Jones, used his dangerous jump shot to lead all scorers with 23 points, while also helping to hold UCLA's Morrie Taft to six-of-23 shooting. In Taft's defense, he was playing with a bad back. He and Naulls both got 16 points.

Game 54

The dyntasy of the present beat the dynasty of the future when the University of San Francisco knocked off UCLA in the first round of the 1956 tournament.

The Bruin 100 Game 55

UCLA 74, Iowa State 73 (Overtime)
March 20, 1997

Steve Lavin reclines in the blue upholstered rocking chair inside his office on the ground floor of the two-story J.D. Morgan Center and gestures with his left hand, to a spot behind the big wooden desk.

To the game ball.

"That ball kind of represents the whole first season," Lavin says.

His first season as coach, the made-for-Disneyland ride that careened from an overtime loss in the opener to the worst loss in school history and then to the recovery, the 12-game winning streak capped this night before 29,231 inside San Antonio's Alamodome.

"The way in which we fought back, which we had done all season," Lavin says, recalling the moment. "When we seemed to be down for the count, we came back."

This was playing the daredevil more than any other time, even more than when they also trailed Oregon and Washington by the same 16 points, because of the implications, a loss meaning the Bruins would be eliminated and not bound for the Elite Eight. Likewise, the two during Pacific 10 Conference play came in March and ended in victory.

"We just never gave up," Charles O'Bannon said that night. "At halftime, we talked about how many times we'd been down this year. And we said we should never give up."

Stepping back out on the ledge, the Bruins were down 46-30 with 16:43 left in regulation. The comeback got them the lead in the final minute, before Dedric Willoughby got Iowa State a tie with a three-pointer with 22 seconds remaining, one of his eight makes from behind the arc that led to 39 points.

Close throughout the five-minute extra period, the game turned in UCLA's favor for good when point guard Cameron Dollar drove the length of the court, then drove right at Iowa State's Kelvin Cato in a very aggressive move. The short bank, a virtual layup, with 1.9 seconds remaining gave Dollar a career-high 20 points and the Bruins a spot in the next round against the region's top-seeded team, Minnesota.

"He doesn't have the greatest physical skills," Lavin said that night. "He couldn't jump over two Ritz crackers. But he's like Jim Plunkett—he has the heart and intelligence of a winner."

"In my mind I was going to go for this," Dollar said, "I saw the big man, but I was going to go at him. If he blocks it, we go home. If we make it, we stay and play. You have to go down swinging when you play this game."

This team, and this player, would know. It was only three games earlier, after all, that Dollar, reviving memories of Tyus Edney's legendary play from the 1995 tournament, got the ball with 4.5 seconds left in the regular-season finale at Washington State and bolted downcourt for a layin with :0.9 showing and an 87-86 victory.

The Bruin 100 Game 56

UCLA 99, Texas 54
December 13, 1969

A legendary coaching career that began thousands of miles away, at Indiana State, reached another benchmark: career victory No. 500 for John Wooden.

Adolph Rupp of Kentucky, Henry Iba of Oklahoma State and Tony Hinkle of Butler were the only active coaches with more wins, though Wooden was in his 24th season, 15 fewer than any of the others. Fittingly, given the Bruins' dominance of the times, it came with ease, the 45-point defeat marking the second-largest in Longhorn history at the time.

"It was just another ballgame, but I'm thankful for every one of those 500 wins," Wooden said, doing his best, as always, to downplay the individual accomplishments. "If anyone had told me that I'd stay in coaching long enough to get that many, I'd have told them they were off their rocker."

It was just another ballgame in one sense, this rout at Pauley Pavilion coming only two nights after the 127-69 thrashing of Miami (Fla.). The Bruins

Coach Wooden is still intense even after 500 wins.

toyed with Texas for about the first 15 minutes, then finished the half with a 12-4 rally that was good for a 42-26 advantage, and followed that up in the first nine minutes after intermission with a 26-7 run to put the game away. The Longhorns were held scoreless for 5:29 of that.

The party broke out right on schedule. The big milestone would come with a big win, so with a couple minutes left the crowd rose for a standing ovation and refused to sit, offering the same stubborness in tribute that Wooden showed in trying to avoid the spotlight.

But he couldn't avoid this. The crowd sat only after he acknowledged the applause, even if that wasn't the same as acknowledging any extra importance to the victory. Just another ballgame, indeed.

The victory came behind 24 points from John Vallely, 20 points and 10 rebounds from Sidney Wicks, and 18 points from Henry Bibby, 16 of which came in what turned out to be the decisive first half. The Bruins were 4-0 on the season, and Wooden was 500-151.

The Bruin 100 Game 57

Penn State 74, UCLA 69
March 18, 1991

Can you hear it? Can you hear the silence?

"We didn't put up," junior guard Gerald Madkins said, "so now we have to shut up."

Not just in what became the season finale, either. Worst of all, as if a first-round upset in the NCAA tournament wasn't enough on its own, the defeat at Syracuse, N.Y. presented lasting evidence that the critics were right to claim the Bruins were an offensive-minded group that showed little interest in defense.

"Those people seem to be very wise now," Madkins said.

Just not very surprised. The Bruins had lost five games during the Pacific 10 schedule alone that came down to the final minute, and here they were again, a club that had lasted three rounds the year before failing to execute at the most critical of moments versus an opponent that likely would not even have made the 64-team field if it hadn't won the Atlantic 10 Conference tournament a week earlier on its home court.

They held only a 44-40 lead, tenuous enough anyway, with 14:45 to play when Don MacLean picked up his fourth foul jostling in the post with Penn State's Dave Degitz and exited. When MacLean returned five minutes later, the Bruins trailed 53-48.

They regained the lead not long after, but then faded badly. Tied at 61 with 4:35 remaining, their next six possessions resulted in two points, four turnovers and a missed three-pointer by Darrick Martin. Penn State, meanwhile, scored nine points and took a 70-63 edge into the final minute.

UCLA's promising draw—opening against Penn State, what would have been a second-round matchup with equally unimposing Eastern Michigan—ended up being worth nothing. The fourth-seeded team in the East Regional now had an especially long trip home, as if there was any other way for the Bruins that had managed only a 10-8 mark over the last two months. Unwelcome perspective for the season-long 23-9 record.

"You never think about something like this, especially with the draw we had," said MacLean, the junior forward who made his first six shots, but not another until only 71 seconds remained.

"I thought the best job was done by Coach [Bruce] Parkhill," Bruins Coach Jim Harrick said of his Penn State counterpart. "I thought he prepared his team tremendously. They played us just perfectly. And, of course, his kids executed."

UCLA's did not. Again.

The Bruin 100 Game 58

UCLA 80, Purdue 67
March 22, 1980

The Bruins had gone from No. 4 in their conference to the Final Four in Indianapolis, to near the top of the college basketball world despite not being ranked in the top 20. Like they were going to hop off the ride at this point.

Help came in that the opponent in their first trip to the semifinals since 1975 was merely 20th in the poll after finishing third in the Big Ten, but the Bruins were through worrying about outside aid during this magical, unlikely journey. They had already knocked off mighty DePaul in the second round, proving their worth at least at the end of the season.

The big concern this time was the big man, 7-foot-1 center Joe Barry Carroll who would get a crack at their Lilliputian front line of 6-5 Mike Sanders, 6-7 James Wilkes and 6-8 Kiki Vandeweghe. And then he was held to 17 points in another great display of team defense, just like in the DePaul game, and UCLA was in the championship game behind 24 points on nine-of-12 shooting from Vandeweghe.

Even more impressively, the young team and their coach making his first Final Four appearance on the sidelines made an emotional stand when the game could have slipped away. The 10-point cushion was all the way down to one with 3:25 remaining, prompting Larry Brown to take a timeout and jump all over his team.

"They were scared to death," he said later. "Just scared to death."

Said Cliff Pruitt, admitting as much: "I can't remember the last time I was scared."

"I don't want to take the credit and say the timeout turned the game around," Brown reasoned. "That would be like me doing this." (He pats himself on the back.) "We weren't attacking. We were being too tentative."

Except that the timeout did turn the game around, or at least turned it back in the Bruins' favor. They held their composure and held on to the win by making 10 of their final 11 free throws, including the last eight, typical for the team that had shot well from the line all season. Vandeweghe, going aggressively at Carroll, iced the game by making four in a row.

"I was trying to take it to him," Vandeweghe said. "I knew if I slowed up and threw up something fancy, he would block it. I think that's the best way to do it when you are facing a shot blocker like Joe Barry. I wanted to get a field goal or get fouled."

The Bruins improved to 22-9 after the night that included ironies and sad contradictions. Vandeweghe played a major role in getting them to the championship

game, then a role in them losing it. Meanwhile, Brown became the first coach since John Wooden to get UCLA back to the Final Four and the final—held in the very same building he would eventually coach Reggie Miller and Pooh Richardson, among others, with the Indiana Pacers.

Kiki Vandeweghe stuck to his plan of taking the ball aggressively at the bigger Purdue players.

Game 58

The Bruin 100 Game 59

UCLA 34, California 32
February 3, 1940

What a strange place for a gutsy, swift young man, this game in Berkeley, California, that was played with such a cautious approach and at such a slow pace that it was 4-4 after about 10 minutes. Things eventually picked up to where the host Bears had built a 21-15 halftime advantage.

The scoring explosion that followed made for a 32-32 tie, and both teams again avoided risks, looking for the perfect opportunity. UCLA got its with a few minutes to go, newspaper accounts of the day tending to be light on things like the time of the winning basket, or even first names, among other details. Typical was the Associated Press dispatch that made a pass at describing the critical elements of the victory, one that included only partial identity of the forward who became the hero:

"Then Robinson broke clear and sank a field goal for the winning points. The Bruins stalled through the final minutes."

Robinson.

Jackie Robinson.

Some seven years before breaking baseball's color barrier, he broke UCLA's 31-game Coast Conference losing streak, scoring 12 points, five more than anyone else, to end a skid that had started with the final two games of 1936-37 and continued through all 12 contests of the next two seasons and then the first five of 1939-40.

In his notes column that ran this day, before the game, Bob Ray observed in *The Sports X-Ray* that the Bruins have "been kicked around so long that they're afraid to stoop over and tie their shoestrings." And, in drawing attention to a recent improvement to Cal, that "it looks as if the Bruins are just destined to keep on losing and losing until further notice." That's how critical Robinson's performance became.

It wasn't just this night, either. UCLA had lost the previous game 39-33, despite a game-high 15 points from Robinson. And two games after snapping the long losing streak, the Bruins won again, versus Stanford in overtime, as Robinson scored 14 points and had the assist on the basket by Harley Humes that proved to be the winning score.

Though better known at UCLA for other sports, Jackie Robinson also starred on the basketball team.

The Bruin 100 Game 60

DePaul 93, UCLA 77
December 27, 1980

Toto, we're not in Japan any more.

In the first game back in the United States after routing Temple in Tokyo, a week earlier according to the calendar but light years in reality, UCLA went to DePaul's new arena, the Horizon, for what was supposed to be a showdown between No. 1 and No. 3 in the nation, only to be smacked back a few time zones. The Blue Demons, affirming their top ranking in overwhelming fashion, went on a 19-3 scoring run about midway through the first half and cruised.

That had only been 9 $1/2$ months in coming for DePaul, still living the tournament defeat at the hands of the Bruins from March. The type of built-up emotions that are sure to produce either a huge victory or an ulcer.

"I was so pumped up that I tried to calm myself down and couldn't," All-America forward Mark Aguirre said.

He finished with 23 points and nine rebounds.

"To see a team that's done us the way they did, I just wanted to destroy them," sophomore center Terry Cummings said.

He contributed 19 points and eight rebounds.

So overwhelming was the defeat for the Bruins, who suffered their first defeat of the season after a 6-0 start,

suffered being the operative word, that they were outscored, 6-0, in one stretch of the opening half without even getting the ball across midcourt. This came just as the party was beginning before 16,702 in suburban Chicago, when Cummings hit two free throws, Bernard Randolph stole the ensuing inbounds pass to set up Dennis Moore's basket, and Aguirre scored again after another UCLA turnover.

It was 47-29 at intermission, and the Bruins, struggling mightily against the zone defense, managed just 38.7% from the field, an especially significant indication of the problems since they came in at 54%. There were others, though, namely foul trouble. A second-half shooting recovery got them up to a respectable 46.4% by the end, which was not to be confused with getting them respect.

"In the second half, no pressure, they shoot beautifully," said DePaul's legendary coach, Ray Meyer.

As if the wounds from the game itself weren't deep enough.

Michael Sanders made just two of 11 attempts and fouled out after 24 minutes. That was the same time Kenny Fields got while playing with four fouls. Darren Daye made it all the way to 28 minutes before getting his fifth.

"I don't think DePaul should be so happy," an obviously frustrated Sanders said. "... I'll give it to them, they played pretty well. But with the officiating on your side, you can't help but play good."

It was hardly shocking that Sanders would be most bothered by the calls that went against him—he was usually the first to admit that he had a tendency of letting referees take him out of games. Plenty of others were willing to be the second to admit it.

"He's a sensitive kid," Coach Larry Brown said. "He was visibly upset by the fouls. When he got his fourth, I looked into his face. He was finished."

That was with 14:06 still left. But, then again, it so happened that all the Bruins were finished.

An emotion-filled Larry Brown patrols the sideline.

Game 60

The Bruin 100 Game 61

UCLA 51, Stanford 45
March 12, 1963

The game the Bruins had to win for later in the week became the game they won for the more-extended future.

Facing Stanford not only for the fourth time this season, but for the fourth time in eight days, they won the playoff game at Santa Monica City College on Tuesday to break the tie in which both teams were 7-5 in the conference and determine the AAWU representative in the NCAA tournament Friday. In the process, they also provided an early look at the Bruin Blitz that just a year later would carry them considerably farther than Provo, Utah, for the West Regional.

Undersized, just the way it would be in winning the national championship in 1964, UCLA had to contend with 6-foot-8 Tom Dose, the Stanford inside presence who had averaged 30 points a game in the three previous meetings against 6-5 Fred Slaughter. Except that this time, John Wooden's defensive adjustment had Slaughter fronting Dose and either forward Jack Hirsch or guard Gail Goodrich collapsing to help when needed.

The strategy worked, with some help from the Indians—Hollis Moore, Clayton Raaka or Bob Sommers, the players usually left alone on the perimeter when the Bruins double-teamed inside, combined for just 11 points.

Raaka made three of seven attempts, and two were on follows. Moore hit a jumper for Stanford's first basket, then missed his six other tries. Sommers went one of four.

"We had the good shots," Indians Coach Howie Dallmar said after his team combined to finish 33.3%. "They left us the outside, but we couldn't hit."

They didn't find much success inside either. Dose scored just 19 points, and Slaughter was positioned so well that he was able to bat away about a half dozen lobs before they could even get to the Cardinal big man. Slaughter also contributed nine points and eight rebounds, while Walt Hazzard scored 19 points and Hirsch 15.

"When I get some help," Slaughter proclaimed, "watch out."

Duly noted. The Bruins—angering many fans when they chose to play at the 2,000-seat "Beach Bungalow" at the junior college near campus instead of the 15,000-seat Sports Arena downtown—had won despite shooting just 36.2% themselves. It capped an amazing turnaround from two weeks earlier, when they were 4-5 in the AAWU and Stanford was 7-3.

Walt Hazzard scored 19 points to help the Bruins beat Stanford in a playoff game at Santa Monica City College to earn a bid to the NCAA tournament.

The Bruin 100 Game 62

Wyoming 78, UCLA 68
March 14, 1987

There was the meltdown, and then there was the meltdown. The one that really cost the Bruins was a terrible second half that resulted in second-round elimination in the NCAA tournament and forever burned the name Fennis Dembo into UCLA lore. The other one merely cost them a few bucks, due to the postgame destruction of some television equipment located in a room next door to the UCLA locker room.

The Bruins, especially Coach Walt Hazzard, would come to believe that the location was a factor, close enough to the Laramie campus and Wyoming in general so that Cowboys fans could pack the Special Events Center. Just not as big a factor as Dembo, the junior forward who made all 16 free throws, seven of 10 three-pointers, nine of 14 shots overall, scored 41 points in one of the greatest offensive performances ever by an opponent and also grabbed nine rebounds. Center Eric Leckner, from just south of Westwood, added 20 points and 14 rebounds.

"Does tradition play any part in the outcome of the game?" Dembo asked afterwards. "I didn't play against no Kareem, no Marques Johnson or no Kiki Vandeweghe."

"Fennis hasn't seen that much room in a long, long time," Wyoming Coach Jim Brandenburg said. "I think maybe I'd have gotten somebody on him a little bit more."

Except that a loose defense was only part of the UCLA problem, especially in the second half. That's when Dembo got 29 of his 41. It came at the same time the Bruins shot a brutal 25.7% and scored 24 points, compared to 40 for Wyoming. Reggie Miller had 24 points, nine rebounds and seven steals, but only two field-goal attempts the final 10:58, an uncharacteristic end to his college career.

It got worse for the Bruins the longer it went. The No. 15 team in the country scored four points in the last 7:58. It missed 12 of the final 13 shots, while Wyoming blew past.

In the end, the UCLA backcourt had outscored its counterparts 27-8. But up front, Dembo and Leckner alone outscored Miller, Jack Haley, Trevor Wilson, Charles Rochelin and Craig Jackson. And other than Miller, no Bruin grabbed more than five rebounds.

"We lost to a physical team," Hazzard said. "They were at home, they had the crowd. We had plenty of opportunities to take the lead we lost, but we missed layups and other shots we normally make."

When UCLA did get brutish, it was in the wrong place and the wrong time, and against a defenseless opponent at that. Someone had kicked and thrown chairs and broke two CBS television monitors in a room adjacent to

the locker room, and a network technician and Utah official both told the *Los Angeles Herald-Examiner* it was the work of Hazzard. To which the author of the story, Bob Keisser, noted: "If so, the Bruins coach was only doing what his team had done on the court moments earlier— lose its poise."

The monitors cost several hundred dollars. The damage from the on-court destruction was far greater.

Walt Hazzard, the Bruin player turned Bruin coach.

Game 62

The Bruin 100 Game 63

UCLA 89, Arizona State 75
March 22, 1975

Illness shadowed him closer than most defenders during the sophomore season of Marques Johnson, who had already shown the capability to be the best forward in the nation—when healthy. That disclaimer, the other thing that always followed.

A bout with hepatitis in the preseason was still doing damage, robbing Johnson of stamina and offering in return the frustration of knowing that he could be a monster, in his words, given the proper endurance. Then came this day, the one that proved, or simply reminded, that the star in the making was just that and not hype. That he had the potential for greatness.

By arrangement with Coach John Wooden, he was allowed to skip practice the day before in Portland, Ore., to rest up to face the Sun Devils. The payoff was that Johnson played 37 of the 40 minutes, and his timing wasn't so bad either. The 35 points—20 in the second half—and 12 rebounds came in the West Regional finals along with 16 points and 12 rebounds from Richard Washington and helped the Bruins earn their 11th trip to the Final Four in the last 12 years.

"Marques just had a great game," Wooden said afterwards. "He was under instructions to let us know when he was ready to come out, and he did so in both halves."

Arizona State Coach Ned Wulk tried to single cover the 6-foot-6 Johnson. Not only that, he tried it with 6-2 Rudy (Lightning) White. Eventually, 6-4 James Holliman, who had said in the Sun Devil media guide that UCLA is his favorite team, took a turn, with similar results.

"Johnson seemed to know just where to be—all the time," Wulk said. "It was just extraordinarily opportunistic play. He must have made half a dozen baskets just by being in the right place at the right time."

It was also extraordinarily inspired play. Former UCLA star Sidney Wicks, who had always been an influence on Johnson's game, even back to grade school as Johnson subconsciously copied some of his moves, stopped by the locker room at halftime. Wicks had the advantage of knowing his way around the Memorial Coliseum, his home arena as a member of the Portland Trail Blazers.

"He shouted obscenities at me—and other forms of encouragement," Johnson said. "That really picked me up."

Bill Walton, likewise a former Bruin standout and current Trail Blazer, visited the team hotel the night before and encouraged Johnson, playing on the talented front line with senior David Meyers and fellow sophomore Washington, not to be afraid to take his shot. Johnson, who obviously wasn't, took 20 of them and made 14, along with seven of eight free throws. The 35 points were 13 more than his previous season high and would come to be topped only by one other performance, the 37 he scored on Feb. 26, 1977.

The Bruin 100 Game 64

USC 86, UCLA 85 (Overtime)
March 3, 1960

Sam Balter, the Bruin star from the late 1920s and member of the 1936 Olympic team that won a gold medal in Berlin, was at this stage of his life a sports columnist in Los Angeles, which was either putting his UCLA education to good use or to waste, depending on your point of view. But he did have the background few could match, that much was certain, so it came with considerable perspective when he wrote the next day of the controversial ending at the beautiful new Sports Arena.

"In 30 years of playing and following this game, I'd never seen it, or heard of it," Balter said in what appeared to be near exclamation. "How can a man interfere with the ball on his own offensive board? It could be called goaltending on the defensive board, but I've never heard of this one."

He wasn't alone. Offensive basket interference was a rare call in these days, and referee Joe Frivaldsky not only made it, but made it with 19 seconds to play in a close game. It cost UCLA the chance to turn a 77-75 lead into what would likely have been a safe four-point advantage and created the opportunity for USC to force overtime when Wells Sloniger hit a 20-footer with six seconds left and for the Trojans to win in the extra period.

The play began when John Berberich got inside and attempted a layup. The ball momentarily bounced on the rim, then got knocked off. A whistle blew.

Offensive goaltending on UCLA's Ron Lawson.

"Lawson touched either the rim or the ball, I'm not sure which, but it was basket interference," Frivaldsky explained. "The other team is awarded the ball."

USC being the other team. The team that now had the chance to tie. Coach Forrest Twogood called timeout and told his players to try and get the ball to star John Rudometkin. But Rudo was, as Jack Disney described in his game report, "being guarded closer than Adolph Eichmann." So it fell to Sloniger, in the game only because Chris Appel had fouled out, to be the hero.

The Trojans led most of the way in overtime. They sealed the victory when Ken Stanley made two free throws with 12 seconds remaining, providing an 86-83 edge and making a basket by UCLA's John Cunningham inconsequential.

The Bruin 100 Game 65

Indiana 106, UCLA 79
March 28, 1992

About that scouting report....

The Bruins had the most reliable of insight on their opponent in the Elite Eight, namely their own 15-point victory against the same team in the season-opener at another neutral site, Springfield, Mass., for the Hall of Fame game. This time, everyone was thousands of miles away, in Albuquerque, N.M., and millions of miles away.

"We got the gap closed a little bit from the first time we played them," Indiana Coach Bob Knight said.

Forty-two points a little bit.

The only significant difference in the Hoosiers between now and then was the addition of junior guard Chris Reynolds, who planned to red-shirt and therefore didn't play in the first game, only to change his mind after talking with Knight on the trip home from Massachusetts. Due respect and all that, but the staggering turnaround wasn't about a complementary piece like Chris Reynolds on a night when Calbert Cheaney scored 23 points and Damon Bailey 22 and Alan Henderson and Eric Anderson out-muscled and intimidated the Bruins inside.

This instead was about a harsh defeat that threatened to make people forget what had come before, the Pacific 10 Conference title and the 28 victories in 32 games. The consideration that the memory of the most wins since 1975-76 would be replaced by the worst postseason loss in school history.

"Once we get away from the defeat, it'll settle in that we had a good year," senior guard Gerald Madkins said. "But before then, we'll be criticized, lambasted because of this game. That's life."

On this night, it was a brief one. Indiana went ahead at 9-8 with six minutes gone and never trailed again, pushing that to 27-13 about seven minutes later and then 44-29 at the break. UCLA scored on six consecutive possessions early in the second half to cut the lead to 12 and show signs of a pulse, but the Hoosiers quickly regained the momentum and an 18-point cushion, en route to shooting 72% after halftime and 57.7% in all.

Madkins had closed his college career with 18 points, but Don MacLean, the leading scorer in UCLA history, went out on a down note, just 12 points while missing nine of 13 shots. Tracy Murray, who would return, had 15 points.

"I was tired from the start," MacLean said. "I couldn't figure it out. I don't know how you can be so mentally ready and want it so badly and come out so flat."

The Bruin 100 Game 66

UCLA 94, Oregon 78
March 11, 1995

"The other day, George [Zidek] asked me about it," Ed O'Bannon said of the moment. "He was like, 'Are you going to be sad, this is the last home game?' I said, 'Naw, I'm pretty excited. I'm happy. I'm glad that I get a chance to get to the final home game.' "

Because it wasn't always a certainty he'd make it. But then O'Bannon battled back from what could have been a career-threatening knee injury, one that required major surgery and about a season and a half away from action, all the way back to where he would soon be named player of the year by many, impress everyone with his maturity and class as well as his talent, and lead the Bruins to the national championship.

So even though this was also the final home game for two other senior starters who would likewise play prominent roles in the tournament ahead, center Zidek and guard Tyus Edney, it became an especially emotional moment for O'Bannon. His family came to Pauley Pavilion to take part in the festivities—including, of course, younger brother Charles, who scored a game-high 25 points and also grabbed 11 rebounds. Coach Jim Harrick also did his part, setting up his star forward for the crescendo.

With 4:48 to play and the game in hand, omm'A Givens was sent in for O'Bannon. The crowd—13,037, a record

at the time—roared. Ed bowed to the student section. He bent down to kiss center court. Coming off the floor, he made it a point to give trainer Tony Spino a long embrace in recognition of all the help during the rehabilitation from the knee injury.

"I didn't plan it, but I'm glad I did it," O'Bannon said of the kiss. "There was so much emotion out there tonight. At that moment it hit me this was my last game in Pauley, that five years were coming to a close and it seemed like the right thing to do."

"I remember it was against Oregon four years ago when Ed played his first game after the injury," Harrick recalled afterwards. "To see it culminate like this, I'll tell you, is a thrill."

It didn't hurt that the moment was accompanied by a performance typical of O'Bannon's season: 24 points and 10 rebounds. Edney, meanwhile, got 22 points and eight assists as the top-ranked Bruins avenged the loss at Oregon that opened the Pacific 10 Conference season. It became a fitting farewell, just not the end. There was still a tournament ahead.

The Bruin 100 Game 67

Washington 95, UCLA 94
March 1, 1998

There was no hint that the day would turn out with Toby Bailey being mentioned in the same breath as Lew Alcindor. Three shots before intermission in Seattle, zero makes.

Then came the rest of the game, or the entire game for Bailey. Seventeen shots, 13 makes, including three of four on three-pointers, for 32 points, tying Alcindor for the most in a half in school history. It was also a career high for the senior swingman.

"I let my team down in the first half and I wanted to redeem myself," Bailey said afterwards. "I was hitting shots and my teammates saw that I was hot, so they kept getting me the ball."

Said one of them, Kris Johnson: "Toby scored 32 in the second half? Thirty-two? That's crazy!"

Not far behind that was the Bruins arriving as the 18th-ranked team in the country at 21-6 to play a team just fighting for a tournament invitation getting buried in the first half. Washington had a 46-30 cushion at intermission, then held on for the victory that would help earn a bid.

The Huskies had to hold on so much, the entire lead was gone when Johnson's three-pointer put UCLA ahead 94-93 with 13 seconds left. After nearly turning the ball over on the ensuing possession, they instead got a break when J.R. Henderson was called for a dead-ball foul on Todd MacCulloch when Washington prepared for another in-bounds play.

Not wasting the gift, MacCulloch hit two free throws with 2.1 seconds remaining. The Huskies had held on. The Bruins had wasted a 64-point explosion in the second half and the greatest half by a UCLA player in 32 years, not to mention Henderson getting 16 of his 20 points in the same span.

"It shows we have the heart to fight back," Bailey said. "I'm proud of our team for that. But it still hurts. It doesn't seem like we're supposed to lose these kind of games, when we're fighting back so hard."

At least Bailey held on to the scoring touch. In a season in which he would average 17.9 points overall, he went on to get 22, 22 and 21 the next three outings, while adding eight, nine and 11 rebounds at the same time.

The Bruin 100 Game 68

UCLA 19, USC 17
January 23, 1932

Braven Dyer, one of the journalists who attended the game at Olympic Auditorium when a sculptor could have offered a much more accurate depiction, explained in the *Los Angeles Times* that "It isn't for this writer to decide which team was at fault. S.C. was ahead and had the ball. The Bruins apparently didn't want it, so that's the way matters stood."

And stood. And stood. And stood.

For 15 minutes in the first half, USC guard Julie Bescos held the ball, virtually motionless. It was a filibuster. Most of the Bruins gathered under the basket, at least better able to converse that way in an attempt to pass the time, though others had their own methods.

The crowd, about 5,000 strong, sang songs, cheered and booed in protest and support of their side. They threw pennies, peanuts and paper on the court.

One such object was a newspaper. UCLA guard Jimmy Soest, according to one account, started reading it and then offered a section to Jerry Nemer of the Trojans. Nemer scanned the pages for a moment, then put it down.

The UCLA band at one point played a funeral dirge.

USC had protected its 5-2 lead all the way to halftime. The pace picked up from there, without any explanation the next day as to why the Trojans would change their game plan so dramatically, especially since UCLA came back from what could have been an insurmountable three-point deficit to win on Bud Rose's basket in the final minute.

"Whether basketball will retain its popularity here with such games remain to be seen," Dyer wrote.

The Bruin 100 Game 69

DePaul 95, UCLA 91
March 17, 1979

The Blue Demons already had a 51-34 lead, so it's not like the game turned at halftime. The crowd did, though, against the Bruins so much because of the strange developments during intermission of the West Regional final in Provo, Utah, that it may have hindered the comeback that ultimately fell just short.

Most unusual of all, it had as much to do with the UCLA band as the UCLA team. So when the comeback started in the second half, fans rallied behind Chicago's Blue Demons, no matter whatever geographical loyalties may originally have rested with the Bruins, all because of a dance routine.

The DePaul folk dance team had such notoriety that the coach of the DePaul basketball team, having already lost to UCLA by 23 points in the second game of the regular season, joked that the Blue Demons' only advantage would come at halftime. Little did Ray Meyer know.

About halfway through the routine, the Bruins returned to the court to prepare for the second half. The UCLA band rose to greet them with the fight song, drowning out the music for the folk dancers even as some members of the band refused to join in, feeling it was rude to play over the DePaul arrangement.

The crowd booed UCLA, at least the ones not there to support the Bruins. The atmosphere had changed on the spot.

"It was like somebody lifted the roof off at halftime, a blimp landed and brought in all new fans," DePaul's Gary Garland said.

"We came out and thought it was a different game," Meyer added. "The way they were yelling, they certainly pumped some adrenaline into the kids."

Which became especially important as the Bruins mounted their major push, cutting a 63-46 deficit with about 15 minutes left all the way down to 93-91 with just 39 seconds remaining. But they did not score again, losing despite 37 points and 10 rebounds from David Greenwood and 16 points and 10 assists from Roy Hamilton. Both scoring numbers marked career bests.

"We've been noted as a second-half ball club all season," Greenwood said after his outstanding career that included two consensus All-America selections ended in disappointment. "Our trademark has been trying to stay close the first half and put them away in the second. But we just got too far behind."

Clearly, these were not the same Blue Demons who got blown out months earlier, not during the transition time that came with the departure of Dave Corzine to the NBA as a first-round pick and the arrival of a promising newcomer named Mark Aguirre. Besides, that game had been played at Pauley Pavilion, eliminating the support homecourt advantage could provide somewhere else. Provo, Utah, for instance.

The Bruin 100 Game 70

UCLA 102, Connecticut 96
March 25, 1995

The Bruins were clearly headed in the right direction, literally and figuratively. North, from Los Angeles to Oakland for the West regional final and hoping to continue up the coastline some more, to Seattle and the Final Four.

"The weight is there," Ed O'Bannon said beforehand, acknowledging the pressure. "We're going to try and deal with it as best as possible."

"That's one thing I want to accomplish," said another senior standout, Tyus Edney. "That's one thing I've always wanted to do, make it to the Final Four."

Edney made it, all right. He largely made it possible, joining with freshmen Toby Bailey and J.R. Henderson in the track meet against another team with impressive athleticism to push the Bruins to the semifinals for the first time in 15 years.

It was the recent past and the immediate future in a capsule. Bailey had 26 points and nine rebounds, two games before starring in the championship-game win over Arkansas. And two games after his historic end-to-end run against Missouri got the Bruins to

Oakland, Edney offered an abbreviated version versus Connecticut, making a dash after getting the ball with 3.6 seconds left that culminated with a pull-up basket. It gave UCLA a 48-41 lead, it gave UCLA the momentum.

Enter the freshmen. Henderson, who contributed 18 points off the bench while making nine of 12 shots, and Bailey had key baskets in the 13-6 run that provided the insurmountable 82-68 advantage with 8:27 remaining. Edney finished with 22 points and 10 assists.

UConn had scored 55 points in the second half and still lost. The 36 points and nine rebounds from Ray Allen, the talented small forward Bruins Coach Jim Harrick would later call the best player UCLA faced, went to waste. The Huskies were going home.

The Bruins were going to the Final Four.

"It's kind of overwhelming at the moment," O'Bannon said. "It's the best view I've ever had. I've been here five years, and it's been up-and-down for me. I'm happy we got a chance for all of us to cut down the nets and go up the ladder."

And up that coastline.

Ed O'Bannon went from a knee injury that could have ruined his career to the top of the college basketball world.

The Bruin 100 Game 71

Duke 120, UCLA 84
February 22, 1998

"At least we didn't just lay down and get blown out by 50," senior J.R. Henderson said.

So much for the good news.

Not to be lost among such positives is that Duke scored more points against UCLA than any team ever, bettering (worsening?) the 116 Stanford hit the Bruins for in double-overtime on Dec. 23, 1987 and the 112 Tulsa got in regulation on March 18, 1994. In terms of margin of defeat, it was the fifth-worst loss.

Of even greater concern to the Bruins, with the tournament starting in just three weeks, is that it made them 1-5 against teams in the top 15, following a pair of losses to Stanford and one each to North Carolina and Arizona. The only victory came against New Mexico.

The two Tobacco Road teams had done the most damage, North Carolina winning by 41 points in the season opener at the Great Alaska Shootout and now Duke by 36 in Durham, N.C. But the latter may have been worse, despite the numbers, because the Tar Heel debacle came in what was the first game for UCLA and the fourth for North Carolina and while both Jelani McCoy and Kris Johnson were serving suspensions.

At least Johnson was back for this game. Sort of. He missed 10 of 15 shots. This came as Henderson was limited to just 18 minutes after picking up three quick fouls, then his fourth with 18:20 remaining in what passed for a game. But he stayed in after that and proceeded to score or assist on the next seven UCLA baskets.

The absence of McCoy and semi-absence of Henderson forced the Bruins to send all able bodies diving to the interior and hope Duke wouldn't beat them from the perimeter. The Blue Devils did. They hit 15 of 28 three-pointers, with Trajan Langdon going six of 10 from behind the arc and 11 of 16 overall en route to a game-high 34 points.

The battle between No. 2 and No. 12 showed far greater distance between the teams. It also marked, probably in black and blue, the conclusion of the UCLA-Duke series after they had met in six of the last seven seasons. An end that obviously came a year too late for the Bruins.

The Bruin 100 Game 72

UCLA 121, Washington State 77
January 4, 1964

The Bruins went to a basketball game and King of the Hill broke out. By the end of the night, they were, destined for the spot as the top-ranked team in the nation for the first time in school history when they cruised to victory at Pullman, Wash., on the same night No. 1 Kentucky lost to Georgia Tech.

"There's no denying it, we like being No. 1," Coach John Wooden said of the move in to what would practically become a permanent home. "It would be wrong to say we didn't like it, and we hope we warrant it.

"But you don't stay on top on what you did last week. As Kentucky found out, you are no better than your next game."

Wooden told his players at halftime that Kentucky had lost, but it was hardly a motivational ploy. The Bruins were already ahead 61-28 at that stage, on the strength of hot shooting and a full-court press that at one stage created five consecutive turnovers without Washington State being able to so much as get the ball past midcourt, each of which became UCLA baskets.

Things didn't get much better for the Cougars after that. The 121 points they allowed also became the most UCLA had ever scored, blowing past the 113, established a few weeks earlier against BYU, even as substitutes played the final 6 $^1/_2$ minutes. Only that limited Gail Goodrich to 21 points and Walt Hazzard to 17, though there was nothing to stop all the Bruins from shooting a combined 59.8%.

They were 11-0. Two days later, they were No. 1.

The big jump had actually come the week before, when the Bruins moved from fourth in the *Associated Press* balloting and fifth by *United Press International* to second in both on the strength of winning the Los Angeles Basketball Classic, most notable being the victory over highly regarded Michigan. Then, when they won and Kentucky lost on this same Saturday, the next move was apparent.

It became official on Monday, getting 31 of a possible 51 first-place votes from the *Associated Press* and 25 of 35 in the *United Press International*. Kentucky, Loyola of Chicago and Michigan followed in that order in both rankings.

High-scoring guard Gail Goodrich drives to the basket, just part of his offensive arsenal.

Game 72

The Bruin 100 Game 73

Cincinnati 72, UCLA 70
March 23, 1962

It was a strange combination after the game in Louisville, Ky., that mixture of disappointment and pride.

The first trip to a Final Four in school history had led to a heartbreaking defeat when Cincinnati's Tom Thacker hit the winning shot with three seconds left to deny the upset bid, but there was UCLA Coach John Wooden after the game, down but literally unable to contain his satisfaction.

"I've never been more proud of any team that won than I am right now," he said.

Tears appeared in Wooden's eyes as he spoke.

"It wasn't quite enough, I guess. Those kinds take the heart out of you."

Cincinnati, the No. 2 team in the country, advanced to face Ohio State in the finals in what amounted to a backyard rumble and a replay of the 1961 title game, but only after surviving against UCLA, unranked all season and big underdogs on this night. A close game might have been enough of a moral victory for the Bruins, untested in such settings, but they got much more.

Two free throws by John Green with 2:27 left earned UCLA a 70-70 tie. The teams then traded turns committing offensive fouls, first by Cincinnati star Paul Hogue and then the Bruins' Walt Hazzard despite his protests to the contrary. The latter gave the Bearcats the ball back with 1:34 remaining.

As expected, they held for the last shot, draining most all the time before calling timeout with just :10 showing to set up for the final push. Cincinnati had control and had options. Hogue, en route to 36 points and 19 rebounds while making 12 of 18 attempts. Ron Bonham, the best shooter. Wooden figured one of them would get the call, and Bearcats Coach Ed Jucker knew this.

So he went to Thacker.

The same Thacker who had missed all six of his shots so far.

"In fact," Wooden said afterwards, "we'd give Thacker that shot again under similar circumstances."

The junior guard took the pass from Tom Sizer when play resumed after the timeout. Thacker dribbled to his right, stopped 25 feet from the basket and launched. Swish.

UCLA had only time for a desperation shot, and Hazzard's length-of-the-court toss was knocked away before it got close. The Bruins got 27 points from Green and 19 from Gary Cunningham, but had to settle for coming close.

"UCLA is a terrific ballclub," Jucker said. "They were a vastly underrated team—but not by us."

Within two years, not by anybody.

The Bruin 100 Game 74

UCLA 82, Kentucky 81
December 3, 1994

How fitting that the inaugural Wooden Classic, held at the Arrowhead Pond of Anaheim, would offer the first indication of the ingredients that would carry the Bruins to an eventual national title and revive memories of Wooden's past classics.

They came 18,307 strong to the new invitational in the new arena about an hour south of UCLA to see four of the top seven teams in the country at the time—the Bruins at No. 5 coming into the early season showdown with No. 3 Kentucky, along with No. 1 Massachusetts and No. 7 Kansas—and instead saw the future on display. The UCLA freshman who would make a major contribution to the very end. Ed O'Bannon offering such an inspired performance that even fans of the opposition Wildcats were commenting in the stands about his play. Solid supporting contributions.

In other words, everything that came into play for the championship run that would eventually follow.

The Bruins trailed by 10 points four different times in the final 11 minutes of the first meeting between two of the most storied programs in the nation since 1975, ironically the final game of John Wooden's coaching career. They were down by as many as eight with 4:18 remaining before the final charge, the 13-4 run that produced a victory and a prideful 2-0 opening to the season with

help from the 16 points and 10 rebounds by George Zidek.

It came down to the last play, a drive-and-dish by Tyus Edney. He looked for O'Bannon for the deciding basket, as if O'Bannon hadn't already carried the Bruins enough, what with the 26 points and leadership that included prodding, encouraging, shouting and cajoling teammates. But Edney found J.R. Henderson instead.

Henderson was in position to dunk, but got fouled by Walter McCarty before he had the opportunity rather to get an uncontested shot. So Henderson—a freshman—went to the line with the outcome in his hands and 0.6 seconds remaining. In the second game of his college career. Before a packed arena and a national-television audience.

Already six of six on free throws that day, he made the first. Henderson, normally laid back, gave a quick pump of his fist.

"That's about as excited as I'll ever get," he said. "Then we went to the bench [after Kentucky called timeout] and I saw in my mind the second one go through. When that happened, I knew I'd make it, too."

And when that happened, when he made the second one, the Bruins had an emotional win. That and an indication of what was to come.

The Bruin 100 Game 75

UCLA 72, Oregon State 71
January 10, 1970

Only a few contests earlier, coaches had picked John Ecker, a slim, seldom-used junior forward, as one of the players to be made available to the media for postgame interviews. But he had played so little and done so little that night that no one could think of anything to ask. He returned to the locker room, appearing embarrassed.

To be sure, Ecker's UCLA career was rarely tracked by spotlight. He ended up taking 80 shots all season, making half. He never scored more than 12 points that campaign, and averaged 3.5 overall. He was known as steady and reliable and unspectacular, usually getting his minutes in blowouts.

And then there was the day steady and reliable and unspectacular saved the Bruins.

UCLA had already dodged serious upset threats from Minnesota, by one point in overtime, and Princeton, by one point in regulation, and this was just the 10th game of the season. But the winning baskets those times came from Henry Bibby and Sidney Wicks, respectively, a pair of standouts. Ecker was the improbable hero of the season that ended 28-2.

He was in the game at Pauley Pavilion only because Wicks had fouled out with 16 seconds remaining, on a rare double-foul with Oregon State's Jeff Haller, and the Beavers holding a 71-70 lead. Coach John Wooden, knowing he had a jump ball coming next with what could be the final possession, wanted size on the court, so he summoned the 6-foot-6 1/2 Ecker.

Ecker had an immediate impact, controlling the tip against Haller. The Bruins' winning streak still had life. A few seconds later, the ball went in to Steve Patterson. He passed to Ecker, who wheeled around Haller for a six-foot driving hook.

"We hadn't planned specifically for John to take the shot," Wooden said afterwards, "but that was one of the options in the offense we were running."

It was Ecker's only shot of the game—and the only chance he needed. When it banked in with six seconds remaining, the Bruins had a 72-71 victory, a 10-0 record despite shooting 41.3 percent and another one-point win. Oh, and a spectacular Ecker.

The Bruin 100 Game 76

Maybe this was a hint? The Bruins won for the 77th time in a row, and for the second time in the young season, but they may also have been put on notice by this game at Pauley Pavilion that moved Coach John Wooden to use such phrases as "We got a lesson without losing" and "They played well, we played sporadically."

Twelve games later, the winning streak was history, to be followed soon after by the Lost Weekend, to be followed soon after by the loss to North Carolina State in the NCAA semifinals that brought great pain as well as tournament elimination. All of which came after the Saturday night contest as the Bruins escaped with the tightest victory to date for the Walton Gang, no one having previously come closer than the five points by Florida State in the 1972 title game. It was also only the second in what would become the 88-game run that UCLA had a one-point win, the other time at Oregon in January of 1971, before the arrival of a certain redheaded center.

Maryland arrived for the East-West clash with size (Tom McMillen and Len Elmore) and an exciting young point guard (sophomore John Lucas), then moved into position for victory. The Terrapins followed the instructions of Coach Lefty Driesell and fouled Richard Washington, a freshman who had just entered the game when Keith

Wilkes fouled out. As if according to the plan, Washington missed the free throw.

Maryland got the rebound, called timeout, and then put the ball back in play with the intention of getting it to McMillen. Lucas dribbled to the right corner. Seconds were disappearing. When the clock was down to just a few, UCLA's David Meyers, called Spider because of his long arms, reached out and knocked the ball away from Lucas.

Had it gone out of bounds, the Terrapins would have had another chance, albeit a hurried one. But Meyers had enough control while falling out of bounds to tip the ball to teammate Tommy Curtis. Curtis sprinted away as time expired. "What a horrible way to end it," McMillen said.

Said Lucas, claiming foul: "I was going up for a shot. Someone just pushed me from the front—I guess Meyers—and then someone came up from behind. When I looked up, the ball was going down court."

UCLA had held on despite shooting a miserable 33.8%, with Bill Walton going eight of 23, Wilkes four of 17 and Curtis five for 17. But Walton still scored 18 points and had 27 rebounds to set a personal best, to be duplicated about seven weeks later against Loyola of Chicago. He got 20 of the 27 against the Terrapins in one half, establishing a Pauley Pavilion record.

"I don't feel bad," Driesell said. "I'll tell you that now. I think my boys know now they can play with any team in the country. Anytime your team plays well against the greatest team in college basketball history, you've got to be proud."

Greatest for the moment, at least.

The defense of David Meyers, here guarding Len Elmore, was in key in UCLA's victory over Maryland.

The Bruin 100 Game 77

UCLA 85, Drake 82
March 20, 1969

In the other semifinal, the first game of the double-header in Louisville, Ky., Purdue fans, with little to worry about in the way of an actual contest as their Boilermakers all but lapped North Carolina, broke into chant.

"We want Lew! We want Lew! We want Lew!"

Created from desire and an assumption, the cries by the boosters were nearly replaced by tears from the Bruins when the No. 1 team in the country, the two-time defending national champions, the 13-point favorites, found themselves on the verge of a shocker that would have ended Lew Alcindor's college career with an unlikely upset despite his 25 points and 18 rebounds. It was survival, and the chance for Purdue rooters to come to regret their request.

As if almost getting beat wasn't bad enough, UCLA almost got beat at its own game, not some gimmick defense or stall but a full-court press

Guard John Vallely had a career-high 29 points in the victory over Drake in the 1969 semifinals.

that forced 20 turnovers. Hell, UCLA almost got beat by its forefathers, a small Drake team that couldn't help but remind observers of the sawed-off group of players who used the Bruin Blitz five years earlier to deliver John Wooden's first championship.

The Bulldogs, a fitting name to be sure, regularly beat the vaunted Bruins down court. Drake's press created so many problems for the UCLA guards that Curtis Rowe was forced to bring the ball up, and Alcindor had to move away from the basket, to the high post, so teammates would have an easier time getting him in the offense.

Making matters worse, if that's possible, UCLA nearly blew what should have been an insurmountable lead, seven points with 29 seconds remaining, with a trip to the title game on the line. Even many inside Freedom Hall headed to the exits as the second game of the double-header seemed finished.

But then Willie McCarter hit two free throws, part of his 24 points.

When he followed that by intercepting an attempted inbounds pass by Sidney Wicks and hit a quick jumper, the deficit was just 83-80. Six seconds had expired. And still the Bruins continued to crumble, this time with Terry Schofield getting fouled only to miss the front end of the one-and-one. Drake jumped on that chance, too, when 6-foot-4 Dolph Pulliam put in McCarter's missed 20-footer with seven seconds left.

The Bulldogs had the momentum and were only down by a point. They just didn't have much time. Forced to foul, they saw the game disappear for good when Lynn Shackelford made two free throws with no time showing. The line had also been kind to junior John Vallely, who went 11 of 14 there en route to his career-high 29 points.

"I feel like I've just had a reprieve," Wooden said. "If John Vallely had not shot so well, we probably would have lost."

Lew Alcindor rose above the crowd as always, but UCLA still struggled past Drake in the 1969 semifinals.

The Bruin 100

The Bruin 100 Game 78

Illinois 110, UCLA 83
December 4, 1964

From 30-0 to 0-1.

The team that the previous season had won the national championship with an undefeated run—and the team that would win it again this season, though with blemishes—received an immediate reality check at the start of 1964-65. Just in case there were any ideas about being invincible.

That it would come from Illinois, and, more specifically, at Illinois, was hardly a surprise. The Illini had, after all, played UCLA tough about a year earlier before falling, 83-79, in the finals of the Los Angeles Basketball Classic and, as a veteran team, returned most every player, and their memories. And then there was history—the University of San Francisco also had its 60-game winning streak, a national record at the time, snapped in dominating fashion at Assembly Hall on Dec. 17, 1956.

Maybe it was a California thing with the Illini. UCLA was only halfway to the Dons' mark of 60 in a row, but still arrived looking imposing in its own way, having been picked about a week earlier as the No. 2 team in the country in the United Press International. Michigan was No. 1, setting the stage early for the championship game three months later that would decide the top club.

But the Bruins barely made it out of Champaign in one piece, let alone to Portland, Ore., in March. Illinois shot 60.5% (46 of 76) for a school record, while the visitors managed 40% in the season opener for both schools. Illinois scored 110 points to set an Assembly Hall record, Skip Thoren getting a team-high 20 and Bill McKeown adding 19 to lead six players in double figures.

It was also the most points UCLA had ever allowed, strange considering it came in a season filled with so much success. Gail Goodrich scored 25 points and Freddie Goss 18, but the defense had let the Bruins down so much that the closest they could come after falling behind 52-38 at intermission was 11 midway through the second half.

"The press just didn't work," Coach John Wooden said of his club's normally reliable approach. "I know it's a gambling defense. Any team that shoots well will kill the press. I could have taken it off to keep the score down once Illinois started hitting from the outside.

"But I wanted to correct our weakness. I wanted our boys to find where they were making their mistakes, so later on in the season they'll be able to use it more efficiently."

Later on in the season, they did. The Bruins responded to this debacle by winning 28 of their last 29 games, the lone loss the rest of the way coming, coincidentally, also in the state of Illinois, otherwise known as their state of disappointment. That was against Iowa on Jan. 29 in a neutral-site contest at Chicago Stadium.

The Bruin 100 Game 79

UCLA 73, Maryland 63
December 9, 1995

Jelani McCoy recorded a triple-double against Maryland the hard way—with blocks.

Back when the might-have-been actually was, back when they spoke more of Jelani McCoy's potential to become a dominating defensive force inside and not his potential for self-destruction, the day belonged to the sultan of swat.

Maryland's Duane Simpkins was the scoring leader with 21 points and Charles O'Bannon of UCLA was solid at 17 points and 10 rebounds, but McCoy was historic. He threw a block party, the Terrapins both invited guests in Anaheim, Calif., for the Wooden Classic and victims, as the 18-year-old freshman center/forward had a triple double the hard way, with 11 rejections to also set a conference record in the process.

The 15 points and 10 rebounds that went along with it made for the first recorded triple-double in Bruins' history, the asterisk being that blocks were not regularly charted even as recently as the Bill Walton era, let alone the years before that with Lew Alcindor. But McCoy was impressive no matter the specific distinction, not merely surpassing the previous conference standard for blocks but trashing it, dropping David Greenwood, Rodney Zimmerman and Mario Bennett and their eight rejections to a distant second in the rankings.

Eight blocks? McCoy had that many in the second half alone.

"I said this earlier in the week and it's true," Coach Jim Harrick said. "It's been a long time since West Coast college basketball has seen a shot blocker like Jelani."

"After a while," McCoy said, "my timing gets down. I'm going to go after every shot I think I can get and let the refs make the call."

Contesting everything close, he still had just two fouls. The added significance of that is that it came after he'd had four personals, one away from disqualification, in two of the previous five games while the Bruins opened defense of their NCAA championship with a 2-3 mark.

Evening their record while McCoy got his, the Bruins took a commanding 36-23 lead into the break. They stretched that to 44-25 in the second half and then held on after Maryland cut the deficit to 47-42, the Terrapins ultimately doing as much damage to their chances as McCoy by shooting a dismal 24.7%.

Nine days later, Toby Bailey joined McCoy in the triple-double club, getting his with points, rebounds and assists versus Stephen F. Austin. By the end of the year, McCoy had set UCLA marks for the most blocks and the highest shooting percentage in a season, the latter of which he topped again in 1996-97. The flameout came soon after, a suspension for "violation of department policies and team rules" and ultimately a departure from the program during his junior season.

The Bruin 100 Game 80

UCLA 104, California 88
February 23, 1995

Hoping to make its season with a shocking upset of the second-ranked team in the nation, Cal, just 4-8 in conference play coming in, cut the deficit to 64-57 with 13:50 remaining, so Ed O'Bannon answered.

Three-pointer from the left corner.

Three-pointer from the top.

Three-pointer from the left wing.

What may have been the greatest day of what was definitely the greatest season of his career included seven makes from behind the arc, in nine tries, to tie Reggie Miller's school record. O'Bannon had received another major boost in what would become a successful run to being named the national Player of The Year, but this was not to be confused with another game.

"I've never shot the ball like that," he said. "I never had the confidence. It was easy for me because I was getting great picks. All I had to do was catch and shoot."

It was the three-point accuracy that set this game in Berkely, Calif., apart from so many that could stand out during O'Bannon's senior season, even from the several that had just come before. It had, after all, come as the end of a string in which he scored 22 points against Arizona State, a career-high 31 versus Arizona and, two days earlier, 22 at Stanford. UCLA won each, improving to 20-2 in the process.

"He was in a zone," teammate Tyus Edney said of the performance against the Bears.

It was, if nothing else, the weekend in the Bay Area that pushed the Bruins to the top spot in the country, coming as it did the same time as No. 1 Kansas lost.

That wasn't the only motivation, though. About a month earlier, Cal had not merely won in Los Angeles, but did so for the third consecutive visit to Pauley Pavilion, what turned out to be the second and last defeat of the Bruin season. Moreover, there seemed to be some bad blood between the teams because the Bears were angered in January with the belief that UCLA players had purposely walked across the court the day before the game to disrupt their practice.

"We feel we owe them a little something," O'Bannon said before the rematch. "It's no secret. They know it."

By the time they faced off again in Harmon Gym, everyone knew it. The Bruins responded with the 16-point victory, helped most obviously when O'Bannon started hitting threes, strange for the guy who only averaged about two attempts per game during his college career. So who was going to tell him those weren't his shots?

134

The Bruin 100

Ed O'Bannon.

The Bruin 100 Game 81

UCLA 73, Duke 69
February 23, 1997

They packed Pauley Pavilion 13,478 strong, the greatest turnout ever for a UCLA home game, generating noise and compliments. As in, it didn't even seem like a UCLA home game.

"My ears actually hurt," Bruins forward J.R. Henderson said. "They usually hurt at other places, but today they were hurting. We had to get close to each other just to hear what we were saying."

Said Chris Roberts, the radio play-by-play man who, in a switch, wore headphones on both ears: "Usually, I keep one off to hear the crowd, but this time they were just too much."

Maybe it was something about the week, right as the Bruins were building momentum for what would become a successful tournament run. Four days earlier, 13,382 came to Pauley for USC and broke the record that had stood for about two years, and then that one lasted only until the next game.

Duke was obviously a lure, but the Blue Devils had been coming through about every other year in a home-and-home series, so it couldn't have been the novelty. And then was No. 6 Duke against No. 17 UCLA, not some mega-showdown. Yet there they all were. One student camped out for tickets at 7 a.m. on Thursday for a Sunday 11 a.m. tipoff.

The fans came. They brought along the power of healing.

Junior Kris Johnson had a very sore ankle that was "killing" him first thing Sunday morning. Then came late morning. "I guess the adrenaline must have jumped right into it, because most of the time I didn't feel a thing," he said. "I just looked over into our crowd and saw all those painted faces and heard them screaming and I'm thinking, 'This looks like a program. Like Duke or Kansas.' "

Johnson gutted out 14 points and eight rebounds, a solid contribution off the bench that went along with 18 points from Henderson, 11 points and 11 rebounds from Jelani McCoy and defensive work from Toby Bailey that helped limit Trajan Langdon to 11 points and three baskets on 14 shots. Henderson had complained about the early start, insisting he wouldn't be ready for the first half, then proved accurate, getting 16 of his points and six of his seven rebounds after intermission.

That was, of course, when the Bruins needed him most because Duke had a 69-67 lead with 2:01 remaining. But the Blue Devils didn't score again, coming up empty on four consecutive possessions and missing a desperation shot on the fifth.

The Bruin 100 Game 82

UCLA 112, Indiana State 76
December 5, 1964

UCLA had already set up a game at Illinois, the season opener, so friends at Indiana State asked John Wooden, the former coach there, to add the Sycamores to the schedule, seeing as the Bruins were going to be in the neighborhood.

"You ought to help people out," Wooden says.

Just maybe not this much.

Wooden made Indiana State part of the trip to the Midwest and the second game of the season Wooden got an easy win. And Wooden hated it.

"Let me put it this way," he says now. "When I speak at coaching clinics, one thing I always say is never play against your alma mater, never play where they're dedicating a new gym, never play when you're coaching against a dear friend or relative. And I did all of those."

He was matched against his brother when both coached high school teams. This game took care of the other two categories, sort of. There was a gym dedication that night in Terre Haute, but he attended another Indiana school, Purdue.

It was close enough, though, because Wooden still had family and friends in the area, and among the 3,750 in attendance. So there was a strong emotional pull anyway as he returned to face the team he had coached the two seasons immediately before accepting the UCLA job, the program he had directed to a 47-14 mark in that time.

Wooden was honored before the game, just before the Bruins charged to a 63-39 halftime lead and put some distance between themselves and the memory of the shocking 110-83 loss the night before at Illinois. Gail Goodrich scored 22 points in the first 15 minutes and 29 in all.

John Wooden, a true Hoosier, played at Purdue and coached at Indiana State, so his return to play the Sycamores was a difficult moment.

The Bruin 100 Game 83

UCLA 106, New Mexico 41
December 22, 1954

The first time the Bruins won by 65 points to set a school record for largest margin of victory was Dec. 20, 1946, against a police club team, when the story in the paper the next day began, "Getting even for any traffic tickets they may have received in the past, the U.C.L.A. Bruins poured it on the Los Angeles Police Department five in the Westwood gym last night and took a lopsided 83-to-18 triumph."

So the alleged game against New Mexico merely tied the mark, but it was especially noteworthy nonetheless. For one thing, it came against another college. For another— and what still sets this one apart even after the Bruins again matched the 65-point difference against Portland on Jan. 20, 1967, at Pauley Pavilion—is that they played New Mexico with an experiment. A yellow ball, manufactured by Voit.

"The ball is expected to be widely used because its brightness makes it easy to follow," Jack Geyer reported in the *Los Angeles Times*.

Which meant that only one part of the game ended up meeting expectations. The Bruins routed the team that had just lost to USC, 103-39, at Pan-Pacific Auditorium and set a school record in the process for most points in a game, in addition to tying the mark for the largest margin of victory. One New Mexico player had 12 points, but no teammate could manage more than six.

This came at the same time as forward John Moore scored 14 to push his career total to 904 points and past Ron Livingston, who had played the previous three seasons, for first place on the all-time UCLA list. Guard Lindy Kell also had 14.

The Bruin 100 Game 84

UCLA 84, Colorado State 74
December 22, 1966

The game that easily could have faded into the oblivion, holding no apparent significance other than being the 500th of John Wooden's career at UCLA, is one that Kareem Abdul-Jabbar still holds close. It will forever be the night that cemented the future of a dynasty, that's all.

"That game, to me, solidified my confidence in Coach Wooden," Abdul-Jabbar says now. "He had a willing student the rest of the way."

The young Lew Alcindor, a sophomore and in just his fourth varsity game, had the natural uncertainties before then, those that predictably came with moving across the country and then stepping into such a disciplined setting as a Wooden team. But this night changed all that.

Alcindor saw Wooden go to a new zone press with about 13 minutes left and top-ranked UCLA clinging to a 65-64 lead, at which point the Bruins built a cushion as the star center moved to the back of the defense. Once they got into the final minutes, Wooden used the Pauley Pavilion court like a chess board. Alcindor remembers sitting in the huddle during a timeout and thinking one thing.

"Just that: 'Hey, I'm with the right guy.'"

"I was really in awe of his knowledge of the game and his insights into all the subtleties."

Alcindor came in averaging 37.7 points a game, then scored 34 on the night he forever became a Wooden devotee, an unspoken moment that would hold such importance in the three consecutive championships that would follow. Another member of that famed sophomore class, Lucius Allen, added 18 points.

The Bruins shot 40 free throws, with Alcindor taking 13 to the dismay of opponents who felt he was getting every call from the referees as Colorado State's big men fell more and more into foul trouble. "Alcindor is great," Coach Jim Williams said. "I don't know what more he could do with the ball once he gets it, but he doesn't need all that protection."

It was just another game in the compliment-and-complaint department, at least. It may also have been the night Wooden reached a milestone, improving to 365-135, but that paled in comparison. He had picked up another victory, yes, but a major new fan in the process.

The Bruin 100 Game 85

UCLA 54, Colorado 48
December 20, 1958

The world's greatest athlete wasn't such a bad basketball player either. Maybe it was just part of the training routine, or something to help pass the time between Olympic greatness, but decathlete-cum-swingman Rafer Johnson impressed enough in the first few games of his senior season that he moved into the opening lineup against the Buffaloes and scored 16 points.

There would be other times when his third sport—track, field, basketball—didn't seem like an alternative, namely when the 17 points and nine rebounds in a two-point win over USC about a month later and 14 points and 12 rebounds in a loss to Stanford about a month after that. But on this Saturday night at Los Angeles' Pan-Pacific Auditorium, Johnson became a starter in basketball, then made eight of 13 shots.

Most were close-range makes, with his strength providing an obvious advantage inside. It was Johnson, after all, who hit four consecutive shots early in the second half to earn the Bruins a 36-36 tie after they shot a dismal 22.5% in the first half and missed their first five attempts after the break.

One night after a 10-point win against the same opponent, Johnson's effort became the start of the escape that culminated when star Walt Torrence hit a pair of free throws with 31 seconds remaining. It gave UCLA a 56-52 advantage and, after Colorado's Gerry Schroeder hit a short jumper with 16 seconds to play, turned out to be the winning points.

If this was a special moment for Johnson—his first start—it was just another for Torrence. Normally paired in the Bruin backcourt with Denny Crum, who would find his real basketball successes in the years ahead, Torrence that season became a consensus All-America and led the team in scoring (21.5) and rebounding (11.6) and finished second in field-goal percentage.

The best shooter?

Johnson, at 50.7%. He had just 72 baskets and 142 attempts, far below the NCAA minimum for consideration in the national rankings, but made a solid contribution in the local scene nonetheless. First on the team in shooting, third in scoring and third in rebounding. And first in balloting—he was also student body president.

The dependable accuracy was especially critical against Colorado because the Bruins, after the miserable start, improved only enough for a terrible 27% finish. It obviously helped that the Buffaloes shot just 30.8%, but UCLA actually won despite the 19.7% by team members besides Johnson. Not bad for a track star.

"Just another basketball player in junior year," it said in conclusion in the program for the banquet, "this world famous athlete became a stand-out cager this past season."

Rafer Johnson, the track star and 6-3 swingman for the basketball team.

The Bruin 100 Game 86

UCLA 72, Oregon State 62
February 13, 1992

Let the record show that the moment came with 6:11 remaining at Gill Coliseum in Corvallis, Ore., in the 19th game of the season and the 113th of his career. Don MacLean made a free throw to help UCLA recover from an unexpected 10-point first-half deficit and made history.

That much can not be disputed, even if the particulars had been before and continued as a matter of debate to this day. Point No. 2,326 pushed him past Lew Alcindor to become the Bruins' all-time leading scorer, a milestone to be sure. It's just that there was no consensus on whether it was an accomplishment.

"Apples and oranges," the now-former record holder, Kareem Abdul-Jabbar, said of the comparison.

A real fruit salad. Alcindor was nothing short of overpowering, averaging 26.4 points while playing in 88 games—because NCAA rules prohibited freshmen from playing on the varsity in his day. MacLean, he was impressive, but more about longevity and consistency in a career that was allowed to run the full four years, ultimately reaching 127 games and 2,608 points, or 20.5 per outing.

"The fact he did it in three years and is one of the greatest players of all time is a little different than what I've done," MacLean said afterwards.

"Breaking the record is a milestone. I've been consistent, put a lot of points on the board. But it doesn't mean I'm better than anybody."

"My record is already broken," Abdul-Jabbar reasoned. "Sean Elliott [of Arizona] broke the Pac-10 record. Three seasons was all I was allowed."

He knows, he knows.

"I see it the same way," MacLean said. "But it means a lot that I've scored more than a lot of great players. And I've scored more than a lot of great players who played only three years."

Maybe because the game was on the road, there was no acknowledgment of the record when MacLean sank an uncontested jumper with 7:23 left to tie at 2,325 or when he hit the free throw 72 seconds later to take the lead. It was left to his teammates to offer congratulatory high-fives after the No. 3 team in the nation had improved to 18-1.

He finished with 22 points and 15 rebounds as the Bruins broke a three-game losing streak at Oregon State. The offensive production had extra importance since Tracy Murray scored just nine points, the first time he had failed to reach double digits in 56 games.

Game 86

Don MacLean became the all-time leading scorer in UCLA history.

The Bruin 100 Game 87

UCLA 87, Indiana 72
November 15, 1991

There was no shortage of difficulties to overcome. UCLA was the No. 11 team in the nation, but was also playing No. 2. The Bruins were without Ed O'Bannon (still recovering from knee surgery) and partly without Don MacLean (limited to 24 minutes by foul trouble). It was the season opener when so many questioned the direction of this team coming off the first-round tournament loss to Penn State in the spring.

Strange that Indiana didn't become one of the obstacles. The Hoosiers, easily the more highly regarded of the teams, with Alan Henderson and Damon Bailey and Calbert Cheaney, went under in a big way, falling behind by 12 at intermission and then really getting left behind early in the second half.

"That game set the tone for that season," Bruins Coach Jim Harrick says in retrospect.

A season in which they would win 28 games, the most since 1975-76, only to have this game boomerang back at them with the eventual blowout loss to Indiana in the tournament. Still, the Bruins couldn't have asked for a much better beginning, especially considering the circumstances in the front court and the opponent. It would come with the help of a new assistant coach named Steve Lavin, who had studied Indiana up close while on Gene Keady's staff at Purdue and helped implement the defensive strategy in his debut on the UCLA bench.

"I thought UCLA was by far the better team," Hoosiers Coach Bob Knight said. "They did a much better job at both ends of the floor."

He should have seen the job they did behind closed doors, after taking a 48-36 lead to the locker room for halftime.

"I've never seen guys climb the walls like that," Harrick said. "They couldn't wait for the second half to begin. Even just for those 15 minutes."

When it did begin—finally—the Bruins responded with a 9-2 run that put them up by 19.

In the end, Cheaney had totaled five points, one rebound and four turnovers against the combined defensive efforts of Mitchell Butler and Gerald Madkins. Indiana shot 48%, nice production, but also allowed 55.9%. MacLean still got 18 points and nine rebounds in his limited action, while Tracy Murray led all scorers with 21 points, which included three makes in four tries from behind the arc. Butler and Darrick Martin provided a boost of enthusiasm that helped early.

Knight's recognition was nice, but the nationwide one was better. A few days later, the Bruins were up to No. 4 in the polls.

The Bruin 100 Game 88

UCLA 149, Loyola Marymount 98
December 2, 1990

The night Pauley Pavilion was used for an indoor track meet.

Paul Westhead was gone, replaced by Jay Hillock, but this remained the Loyola Marymount that fans had come to love and opposing coaches had come to dread, Jim Harrick among the latter. A "disease" he called the Lions' up-tempo offense, sort of Empire State Building up, as in *way* up.

Harrick got what he feared, but at least he also got an easy win, along with it a spot in the UCLA record books for the most points in a game and the most combined points by two teams and the Pauley mark for the most in a half (84, in the second). Imagine if the Bruins actually needed to go all out.

"It's not really basketball to me," junior forward Don MacLean said. "They come down the floor and just throw it up."

The Lions threw it up 105 times, to be exact, a number that would have been staggering enough on its own but was compounded in that they continued despite making just 36.2% of the attempts. UCLA, meanwhile, got off 89 shots, 24 more than what would become its season-long average.

It was a joke. The Bruins had a 16-0 run in the first half, then an 11-2 rally early in the second, the latter worth an 85-56 lead. They hit triple digits with 12:25 remaining. Rodney Zimmerman's dunk broke the school scoring mark of 134 from just nine days earlier against UC-Irvine in the Great Alaska Shootout, and 4:03 still remained. It ended as the most-lopsided UCLA win since the 111-58 triumph over Arizona at the end of the 1982-83 season.

"I was hoping we'd crack them a little bit," Hillock said, "but we tended to crack ourselves. I expected to play a little better. I thought it would be a little closer."

Said MacLean: "I played only 24 minutes tonight and we still won by 50. We just blew them out."

Those 24 minutes were still long enough for MacLean to score 33 points, meaning a close game and regular minutes would have meant a new career high, better than the 41 set against North Texas two years earlier. Mitchell Butler had 18 points in 27 minutes, Darrick Martin 17 in 25, Shon Tarver 16 in 21, and so on. In all, eight Bruins were in double figures.

The Bruin 100 Game 89

UCLA 74, UC Santa Barbara 61
January 30, 1971

This was not a good start—an underwhelming victory—but it was a start nonetheless.

A week after the loss at Notre Dame as Austin Carr scored 46 points, UCLA returned to the court and the win column, obviously more concerned about the future than this day, and, of course, having no idea what the future would really hold. That this would turn out to be victory No. 1 in the 88-game winning streak.

The Bruins improved to 15-1 as Curtis Rowe had 28 points and 11 rebounds and Steve Patterson added 13 boards, but there was no cause for celebration. It became not so much a recovery from the Notre Dame loss as warm-ups for a showdown with USC, a continuation of the cross-town rivalry that held even greater importance this time because both were highly ranked teams, and that caused trouble. Some from their opponent, mostly from their coach.

"I'm going to initiate this conversation by saying I am not at all pleased," John Wooden said when he arrived for his postgame press conference. "Part of the reason we looked bad was the way Santa Barbara played and part of it was just that we were not sharp."

Added Rowe: "We really just weren't up for this game. USC is on everybody's mind."

More than just that, it again exposed the season-long problem of inconsistent play from the backcourt. Terry Schofield had played well enough of late to earn a spot in the opening lineup, then started ahead of Kenny Booker for the first time and responded by missing five of six shots; Schofield returned to a reserve role against USC. Meanwhile, Henry Bibby continued to struggle, so seldom-used Andy Hill got minutes.

The Bruins finally pulled away in the final 10 minutes. Rowe scored 12 of his points during the 14-3 run that turned a 56-52 edge into a comfortable 70-55 advantage.

Jack Hirsch (50) averaged 12.5 points a game during his UCLA career, but it was his defense on Michigan star Cazzie Russell that made the major contribution in the win over the Wolverines. Gail Goodrich (25) led the offense with 30 points.

148

The Bruin 100 Game 90

UCLA 96, Michigan 80
December 27, 1963

In a time the Bruins still needed to prove they were of championship caliber, unlike the years that would follow when such a status was assumed and even taken for granted, this proved to be a pivotal night, this semifinal game of the Los Angeles Basketball Classic at the Sports Arena.

Both teams came in 7-0, with Michigan No. 2 in the *United Press International* rankings and No. 3 in *Associated Press* and UCLA No. 5 and No. 4, respectively, a logjam to be sorted out as everyone trailed Loyola of Chicago, the defending NCAA champion. The Wolverines also brought a star to Los Angeles, Cazzie Russell, a 6-foot-5 1/2 sophomore guard. Bill Buntin, the All-Big Ten center, was another serious concern for the Bruin defense.

John Wooden opted to go with forward Jack Hirsch on Russell, even if it was a positional switch for Hirsch, and was rewarded with a 44-41 lead at halftime as Russell managed just five shots, two makes, four points and eight rebounds, a contribution far behind the 19 points UCLA had gotten from Gail Goodrich in the same stretch. And when the Bruins followed that with an overwhelming first nine minutes after intermission, the Wolverines were done.

Then there was the bonus. With a little more than four minutes left, and UCLA ahead 87-70, the public-address announcer informed the crowd that Loyola had lost to Georgetown. Chants of "We're No. 1!" erupted from the Bruin rooting section.

In the end, Russell had finished with just 11 points on five-of-nine shooting and 10 rebounds, and Buntin got 11 points, seven rebounds and missed 11 of 15 attempts. Forward Oliver Darden had 25 points and 17 rebounds, but that couldn't offset the virtual elimination of Russell.

"Since Russell is a guard, but plays the post, we decided to have Jack guard him because he played there in high school and junior college," Wooden said afterwards.

"Hirsch was in Russell's T-shirt all night," Hazzard said.

More than that, actually. Goodrich finished with 30 points, but Hirsch, the defensive hero, also contributed 16 points and 15 rebounds, while Fred Slaughter added 16 points and 13 rebounds.

A few days later, UCLA was voted No. 2 in both polls—behind Kentucky—making the victory over Michigan one of the most significant early wins for the Wooden era. A few days after that, on Jan. 4, Georgia Tech beat Kentucky and UCLA crushed Washington State on the road to earn the top spot in the country, a ranking the Bruins would not relinquish.

The Bruin 100 Game 91

UCLA 57, Long Beach State 55
March 20, 1971

Any thoughts that these were the invincible Bruins of old—or, as it would turn out, the future—had long ago disappeared, overtaken instead by the image of a team that already had six victories by five points or less before even coming to Salt Lake City for the second-round matchup with Long Beach and its emerging coach, Jerry Tarkanian. UCLA was 26-1 and No. 1 in the country... and vulnerable.

By the second half, they had been downgraded to desperate. The Bruins trailed by 11 points with 14:40 remaining. Their outside shooting was nonexistent. Their coach was contemplating attending the Final Four as a spectator—"At that moment, I thought that Mrs. Wooden and I could leave for Houston a day early next week and just have a good time," Mr. Wooden said.

That's when UCLA ran off nine unanswered points, all from Henry Bibby and Steve Patterson. It got a new game—a tie—at 50-50, and better than half a chance to win as sophomore guard Ed Ratleff fouled out after scoring 18 points. The Bruins, meanwhile, were forced to leave Sidney Wicks on the bench with four fouls.

The intentional shakeup came when Wooden replaced 6-foot-3 Terry Schofield with 6-foot-6 John Ecker, leaving Bibby as the only true backcourt player in the lineup with Ecker, Patterson, Curtis Rowe and Larry Farmer.

Ecker made the Bruins stronger on defense, and the coach wanted to attack Long Beach's zone with a one-guard alignment.

It was still tied at 53-53. Tarkanian called for the stall. When the 49ers took a shot, a jumper from near the corner by Dwight Taylor, Ratleff's replacement, it bounced off the rim. UCLA got the rebound, then went into its own stall.

Finally, with 25 seconds left, Taylor fouled Wicks. The senior forward, a two-time All-American by the time he left school, went to the line, got a helpful bounce on the first attempt and a clean make on the second, and the Bruins got a two-point lead. When Long Beach missed on the ensuing possession, Wicks was fouled again and, with 12 seconds remaining, made two free throws again to clinch the victory.

They were heading to Houston and the Final Four for a semifinal meeting with Kansas and the chance for their fifth consecutive national championship, despite Bibby going just four of 18 from the field, Wicks five of 13 and the Bruins as a whole a dreadful 29%. A fitting way for this group to advance.

John Wooden (left) put the ball on Henry Bibby's hands at the critical stage of the game against Cal State Long Beach, shifting the lineup to make Bibby the only UCLA guard on the court.

The Bruin 100 Game 92

UCLA 87, Stanford 68
February 8, 1997

OK, so it wasn't exactly a massacre, but it was a considerable victory at a time when one of any kind was desperately needed.

It was meaningful for all Bruins—even the one of old who took a very personal interest—but especially for Coach Steve Lavin, still trying to work off the interim tag and getting little help from his roots in the Bay Area. Stanford, after all, had just hammered them about a month earlier, so bad that it became the worst loss in UCLA history by margin of defeat, so bad that it had its own name, the Maples Massacre. And Cal had just won by three points at Pauley Pavilion, closing with an 11-2 run to claim victory, two days before the Cardinal came in on this Saturday.

The latter made it as much about survival as revenge, the Bruins at 12-7 overall at the start of the day, in a battle in the conference for a tournament bid, and heading to Arizona next. Just in case anyone within missed the urgency, Ed O'Bannon, nearly two seasons removed from his UCLA playing days, delivered what was described as a "bristling" pre-game speech.

"I've watched a few of their games," he explained later, "and what I've seen is a team that just needed a little kick or something. I guess that's what I was trying to give them today."

Said younger brother Charles, a senior forward: "I tried to block it out, not let myself get carried away by the emotion. But Ed came in here and gave a pregame speech, and he had us all sweating and fired up."

Carrying that energy to the court, the Bruins responded with a powerful performance and the first of what became eight consecutive wins to claim the Pacific 10 Conference title. They combined to outrebound the Cardinal, 36-28, after having lost the battle of the boards, 45-26, at Maples Pavilion, and Charles O'Bannon finished with 23 points and 12 rebounds.

Two days later, on Monday, Athletic Director Pete Dalis told Lavin the interim label was being removed. A day after that, UCLA held a press conference to make the announcement. But to say Lavin got the job because of the victory over Stanford would be oversimplifying the situation, seeing as the Bruins were hardly on a great roll at the time, having just folded in the final minutes to lose to Cal. It's more likely that the promotion may have come eventually because school officials liked the discipline Lavin had brought to the program, though the contrast between the Cardinal games probably didn't hurt.

"That was probably a key factor in me becoming the head coach at that point in the season," Lavin says now. "They didn't see the need to delay it or continue the search.

"To come back against that very same team a month or five weeks later, it was such a clear, dramatic statement of how much we had improved."

The Bruin 100 Game 93

UCLA 75, Oregon 58
January 9, 1970

Through all the cheers and the applause and the ovations and the adulations for the No. 1 team in the country, the team that improved to 9-0 with this win, a different kind of reaction forced its way through.

Boos.

At home, even.

It was the strangest of sounds, the Bruins as the target of disgust while playing before 12,703 at Pauley Pavilion. Of course, it came because of a pretty strange sight: a John Wooden team employing the stall.

Wooden disdained the slowdown game; he hadn't used it since UCLA played the same Ducks in Eugene during Lew Alcindor's sophomore season, three years earlier. But he opted for it this time with about four minutes left in the first half and the Bruins leading, 45-33, hoping to pull Oregon out of its zone defense, first the 1-2-2, followed by the 3-2 and then the 2-1-2. The decision came even though his team was handling it without too much difficulty.

And there was the future to consider—Wooden wanted to get in some work playing at that speed in anticipation of the next game, a day later, against an Oregon State squad he figured would stall. So the Bruins stayed in first gear for the rest of the half, then came back out after intermission and took one shot in the first nine minutes. One.

The home fans were quiet at first, maybe even stunned into silence. But the boos started after a few minutes. Finally, knowing his Ducks had to start getting some quick scores if hopes for the unlikely comeback were to remain, Oregon Coach Steve Belko abandoned the zones with about nine minutes left in the game and UCLA ahead 56-42.

Belko was asked afterwards why he didn't go man sooner. "We though the stall might hurt their tempo, too," came the reply. Hardly. The Bruins shot 52.6% in all, with Henry Bibby going seven of 12 from the field and Curtis Rowe seven of 11. The tactic was only noticeable in that UCLA scored about 28 points below its season average to date and in one stretch had gone 10 minutes without a field goal and 13 minutes with only three attempts.

Battling an opponent and public opinion in their own building, the Bruins had won easily to improve to 9-0. But they did not, even with the result, change Wooden's mind about the offensive tactic. That much became obvious when someone asked him in the aftermath if his opinion of the slowdown was still the same.

"It sure is," he responded, enunciating each word carefully, his voice steadily rising.

Soon enough, Wooden didn't even have the fallback reasoning. Oregon State did not stall the next day.

The Bruin 100 Game 94

California 100, UCLA 93
January 28, 1995

Ten years earlier, maybe. But Cal had certainly earned the respect by this point, what with wins in the two previous meetings in the series and three of the last four. Even with two in a row at Pauley Pavilion, after having lost 52 in a row in any building from 1961-85.

But there the Bears were, feeling dissed and using it as fuel on this Saturday, building a 14-point lead in the first half and then later reeling off nine unanswered points to put the game away when UCLA got within two points. All because of what happened the day before.

"They probably don't think it was a big deal," Cal's Jelani Gardner said. "But to us, it was a big deal. It made us emotional for the game."

He was right. UCLA didn't think it was a big deal. But the Bears were offended when some Bruins, including coaches, interrupted the visitor's practice on Friday at Pauley Pavilion, becoming a distraction at the very least and maybe even disrespectful. Cal said there was no maybe about it.

The Bears' workout was supposed to run from 1 to 3 p.m., but UCLA Coach Jim Harrick, according to his counterpart, walked by the court around 2:30. Ten minutes later, it was assistant Steve Lavin. Eventually, Todd Bozeman said, Bruins players started hovering around the periphery of the court, one even running along the baseline to warm up and another jogging the sideline.

So much for the closed practice.

"I had never seen that before," Bozeman said. "They showed us no respect, and we always respect our opponent. We give them respect until they don't deserve it, and we have to thank [the Bruins] for that."

Added Cal player Tremaine Fowlkes: "Yeah, we talked about that. It was a lack of respect."

The Bruins, meanwhile, disputed the events and definitely denied the significance. Easy for them to say.

"We didn't mean any disrespect," J.R. Henderson said. "We have more class than that."

"I think he's just saying that to write some articles," Ed O'Bannon said of Bozeman. "There was no disrespect on our side. This is our gym, and we usually practice at 2:50."

Led by Fowlkes' 24 points, Cal's bench outscored UCLA's by a stunning 52-3. It was also Fowlkes who dominated that 9-0 run to end the threat by the Bruins and restored the lead to 11; being defended by Charles O'Bannon, playing with four fouls, he had two free throws, a dunk, a three-pointer and an eight-foot hook. It turned out to be the last loss of the season.

The Bruin 100 Game 95

UCLA 74, Washington 66
February 9, 1995

Anyone wanna buy a Winnebago?

Because they happened to be in the neighborhood, heading back to the Seattle hotel after the shootaround earlier in the day at Hec Edmundson Pavilion, the Bruins stopped by the Kingdome, site of the Final Four about two months later, in a quick trip arranged by Coach Jim Harrick. They found an RV show, but that didn't really matter. They also found motivation for a long journey of another kind.

"Just trying to put a little picture in their mind, you know?" assistant coach Lorenzo Romar said that night. "I think they enjoyed it."

You could say that.

"I just imagined us coming back in seven weeks," sophomore Charles O'Bannon said. "Whatever message he [Harrick] was trying to send us, it registered. I got a taste of it. Now I want the whole thing."

Said George Zidek, the senior center who liked to stare at a poster of the Kingdome that hung in the UCLA locker room back home: "It was great, especially for me. I'll keep the real picture of that building in the back of my mind for the rest of the season. To play in that place would be the top of my basketball career."

Harrick set up the detour through Vern Wagner, the director of building operations at the Kingdome, once known as the football coach at Morningside High School in Inglewood, Calif., in the early 1970s when Harrick coached basketball there. Wagner unlocked the doors to let the Bruins in for a peek that lasted 15 or 20 minutes in actuality and much longer considering the emotional carryover. Those seven weeks later, of course, they came in the participant's entrance, Zidek was at the top of his basketball career, and Harrick came off as the master motivator because of a February side trip.

The game a few hours later back at Hec Edmundson was not nearly as eventful. The No. 6 team in the country didn't play that well, but still built a 32-21 lead in the first half as J.R. Henderson scored 10 consecutive points in one stretch, then pushed that to a 17-point advantage early in the second half. Washington made a run to close within 61-58 with 8:31 remaining as Bryant Boston scored 13 of his 18 points after intermission, but got no closer.

Both O'Bannons played key roles, Ed scoring 17 points and Charles blocking five shots, including one that doused the Huskies rally. Zidek made eight of 10 shots and also had 17 points. UCLA was 15-2, and envisioning another Kingdome visit.

The Bruin 100 Game 96

UCLA 87, DePaul 77
February 3, 1990

The Bruins took care of the present about midway through the first half, claiming a lead they would not relinquish, then looked to the past.

Bill Walton took the court. And Kareem Abdul-Jabbar. And Ann Meyers and Denise Curry, the former superstars from the UCLA women's team. The day had finally come for the Bruins to retire jersey numbers, what the school called the key moment in its "Pauley at 25" celebration and an obvious lure that drew 12,668.

"It's a tremendous honor and brings back a lot of memories for me," Walton said.

"It's a great honor to be one of the first to get this honor," Abdul-Jabbar added. "I was looking for good things to happen when I got to UCLA, but I couldn't expect this."

John Wooden, who coached both, was given a 50-second standing ovation when he walked on the floor to make the presentations, first giving Walton his framed jersey No. 32 and then Abdul-Jabbar his No. 33. It was a great off-the-court moment for a program that had enjoyed so many in competition.

Meyers, the first four-time All-American in women's basketball and the 1978 national player of the year, was saluted with her No. 15. Curry, who set 14 school records and still ranks first in scoring and rebounding, was given her proper place in history with her No. 12.

All four honorees were consensus All-America at least three times, and all four either were then in the basketball Hall of Fame or bound for future induction in Springfield, Mass.

Six years later, on Feb. 1, 1996, the Bruins retired their second set of uniforms, marking the occasion with a ceremony at halftime of the game at Pauley Pavilion against Oregon: No. 42 Walt Hazzard, No. 35 Sidney Wicks, No. 54 Marques Johnson and No. 31 Ed O'Bannon. All were named national Player of The Year during their careers.

Lew Alcindor (left), John Wooden and Bill Walton gather to commemorate the players having their jerseys retired.

Sidney Wicks (35), Marques Johnson (54), Walt Hazzard (42) and Ed O'Bannon (31) had their uniforms retired on Feb. 1, 1996.

The Bruin 100

The Bruin 100 Game 97

UCLA 65, Miami (Fla.) 62
March 13, 1998

Nearly taking a turn in that other UCLA basketball tradition of the '90s, these Bruins came perilously close to ending up a head on the wall in the trophy room of some program that went big-game hunting in the tournament with little more than BB guns. It was Miami's Hurricanes who lined up the first-round crosshairs this time, eventually to go into the final seconds with a very good chance to join the names of Princeton, Tulsa and Penn State as eternal tormentors around Westwood.

Not that anyone was having flashbacks or anything.

"I remembered the first-round loss to Princeton and I didn't want to go out like this," Toby Bailey said.

The Bruins didn't, escaping instead with a victory but little else to feel good about. They couldn't so much as hold a 10-point lead with 10:52 remaining against the 11th-seeded team in the South regional that went on a 20-9 run to move ahead at 59-58 with 3:03 left, and then at 62-59 with 1:55 to go.

J.R. Henderson got the heavy favorites back within a point on a 12-foot bank. Miami took timeout, but found no more miracles. Its offense was tapped out, setting the stage for the Bruins to get the lead back on Henderson's

two free throws with :41 showing, and then for them to get the 65-62 cushion when Bailey hit two from the line with seven seconds remaining. The latter almost became critical, but Johnny Helmsley and Charles Wiseman each missed open three-pointers in the final moments that would have meant overtime.

"It was a hold-your-breath end to a hold-your-nose game," Tim Kawakami began his story in the *Los Angeles Times*.

"This was basketball in a green and orange straight jacket, a grinding, grueling game that was as painful to watch as it was to play," Jon Wilner wrote in the *Los Angeles Daily News*.

It wasn't just media bashing, either. Henderson scored 26 points despite fighting a virus that made him dizzy at times and Bailey added 21, but the Bruins seemed to pay the price for practicing only twice in the previous five games, thinking it would make them fresher but instead coming out sluggish. Kris Johnson, in particular, was, in his own words, "worse than doo doo," managing just three points while missing five of six shots and needing the other two seniors to pick him up and avoid what could have been their final college games ending in disaster.

"I wasn't going to lose leaving anything out there," Bailey said. "It feels great to get past this game. We were a little rusty at first, but we fought back and in clutch time we dug down like we have so many times in our career."

There's that theory. Or there's always the one offered by Henderson.

"I was worried. I felt like we had a little help from upstairs on this one."

J.R. Henderson hits a key shot in Bruin victory.

The Bruin 100 Game 98

UCLA 64, St. Louis 57
December 23, 1996

The Bruins had just lost at Illinois in a terrible performance. Three games before that, Kansas beat them badly at Pauley Pavilion, needing only until near the end of the first half to go up by 28 points and then breeze in from there to win by 13. And two games before that, they lost in overtime to Tulsa in the season opener. The victories dotted in between offered only faint contrast—Cal State Northridge, Jackson State and Ohio State.

That intersection UCLA passed through on the short journey from Champaign, Ill., to St. Louis was likely the crossroads of its season. A loss to the Billikens and the resulting 3-4 record would have been bad enough, but this would have been 3-4 with the Christmas break coming next.

"They would probably have gone home with a lot of doubt, a lot of uncertainty about which direction we were going," Coach Steve Lavin says now of his players. "In L.A., that would have been a week for the vultures—the talk-radio shows, the letters to the editor, the Internet.

"We were in desperate need. That was one we had to have."

The argument could be made that the victory they got at the Kiel Center, with help from the emotional release from the players'-only meeting after the loss to Illinois, was the turning point of the season that became a huge success, the same team that was in danger of going under in late December having come all the way back to reach the round of eight in late March. Fittingly, the game itself also came with a gut check in the second half, perhaps bringing the future of 1996-97 to a head at a specific moment, when the Bruins had their 11-point cushion with 11:44 to play cut to one a little more than six minutes later.

It was 54-53 with 5:28 remaining. It was, Lavin said afterwards, the moment of truth.

"Instead of folding like an accordian," he said, "we withstood the run."

They did by making each of their next 10 foul shots, en route to finishing 20 of 26 from the line a game after the horrible 10-of-21 showing against Illinois. Cameron Dollar, replaced in the starting lineup by Kris Johnson, had the two biggest, the ones that made it 62-57. Johnson, meanwhile, scored 20 points.

"Everybody will say we should have won and they'll wonder why we're so happy," UCLA's Toby Bailey said. "But we have to start somewhere. The way we were going kind of humbled us. We know we have great players, but we're not a good team. We have the potential to be great, and hopefully we made the first step tonight."

The Bruin 100 Game 99

UCLA 73, Temple 49
December 21, 1980

It was a Sunday afternoon tipoff, but a Saturday night following. The Bruins, No. 3 in the *Associated Press* poll, had gone to Tokyo to play a regular-season game as part of a six-day swing through the Orient, hardly a milestone for competitiveness but historical nonetheless because it marked the first NCAA contest outside the United States.

Game time came about 8 p.m. back in Los Angeles, across the international dateline, this for a school that hadn't even scheduled any trip farther away than South Bend, Ind., the previous three seasons. This journey came about when Suntory, a huge Japanese food and beverage corporation, wanted to stage a tournament that would also include the likes of North Carolina, Indiana and Kentucky, but had to downgrade the sights to the more-realistic one game.

So Suntory got the Bruins and Owls, got each to also play an exhibition against a group of Japanese all-stars, and UCLA got a hefty payout to move the contest that was originally scheduled for Pauley Pavilion. Athletic Director Robert A. Fischer wouldn't discuss specifics of the financial incentives, admitting only that it was a "very substantial guarantee."

"Let's just say it was sufficient to make it worthwhile for us to move a home game," he added.

In many ways. Along with the actual payout, Suntory also had to earmark a sizable contribution for UCLA research projects, so the decision went far beyond sports. It went all the way to marketing, in fact, after the Bruins had already made inroads into Asia with the recent football game against Oregon in Tokyo.

"I would equate it today like the NBA playing every other year in Japan," Don Casey, then the Temple coach, says now. "Cementing the relationship, building on it. I don't exactly know what was the reason, but UCLA was huge in Tokyo. Just huge. I even think they had a gift shop there.

"The Japanese had such an affinity for UCLA, it was almost like an extension campus."

There were other connections—Bruin Coach Larry Brown had played in the same building as a member of the U.S. Olympic team that won a gold medal in 1964. His return to Yoyogi Sports Center came with about 5,000 people crammed into the arena that supposedly had a capacity of 3,500, and with UCLA using its superior quickness for an early 17-2 run and 21-8 lead. Temple never got closer than 15 points in the second half.

Kenny Fields and Michael Sanders finished with 14 points each to lead the easy win. Brown got just as much

attention, prompting a Japanese announcer to ask him after the game why the coach was so active on the sideline, a contrast for the fans not used to seeing such animated behavior.

"Well," Brown said, smiling, "I like to encourage my players a lot."

Added one wire dispatch sent back to the States: "Fortunately for Brown, the Japanese audience could not interpret some of the standard slogans Brown yelled at the officials."

The emotion of Coach Larry Brown has always been evident.

Game 99

The Bruin 100 Game 100

UCLA 109, CAL 95
February 28, 1970

It's likely the passing comment was the product of desperation, given that dead air didn't seem like much of an option, or boredom, or both, and therefore excusable. But then it developed a life of its own and, well, he was stuck.

Dick Enberg would have to sing standing on the court in Pauley Pavilion.

Oh, my!

It all started about seven weeks earlier, during the Jan. 9 game against Oregon as lengthy stall tactics left the play-by-play man for UCLA's flagship station, KMPC, with little action to give his listeners. So Enberg recapped the scoring, as if this was a baseball game and down time for a pitching change. He recapped the previous meetings between the Bruins and Ducks. He looked ahead to next week's schedule.

So desperate to fill was Enberg that he even mentioned that the theme from a recently released movie, *Butch Cassidy and the Sundance Kid*, was going through his head because of all the play time it had been getting. And then he started humming the tune for the radio audience.

The next night, when Oregon State came to Pauley, several students brought him the lyrics for "Raindrops Keep Fallin' on My Head." And when UCLA escaped

near defeat on John Ecker's driving hook with six seconds left, Enberg used the analogy of dodging the downpour of opponents constantly aiming for the defending national champions... and said just before signing off that he would sing the song at center court if and when the Bruins won the conference title.

"And of course that became the Red Auerbach [victory] cigar," Enberg told David Smale for the book *Pauley Pavilion: College Basketball's Showcase*. "Every time UCLA would get ahead by 20 points late in the game, the band played a rendition of 'Raindrops.' And the kids would turn around and say, 'You'll sing. You'll sing.' Of course I had to pay off the bet at the end of the year, much to the chagrin of anyone who has any musical sense or ear."

Two games still remained in the regular season, and then another successful tournament run, but this still qualified as one end because the victory over Cal combined with the loss by second-place Oregon at Washington a few hours earlier clinched the Pacific 8 crown for the Bruins. That was Enberg's cue.

"When I finally paid off the bet, I had to go out to center court," he told Smale. "I delayed for half an hour, hoping everyone would leave. And nobody did ... .

"As I started to sing, I was facing the student body, and they all opened up their umbrellas. It was really nice.

they all opened up their umbrellas. It was really nice. They were saying, 'We're all on the same page.' I was nervous and it was their way of saying, 'Hey, we enjoyed it.' I've only played Pauley once, not basketball, but trying to sing. And I could tell everyone I had sung once in public, but I did it in front of 10,000 people."

Dick Enberg makes good on his promise.

Game 100

The Pauley Pavilion crowd gets in the spirit.

The Bruin 100

UCLA Coaches Records

UCLA goes into the 1998-99 season with a 79-year all-time basketball record of 1,428 wins and 613 defeats for a .700 winning percentage.

Season	Captain	Overall			Conference		
		W	L	Pct	W	L	Pct
Fred W. Cozens, Coach							
1919-20	Si Gibbs	12	2	.957	—	—	—
1920-21	Raymond McBurney	8	2	.800	—	—	—
Caddy Works, Coach							
1921-22	Si Gibbs	9	1	.900	—	—	—
1922-23	Buck Beeson	12	4	.750	—	—	—
1923-24	Bill Goertz	8	2	.800	—	—	—
1924-25	Wilbur Johns	11	6	.647	—	—	—
1925-26	Horace Bresee	14	2	.875	—	—	—
1926-27	Jim Armstrong	12	4	.750	—	—	—
1927-28	Jack Ketchum	10	5	.667	5	4	.505
1928-29	Sam Balter	7	9	.438	1	8	.111
1929-30	Larry Wildes	14	8	.636	3	6	.333
1930-31	Carl Knowles	9	6	.600	4	5	.444
1931-32	Dick Linthicum	9	10	.474	4	7	.363
1932-33	Ted Lemcke	10	11	.476	1	10	.091
1933-34	Don Piper	10	13	.435	2	10	.166
1934-35	Cordner Gibson	11	12	.478	4	8	.333
1935-36	Don Ashen	10	13	.435	2	10	.166
1936-37	Orv Appleby	6	14	.300	2	10	.166
1937-38	Jack Cooper	4	20	.167	0	12	.000
1938-39	Bob Calkins	7	20	.259	0	12	.000
Wilbur Johns, Coach							
1939-40	Alex Rafalovich	8	17	.320	3	9	.250
1940-41	Bob Null and						
	Lloyd Anderson	6	20	.231	2	10	.166
1941-42	Bob Alshuler and						
	Ernie Handelsman	5	18	.217	2	10	.166
1942-43	John Fryer	14	7	.667	4	4	.500
1943-44	Dick West	10	10	.500	3	3	.500
1944-45	Bill Putnam and						
	Bill Rankin	12	12	.500	3	1	.750
1945-46	Dick Hough and						
	Hal Michaels	8	16	.333	5	7	.417
1946-47	Dick Perry	18	7	.720	9	3	.750
1947-48	John Stanich	12	13	.480	3	9	.250
John R. Wooden, Coach							
1948-49	Ron Pearson	22	7	.759	10	2	.833
1949-50	Alan Sawyer	24	7	.774	10	2	.833
1950-51	Eddie Sheldrake	19	10	.655	9	4	.692
1951-52	Don Johnson and						
	Jerry Norman	19	12	.613	8	4	.667
1952-53	Barry Porter	16	8	.667	6	6	.500
1953-54	Ron Livingston	18	7	.720	7	5	.583
1954-55	Don Bragg and						
	John Moore	21	5	.808	11	1	.917
1955-56	Willie Naulls	22	6	.786	16	0	1.000
1956-57	Dick Banton	22	4	.846	13	3	.813
1957-58	Ben Rogers	16	10	.615	10	6	.625
1958-59	Walt Torrence	16	9	.640	10	6	.625
1959-60	Cliff Brandon	14	12	.538	7	5	.583
1960-61	Bill Ellis and						
	John Berberich	18	8	.692	7	5	.583
1961-62	John Green and						
	Gary Cunningham	18	11	.621	10	2	.833
1962-63	Jim Milhorn	20	9	.690	8	5	.615
1963-64	Walt Hazzard and						
	Jack Hirsch	30	0	1.000	15	0	1.000
1964-65	Keith Erickson and						
	Gail Goodrich	28	2	.933	14	0	1.000
1965-66	Doug McIntosh	18	8	.692	10	4	.714
1966-67	Mike Warren	30	0	1.000	14	0	1.000
1967-68	Mike Warren	29	1	.967	14	0	1.000
1968-69	Lew Alcindor and						
	Lynn Shackelford	29	1	.967	13	1	.929
1969-70	John Vallely	28	2	.933	12	2	.857
1970-71	Curtis Rowe and						
	Sidney Wicks	29	1	.967	14	0	1.000
1971-72	Henry Bibby	30	0	1.000	14	0	1.000
1972-73	Larry Farmer	30	0	1.000	14	0	1.000
1973-74	Bill Walton,						
	Keith Wilkes	26	4	.867	12	2	.857
1974-75	David Meyers	28	3	.903	12	2	.857

Gene Bartow, Coach

Year	Player(s)						
1975-76	Marques Johnson and Richard Washington	28	4	.875	13	1	.929
1976-77	Marques Johnson	24	5	.831	11	3	.786

Gary Cunningham, Coach

1977-78	Raymond Townsend	25	3	.893	14	0	1.000
1978-79	David Greenwood	25	5	.833	15	3	.833

Larry Brown, Coach

1979-80	Kiki Vandeweghe and James Wilkes	22	10	.688	12	6	.667
1980-81	Mike Sanders and Tony Anderson	20	7	.741	13	5	.722

Larry Farmer, Coach

1981-82	Mike Sanders, Tony Anderson	21	6	.778	14	4	.778
1982-83	Michael Holton	23	6	.793	15	3	.833
1983-84	Ralph Jackson	17	11	.607	10	8	.556

Walt Hazzard, Coach

1984-85	Gary Maloncon	21	12	.636	12	6	.667
1985-86	Reggie Miller, Montel Hatcher	15	14	.517	9	9	.500
1986-87	Reggie Miller	25	7	.781	14	4	.778
1987-88	Craig Jackson, Dave Immel	16	14	.533	12	6	.667

Jim Harrick, Coach

1988-89	Pooh Richardson	21	10	.677	13	5	.722
1989-90	Trevor Wilson	22	11	.667	11	7	.611
1990-91	Game Captains	23	9	.719	11	7	.611
1991-92	Gerald Madkins	28	5	.848	16	2	.889
1992-93	Mitchell Butler	22	11	.667	11	7	.611
1993-94	Shon Tarver and Rodney Zimmerman	21	7	.750	13	5	.722
1994-95	Ed O'Bannon, Tyus Edney and George Zidek	32	1	.979	17	1	.944
1995-96	Charles O'Bannon and Cameron Dollar	23	8	.742	16	2	.889

Steve Lavin, Coach

1996-97	Charles O'Bannon and Cameron Dollar	24	8	.750	15	3	.833
1997-98	Toby Bailey and J.R. Henderson	24	9	.727	12	6	.667

UCLA's All-Time Head Coaching Records

Coach	Yrs.	Won	Lost	Pct.
Fred W. Cozens	2	20	4	.833
Pierce "Caddy" Works	18	173	159	.521
Wilbur Johns	9	93	120	.437
John Wooden	27	620	147	.808
Gene Bartow	2	52	9	.852
Gary Cunningham	2	50	8	.862
Larry Brown	2	42	17	.712
Larry Farmer	3	61	23	.726
Walt Hazzard	4	77	47	.621
Jim Harrick	8	192	62	.756
Steve Lavin	2	48	17	.739
Totals	79	1428	613	.700

John Wooden (left) and Jim Harrick, two title-winning coaches, share a light moment at Pauley Pavilion.

The Bruin 100

UCLA Individual Records

Individual—Career

Most Games: 130 by Mitchell Butler, 1990-93.

Most Starts: 127 by Don MacLean, 1989-92.

Most Points: 2,608 by Don MacLean, 1989-92.

Highest Scoring Average: 26.4 by Lew Alcindor, 1967-69.

Most Rebounds: 1,370 by Bill Walton, 1972-74.

Highest Rebounding Average: 15.7 by Bill Walton, 1972-74.

Most Field Goals: 943 by Lew Alcindor, 1967-69 and Don MacLean, 1989-92.

Most Field Goal Attempts: 1,776 by Don MacLean, 1989-92.

Highest Field Goal Percentage: 69.4% by Jelani McCoy, 1996-98.

Most Three-Point Field Goals: 197 by Tracy Murray, 1990-92.

Most Three-Point Field Goal Attempts: 501 by Toby Bailey, 1995-98.

Highest Three-Point Field Goal Percentage: 46.4% by Pooh Richardson, 1986-89.

Most Free Throws: 711 by Don MacLean, 1989-92.

Most Free Throw Attempts: 827 by Don MacLean, 1989-92.

Highest Free Throw Percentage: 88.0% by Rod Foster, 1980-83.

Most Assists: 833 by Pooh Richardson, 1986-89.

Most Steals: 224 by Tyus Edney, 1992-95.

Most Blocked Shots: 188 by Jelani McCoy, 1996-1998.

Most Minutes Played: 4,297 by Pooh Richardson, 1986-89.

Most League Points: 1,486 by Don MacLean, 1989-92.

Most League Rebounds: 687 by Bill Walton, 1972-74.

Individual—Season

Most Games: 33 by J.R. Henderson, Toby Bailey and Earl Watson(all, 1998); Ed O'Bannon, Charles O'Bannon, George Zidek, Toby Bailey, J.R. Henderson and Cameron Dollar (all, 1995); Ed O'Bannon, Tyus Edney, Richard Petruska, Rodney Zimmerman (all, 1993); Mitchell Butler, Darrick Martin, Tracy Murray and Shon Tarver (all, 1992); Mitchell Butler, Don MacLean, Gerald Madkins, Darrick Martin, Tracy Murray and Trevor Wilson (all, 1990); Montel Hatcher, Gary Maloncon, Nigel Miguel, Reggie Miller and Brad Wright (all, 1985).

Most Starts: 33 by Earl Watson, 1998; Ed O'Bannon, 1995; George Zidek, 1995; Charles O'Bannon, 1995; Richard Petruska, 1993; Tyus Edney, 1993; Tracy Murray, 1992; Don MacLean, 1990; Gerald Madkins, 1990; Darrick Martin, 1990; Trevor Wilson, 1990; Nigel Miguel, 1985; Brad Wright, 1985.

Most Points: 870 by Lew Alcindor, 1967.

Highest Scoring Average: 29.0 by Lew Alcindor, 1967.

Most League Points: 500 by Reggie Miller, 1986.

Highest League Scoring Average: 27.8 by Reggie Miller, 1986.

Most Rebounds: 506 by Bill Walton, 1973.

Highest Rebounding Average: 16.9 by Bill Walton, 1973.

Most Field Goals: 346 by Lew Alcindor, 1967.

Most Field Goal Attempts: 582 by Willie Naulls, 1956.

Highest Field Goal Percentage: 75.6% by Jelani McCoy, 1997.

Most Three-Point Field Goals: 78 by Tracy Murray, 1992.

Most Three-Point Field Goal Attempts: 189 by Tracy Murray, 1991.

Highest Three-Point Field Goal Percentage: 50.0% by Tracy Murray, 1992.

Most Free Throws: 202 by Reggie Miller, 1986.

Most Free Throw Attempts: 274 by Lew Alcindor, 1967.

Highest Free Throw Percentage: 95.0% by Rod Foster, 1982.

Most Assists: 236 by Pooh Richardson, 1989.

Most Steals: 82 by Cameron Dollar, 1997.

Most Minutes (Since 1979): 1207 by Tyus Edney, 1993.

Most Blocked Shots (Since 1979): 102 by Jelani McCoy, 1996.

Most Turnovers (Since 1979): 115 by Tyus Edney, 1993.

Consecutive Free Throws: 36 by Henry Bibby, 1972 (Five Games).

Consecutive Free Throws, League Play and Best League Percentage: 28 of 28 (100%) by Gary Cunningham, 1960 (12 Games).

Individual—Game

Most Points: 61 by Lew Alcindor (vs. Washington State, 2/25/67).

Most Rebounds: 28 by Willie Naulls (vs. Arizona State, 1/28/56).

Most Field Goals: 26 by Lew Alcindor (vs. Washington State, 2/25/67).

Most Three-Point Field Goals: 7 by Ed O'Bannon (at California, 2/23/95); Reggie Miller (at Washington State, 12/19/86).

Most Three-Point Field Goal Attempts: 15 by Reggie Miller (at Washington, 12/19/86).

Most Free Throws: 21 by John Green (vs. Washington, 1/6/62).

Most Assists: 15 by Darrick Martin, (vs. Pittsburgh, 2/2/91).

Most Steals: 11 by Tyus Edney (vs. George Mason, 12/22/94).

Most Blocked Shots: 11 by Jelani McCoy (vs. Maryland, 12/9/95)

Team—Season

Most Points: 2,954, 1991.

Highest Scoring Average: 94.6, 1972.

Most Rebounds: 1,670, 1964.

Highest Rebound Average: 55.7, 1964.

Stats

Most Field Goals: 1,161, 1968.

Most Field Goal Attempts: 2,335, 1950.

Highest Field Goal Percentage: 55.5%, 1979.

Most Three-Point Field Goals: 173, 1992.

Most Three-Point Field Goal Attempts: 490, 1998.

Highest Three-Point Field Goal Percentage: 42.6%, 1989.

Most Free Throws: 642, 1956 and 1991.

Most Free Throw Attempts: 963, 1964.

Highest Free Throw Percentage: 75.6%,1979.

Most Assists: 673, 1974.

Most Steals: 312, 1995.

Biggest Scoring Margin: 30.3, 1972.

Best Record: 30-0, 1964, 1967, 1972, 1973.

Most Victories: 32, 1995.

Team–Game

Most Points: 149 vs. Loyola, 12/2/90.

Most Points By Two Teams: 247 — UCLA 149, Loyola 98.

Most Field Goals: 58 vs. Loyola, 12/2/90.

Highest Field Goal Percentage: .731 (38-52) vs. USC, 1/24/96.

Most Three-Point Field Goals: 11 at Oregon,   2/22/87.

Most Three-Point Field Goal Attempts: 23 vs. North Carolina, 11/27/97, USC, 2/25/93, California, 2/15/90 and Tulsa, 3/18/94.

Highest Three-Point Field Goal Percentage: .769 (10 of 13) at California, 1/21/90.

Most Rebounds: 84 vs. Texas, 12/29/71.

Most Free Throws Made and Attempted: 47 of 61 attempts vs. USC, 3/10/56.

Highest Free Throw Percentage: .964 (27 of 28) vs. San Diego State, 12/29/90.

Largest Winning Margin: 65 vs. Portland, 1/20/67 (Pauley Pavilion); vs. New Mexico, 12/22/54 (Men's Gym); vs. Los Angeles Police, 12/20/46 (Men's Gym).

Largest Losing Margin: 48— 61-109 at Stanford, 1/9/97.

Streaks

Longest Winning Streak: 88 (last 15 games of 1970-71, 30-0, both 1971-72 and1972-73 and first 13 games of 1973-74). This is an NCAA record.

Longest Winning Streak, Pauley Pavilion: 98 (15-0, 1970-71, 17-0, 1971-72, 17-0, 1972-73, 16-0, 1973-74, 16-0, 1974-75 and first 17 games of 1975-76).

Longest Winning Streak, NCAA Tournament Play: 38 (4-0, 1964, 1965, 1967, 1968, 1969, 1970, 1971, 1972, 1973 and 2-0, 1974). This is an NCAA record.

Longest Conference Winning Streak: 50 (last game of 1970, 14-0, 1971, 1972, 1973 and first seven games of 1974). This is a Pacific-10 record.

Longest With One Loss: 107 of 108 (won last five games of 1969-70, won first 14 games of 1970-71, lost to Notre Dame, won final 15 games of 1970-71 season, 30-0, both 1971-72 and 1972-73 and won first 13 games of 1973-74).

Most Consecutive Winning Seasons: 50 — longest current streak, the nation (1948-49 to present).

Most Consecutive 100-Point Games: 7 (1971-72).

Pauley Pavilion Records
Individual

High Points:

Game 61, Lew Alcindor (UCLA) vs. WSU, 2/25/67

Half 32, Lew Alcindor (UCLA) vs. USC, 12/ 3/66; Litterial Green (Georgia), 1/4/92

Field Goal Attempts:

Game 42, Pete Maravich (LSU) vs. UCLA, 12/23/69

Half 22, Pete Maravich (LSU) vs. UCLA, 12/23/69

Field Goals Made:

Game 26, Lew Alcindor (UCLA) vs. WSU, 2/25/67

Half 13, TIE — Lew Alcindor (UCLA) vs. USC, 12/ 3/66; Lew Alcindor (UCLA) vs. WSU, 2/25/67

Three-Point Field Goal Attempts:

Game 17, Stevin Smith (ASU), 1/9/93

Game 14, Reggie Miller (UCLA) vs. Washington, 1/29/87

Three-Point Field Goals Made:

Game 8, Don Leary (CSUF), 12/30/92

Game 6, TIE — Kevin Walker (UCLA) vs. Washington, 2/23/89; Dave Immel (UCLA) vs. Louisville, 2/28/87; Reggie Miller (UCLA) vs. USC, 2/26/87

Free Throw Attempts:

Game 18, Lew Alcindor (UCLA) vs. WSU, 2/25/67

Half 13, Darren Daye (UCLA) vs. San Jose State, 12/11/82

Reggie Miller (UCLA) vs. Arizona State, 1/16/86

Free Throws Made:

Game 17, Reggie Miller (UCLA) vs. Arizona State, 1/16/86

Half 13, Reggie Miller (UCLA) vs. Arizona State, 1/16/86

Rebounds:

Game 28, Elvin Hayes, (Houston) vs. University of Pacific 3/12/66; 27, Bill Walton (UCLA) vs. Maryland, 12/ 1/73

Half 20, Bill Walton (UCLA) vs. Maryland, 12/1/73

Assists: Game 15, Darrick Martin, (UCLA) vs. Pittsburgh, 2/2/91

Lew Alcindor needed just three seasons to take UCLA to unprecedented heights.

Team

High Points: (One Team)

Game 149, by UCLA vs. LMU (149-98), 12/2/90
Half 84, by UCLA vs. LMU (84-55), 12/2/90

High Points: (Two Teams)

Game 247, UCLA vs. LMU (149-98), 12/2/90
Half 139, UCLA vs. LMU (84-55), 2/2/90

Low Points: (UCLA)

Game 44, vs. USC (44-46), 3/ 8/69
Half 14, vs. Oregon (14-30), 2/21/76

Low Points: (Other)

Game 35, by Oregon State (35-79), 1/ 7/66
Half 9, by Howard (9-29), 12/19/83

Field Goal Attempts:

Game 103, by UCLA vs. Iowa State, 12/ 9/67
Half 56, by UCLA vs. Iowa State, 12/ 9/ 67

Field Goals Made:

Game 58, by UCLA vs. LMU, 12/2/90
Half 35, by UCLA vs. LMU, 12/2/90

Three-Point Field Goal Attempts:

Game 34, by ASU, 1/9/93
Game 33, by Oregon, 3/11/95

Three-Point Field Goals Made:

Game 13, by ASU, 1/9/93
Game 10, by UCLA, four times, last vs. San Diego 12/12/92

Free Throw Attempts:

Game 52, by UCLA vs. Colorado, 12/ 2/77
Half 32, by UCLA vs. Texas, 12/13/69

Free Throws Made:

Game 42, by UCLA vs. Colorado, 12/ 2/77
Half 25, by UCLA vs. Texas, 12/13/69

Rebounds:

Game 84, by UCLA vs. Texas, 12/29/71
Half 48, by UCLA vs. Texas, 12/29/71
UCLA's Largest Winning Margin: 65, over Portland (122-57), 1/20/67
UCLA's Largest Losing Margin: 22, by California (104-82), 1/24/93
Attendance: 13,478, Duke vs. UCLA, 2/23/97

Stats

Individual Career Records

Total Points*

Name	Years	G	Points Per Year	Total Points	Avg
Don MacLean	1989-92	127	577-656-714-661	2608	20.5
Lew Alcindor	1967-69	88	870-734-721	2325	26.4
Reggie Miller	1984-87	122	130-503-750-712	2095	17.2
Toby Bailey	1995-98	129	347-458-450-591	1846	14.3
Ed O'Bannon	1992-95	117	83-550-509-673	1815	15.5
J.R. Henderson	1995-98	127	305-418-452-626	1801	14.2
Trevor Wilson	1987-90	126	199-463-570-586	1798	14.3
Tracy Murray	1990-92	98	407-679-706	1792	18.3
Charles O'Bannon	1994-97	124	444-449-326-527	1784	14.4
Bill Walton	1972-74	87	633-612-522	1767	20.3
David Greenwood	1976-79	118	152-484-489-596	1721	14.6
Gail Goodrich	1963-65	89	300-646-744	1690	19.0
Marques Johnson	1974-77	115	194-335-552-578	1659	14.4
Kenny Fields	1981-84	109	253-376-523-486	1638	15.0
Shon Tarver	1991-94	124	288-349-550-388	1575	12.7
Tyus Edney	1992-95	125	179-450-430-456	1515	12.1
Pooh Richardson	1986-89	122	307-336-348-470	1461	12.0
Sidney Wicks	1969-71	90	226-559-638	1423	15.8
Walt Hazzard	1962-64	87	370-473-558	1401	16.1
Kiki Vandeweghe	1977-80	113	82-248-427-623	1380	12.2
Curtis Rowe	1969-71	90	387-459-525	1371	15.2
Rod Foster	1980-83	113	368-308-279-410	1365	12.1
Roy Hamilton	1976-79	108	25-344-481-505	1355	12.5
Keith Wilkes	1972-74	90	406-433-500	1349	15.0
Kris Johnson	1995-98	112	54-388-319-533	1294	11.6
Henry Bibby	1970-72	90	468-355-470	1293	14.4
Richard Washington	1974-76	87	99-492-644	1235	14.2
Willie Naulls	1954-56	79	212-352-661	1225	15.5
Mike Sanders	1979-82	109	43-360-417-390	1210	11.1
John Moore	1952-55	108	230-315-277-280	1202	11.1
Darrick Martin	1989-92	129	265-374-371-185	1195	9.3
Walt Torrence	1957-59	77	321-323-537	1181	15.3
Mike Warren	1966-68	86	432-382-362	1176	13.7
Darren Daye	1980-83	114	161-325-207-456	1149	10.1
John Green	1960-62	108	265-324-559	1148	10.6
Montel Hatcher	1984-87	119	148-278-388-301	1115	9.4
Dave Meyers	1973-75	89	138-342-566	1046	11.8
Mitchell Butler	1990-93	130	203-252-263-305	1023	7.9
Don Bragg	1952-55	108	310-236-280-195	1021	9.5

(1,000 points or more)

Rebounds

Name	Years	G	Rebs Per Year	Total Rebs	Avg
Bill Walton	1972-74	87	466-506-398	1370	15.7
Lew Alcindor	1967-69	88	466-461-440	1367	15.5
David Greenwood	1976-79	118	114-280-319-309	1022	8.7
Trevor Wilson	1987-90	126	152-281-269-299	1001	7.9
Don MacLean	1989-92	127	231-287-226-248	992	7.8
Willie Naulls	1954-56	79	197-293-410	900	11.4
Marques Johnson	1974-77	115	90-205-301-301	897	7.8
Sidney Wicks	1969-71	90	153-357-384	894	9.9
Ed O'Bannon	1992-95	117	70-230-245-275	820	7.0
J.R. Henderson	1995-98	127	138-202-219-259	818	6.4
Charles O'Bannon	1994-97	124	189-201-186-221	797	6.4
Curtis Rowe	1969-71	90	237-260-299	796	9.1
Fred Slaughter	1962-64	87	268-281-242	791	6.4
Don Bragg	1952-55	108	186-217-185-163	751	7.0
Steve Patterson	1969-71	90	112-300-294	706	7.8
Keith Erickson	1963-65	87	170-272-255	697	8.0
Toby Bailey	1995-98	129	158-134-183-195	670	5.2
Kenny Fields	1981-84	109	122-160-192-193	667	6.1
Keith Wilkes	1972-74	90	245-220-198	663	7.4
Walt Torrance	1957-59	77	184-180-289	653	8.5
John Moore	1952-55	108	155-174-141-180	650	6.0
Tracy Murray	1990-92	98	182-213-232	627	6.4

Field Goal Percentage*

Player	Years	FG-FGA	Pct
Jelani McCoy	1996-98	347-500	.694
Bill Walton	1972-74	747-1147	.651
Lew Alcindor	1967-69	943-1476	.639
Stuart Gray	1982-84	242-422	.573
Kiki Vandeweghe	1977-80	536-941	.570
Marques Johnson	1974-77	688-1211	.568
Darren Daye	1980-83	452-815	.555
J.R. Henderson	1995-98	677-1234	.549
Reggie Miller	1984-87	769-1405	.547
Kenny Fields	1981-84	686-1260	.544

* Minimum 400 attempts

Field Goals Scored

Player	Years	FGM
Lew Alcindor	1967-69	943
Don MacLean	1989-92	943
Reggie Miller	1984-87	769
Bill Walton	1972-74	747
David Greenwood	1976-79	707
Trevor Wilson	1987-90	706
Marques Johnson	1974-77	688
Kenny Fields	1981-84	686
C. O'Bannon	1994-97	684
Toby Bailey	1995-98	679
Ed O'Bannon	1992-95	678
J.R. Henderson	1995-98	677

Field Goals Attempted

Player	Years	FGA
Don MacLean	1989-92	1776
Toby Bailey	1995-98	1479
Lew Alcindor	1967-69	1476
Trevor Wilson	1987-90	1417
Reggie Miller	1984-87	1405
Gail Goodrich	1963-65	1338
Ed O'Bannon	1992-95	1321
David Greenwood	1976-79	1302
C. O'Bannon	1994-97	1271
Tracy Murray	1990-92	1267

Three-Point Field Goal Percentage*

Player	Years	3FG-FGA	Pct
Pooh Richardson	1986-89	52-112	.464
Reggie Miller	1984-87	69-157	.439
Tracy Murray	1990-92	197-479	.411
Kevin Dempsey	1993-96	58-142	.408
Kevin Walker	1987-90	116-286	.406
Gerald Madkins	1988-92	118-296	.399
Ed O'Bannon	1992-95	91-231	.394
Montel Hatcher	1984-87	19-49	.388
Tyus Edney	1992-95	97-253	.383
Kris Johnson	1995-98	64-172	.372
Dave Immel	1984-88	77-207	.372

* Minimum 40 Attempts

Three-Point Field Goals Scored

Player	Years	3 Pt FG
Tracy Murray	1990-92	197
Toby Bailey	1995-98	171
Gerald Madkins	1988, 90-92	118
Kevin Walker	1987-90	116
Tyus Edney	1992-95	97
Ed O'Bannon	1992-95	91
Dave Immel	1984-88	77
C. O'Bannon	1994-97	73
Kris Johnson	1995-98	70
Shon Tarver	1991-94	70

Three-Point Field Goals Attempted

Player	Years	3 Pt FGA
Toby Bailey	1995-98	501
Tracy Murray	1990-92	479
Gerald Madkins	1988, 90-92	296
Kevin Walker	1987-90	286
Tyus Edney	1992-95	253
Ed O'Bannon	1992-95	231
Shon Tarver	1991-94	225
Darrick Martin	1989-92	214
C. O'Bannon	1994-97	213
Dave Immel	1984-88	207

Free Throw Percentage*

Player	Years	FT-FTA	Pct.
Rod Foster	1980-83	309-351	.880
Don MacLean	1989-92	711-827	.860
Reggie Miller	1984-87	488-584	.836
Gary Cunningham	1960-62	201-244	.824
Henry Bibby	1970-72	275-334	.823
Kris Johnson	1995-98	302-374	.807
Tyus Edney	1992-95	450-559	.805
Greg Lee	1972-74	134-167	.802
Tracy Murray	1990-92	329-416	.791
Brad Holland	1976-79	146-186	.785
Pete Blackman	1960-62	193-247	.781

* Minimum 150 Attempts

Free Throws Scored

Player	Years	FTM
Don MacLean	1989-92	711
Reggie Miller	1984-87	488
Tyus Edney	1992-95	450
Lew Alcindor	1967-69	439
J.R. Henderson	1995-98	435
Gail Goodrich	1963-65	416
John Green	1960-62	404
Walt Hazzard	1962-64	385
Trevor Wilson	1987-90	384
Ed O'Bannon	1992-95	368

Free Throws Attempted

Player	Years	FTA
Don MacLean	1989-92	827
Lew Alcindor	1967-69	699
J.R. Henderson	1995-98	682
Trevor Wilson	1987-90	654
Gail Goodrich	1963-65	595
Reggie Miller	1984-87	584
Tyus Edney	1992-95	559
Walt Hazzard	1962-64	545
John Green	1960-62	543
John Moore	1952-55	536

Assists

Player	Years	A
Pooh Richardson	1986-89	833
Tyus Edney	1992-95	652
Darrick Martin	1989-92	637
Ralph Jackson	1981-84	523
Roy Hamilton	1976-79	512
Toby Bailey	1995-98	458
Cameron Dollar	1994-97	451
Gerald Madkins	1988, 90-92	404
Andre McCarter	1974-76	376
Bill Walton	1972-74	316

Steals

Player	Years	S
Tyus Edney	1992-95	224
Cameron Dollar	1994-97	214
Pooh Richardson	1986-89	189
Darrick Martin	1989-92	179
Reggie Miller	1984-87	158
Ed O'Bannon	1992-95	146
Gerald Madkins	1988, 90-92	146
Shon Tarver	1991-94	145
Ralph Jackson	1981-84	145
J.R. Henderson	1995-98	142
C. O'Bannon	1994-97	142

Games Played

Player	Years	G
Mitchell Butler	1990-93	130
Toby Bailey	1995-98	129
Darrick Martin	1989-92	129
J.R. Henderson	1995-98	127
Don MacLean	1989-92	127
Trevor Wilson	1987-90	126
Tyus Edney	1992-95	125
C. O'Bannon	1994-97	124
Shon Tarver	1991-94	124
Cameron Dollar	1994-97	123
Gerald Madkins	1988, 90-92	123

Stats

Individual Season Records

Points Scored

Player	Year	Pts	Avg
Lew Alcindor	1967	870	29.0
Reggie Miller	1986	750	25.9
Gail Goodrich	1965	744	24.8
Lew Alcindor	1968	734	26.2
Lew Alcindor	1969	721	24.0
Don MacLean	1991	714	23.0
Reggie Miller	1987	712	22.3
Tracy Murray	1992	706	21.4
Tracy Murray	1991	679	21.2
Ed O'Bannon	1995	673	20.4
Don MacLean	1992	661	20.7
Willie Naulls	1956	661	23.6
Don MacLean	1990	656	19.9
Gail Goodrich	1964	646	21.5
Richard Washington	1976	644	20.1
Sidney Wicks	1971	638	21.3
Bill Walton	1972	633	21.1
J.R. Henderson	1998	626	19.0
Kiki Vandeweghe	1980	623	19.5
Bill Walton	1973	612	20.4
David Greenwood	1979	596	19.9
Toby Bailey	1998	591	17.9
Marques Johnson	1977	578	21.4
Don MacLean	1989	577	18.6
Trevor Wilson	1989	570	18.4
Trevor Wilson	1990	566	17.2
David Meyers	1975	566	18.3
Charles O'Bannon	1997	565	17.7
Sidney Wicks	1970	559	18.6
John Green	1962	559	19.3
Walt Hazzard	1964	558	18.6
Marques Johnson	1976	552	17.3
Shon Tarver	1993	550	17.2
Ed O'Bannon	1993	550	16.7
Walt Torrence	1959	537	21.5
Kris Johnson	1998	533	18.4
Brad Holland	1979	526	17.5
Curtis Rowe	1971	525	17.5
Kenny Fields	1983	523	18.0
Bill Walton	1974	522	19.3
Ed O'Bannon	1994	509	18.2
Roy Hamilton	1979	505	16.8
Reggie Miller	1985	503	15.2
Keith Wilkes	1974	500	16.7

Rebounds

Player	Year	Rebs	Avg
Bill Walton	1973	506	16.9
Bill Walton	1972	466	15.5
Lew Alcindor	1967	466	15.5
Lew Alcindor	1968	461	16.5
Lew Alcindor	1969	440	14.7
Willie Naulls	1956	410	14.6
Bill Walton	1974	398	14.7
Sidney Wicks	1971	384	12.8
Sidney Wicks	1970	357	11.9
David Greenwood	1978	319	11.4
David Greenwood	1979	309	10.3
Marques Johnson	1977	301	11.1
Marques Johnson	1976	301	9.4
Steve Patterson	1970	300	10.0
Trevor Wilson	1990	299	9.1
Curtis Rowe	1971	299	10.0
Edgar Lacey	1965	295	9.8
John Berberich	1961	296	11.4
Steve Patterson	1971	294	9.8
Willie Naulls	1955	293	11.3
Walt Torrence	1959	289	11.6
Don MacLean	1990	287	8.7
Brad Wright	1985	287	8.7
Trevor Wilson	1988	281	9.4
Fred Slaughter	1963	281	9.7
David Greenwood	1977	280	9.7

Field Goal Percentage

Player	Year	FG-FGA	Pct.
Jelani McCoy	1997	152-201	.756
Jelani McCoy	1996	138-204	.676
Lew Alcindor	1967	346-519	.667
Bill Walton	1974	232-349	.665
Bill Walton	1973	277-426	.650
Bill Walton	1972	238-372	.639
Lew Alcindor	1969	303-477	.635
Kiki Vandeweghe	1979	166-267	.622
Lew Alcindor	1968	294-480	.613
Kelvin Butler	1988	107-176	.608

Field Goals Scored

Player	Year	FGM
Lew Alcindor	1967	346
Lew Alcindor	1969	303
Lew Alcindor	1968	294
Bill Walton	1973	277
Gail Goodrich	1965	277
Richard Washington	1976	276
Reggie Miller	1986	274
Don MacLean	1991	259
Tracy Murray	1991	247
Reggie Miller	1987	247
David Greenwood	1979	247
Ed O'Bannon	1995	247

Field Goals Attempted

Player	Year	FGA
Willie Naulls	1956	582
Richard Washington	1976	538
Gail Goodrich	1964	530
Gail Goodrich	1965	528
Lew Alcindor	1967	519
Walt Torrence	1959	516
Reggie Miller	1986	493
Tracy Murray	1991	491
Lew Alcindor	1968	480
Alan Sawyer	1950	479

Three-Point Field Goal Percentage*

Player	Year	3FG-FGA	Pct
Tracy Murray	1992	78-156	.500
Pooh Richardson	1989	48-97	.495
Dave Immel	1987	43-94	.457
Kevin Walker	1989	57-125	.456
Reggie Miller	1987	69-157	.439
Ed O'Bannon	1995	55-127	.433
Kevin Walker	1988	34-79	.430
Gerald Madkins	1990	38-90	.422
Tyus Edney	1993	34-82	.415
Kris Johnson	1998	47-115	.409

* Minimum one made per game

Three-Point Field Goals Scored

Player	Year	3-FGM
Tracy Murray	1992	78
Tracy Murray	1991	73
Reggie Miller	1987	69
Toby Bailey	1996	62
Kevin Walker	1989	57
Ed O'Bannon	1995	55
Pooh Richardson	1989	48
Toby Bailey	1998	47
Kris Johnson	1998	47
Tracy Murray	1990	46

Three-Point Field Goals Attempted

Player	Year	3-FGA
Tracy Murray	1991	189
Toby Bailey	1996	157
Reggie Miller	1987	157
Tracy Murray	1992	156
Toby Bailey	1998	145
Tracy Murray	1990	134
Ed O'Bannon	1995	127
Toby Bailey	1997	126
Kevin Walker	1989	125
Kris Johnson	1998	115

Free Throw Percentage

Player	Year	FT-FTA	Pct
Rod Foster	1982	95-100	.950
Don MacLean	1992	197-214	.921
Rod Foster	1981	60-66	.909
Reggie Miller	1986	202-229	.882
Keith Wilkes	1974	82-94	.872
Michael Holton	1983	64-75	.853
Jim Spillane	1977	58-68	.853
Don MacLean	1990	179-211	.848
Don MacLean	1991	193-228	.846
Rod Foster	1980	80-95	.842

Free Throws Scored

Player	Year	FTM
Reggie Miller	1986	202
Don MacLean	1992	197
John Green	1962	201
Don MacLean	1991	193
Gail Goodrich	1965	190
Willie Naulls	1956	185
Don MacLean	1990	179
Lew Alcindor	1967	178
J.R. Henderson	1998	166
Walt Torrence	1959	165

Free Throws Attempted

Player	Year	FTA
Lew Alcindor	1967	274
Gail Goodrich	1965	265
John Green	1962	262
J.R. Henderson	1998	260
Willie Naulls	1956	242
Lew Alcindor	1968	237
Reggie Miller	1986	229
Don MacLean	1991	228
Sidney Wicks	1971	227
Gail Goodrich	1964	225

Assists

Player	Year	G	Ast
Pooh Richardson	1989	31	236
Darrick Martin	1991	32	217
Tyus Edney	1995	32	216
Pooh Richardson	1988	30	210
Pooh Richardson	1987	32	208
Roy Hamilton	1979	30	201
Darrick Martin	1990	33	199
Tyus Edney	1993	33	186
Pooh Richardson	1986	29	179
Bill Walton	1973	30	168

Steals

Player	Year	G	St
Cameron Dollar	1997	32	82
Baron Davis	1998	32	77
Tyus Edney	1995	32	74
Earl Watson	1998	33	64
Ed O'Bannon	1995	33	64
Reggie Miller	1987	32	64
Tyus Edney	1993	33	63
Pooh Richardson	1989	31	57
Cameron Dollar	1995	33	54
Shon Tarver	1993	32	53
Tracy Murray	1992	33	53
Roy Hamilton	1979	30	53

Minutes Played*

Player	Year	G	Min
Tyus Edney	1993	33	1207.0
Toby Bailey	1998	32	1177.0
Reggie Miller	1985	33	1173.5
Pooh Richardson	1989	31	1167.0
Reggie Miller	1987	32	1166.0
Toby Bailey	1997	32	1148.0
Ed O'Bannon	1995	33	1130.0
C. O'Bannon	1997	32	1128.0
Shon Tarver	1993	32	1119.0
Pooh Richardson	1987	32	1112.0
Reggie Miller	1986	29	1112.0

*Since 1979

Blocked Shots*

Player	Year	G	BS
Jelani McCoy	1996	31	102
David Greenwood	1979	30	76
Jelani McCoy	1997	32	61
Keith Owens	1991	32	61
Richard Petruska	1993	33	58
Brad Wright	1985	33	44
Rodney Zimmerman	1993	33	41
Charles O'Bannon	1995	33	38
Charles O'Bannon	1994	28	38
Charles Rochelin	1988	30	36

*Since 1979

Stats

Miscellaneous Season Records

Career 20-Point Games

Don MacLean	68
Lew Alcindor	65
Gail Goodrich	47
Reggie Miller	47
Tracy Murray	46
Bill Walton	44
Ed O'Bannon	38
Sidney Wicks	37
Trevor Wilson	31
David Greenwood	31
Marques Johnson	28
J.R. Henderson	27
Richard Washington	25
Kenny Fields	24
Roy Hamilton	23
Willie Naulls	22
Toby Bailey	22

Career 30-Point Games

Lew Alcindor	27
Reggie Miller	16
Don MacLean	12
Bill Walton	11
Marques Johnson	7
Gail Goodrich	7

Single-Season 20-Point Games

Gail Goodrich	25	1965
Tracy Murray	24	1992
Lew Alcindor	24	1967
Reggie Miller	23	1986
Lew Alcindor	22	1968
Gail Goodrich	22	1964
Don MacLean	21	1991
Sidney Wicks	20	1971
Willie Naulls	20	1956
Ed O'Bannon	19	1995
Tracy Murray	19	1991
Lew Alcindor	19	1969
Don MacLean	18	1992
Reggie Miller	18	1987
Bill Walton	18	1974
Don MacLean	17	1990
Richard Washington	17	1976
J.R. Henderson	17	1998

Single-Season 30-Point Games

Lew Alcindor	11	1967
Lew Alcindor	9	1968
Reggie Miller	8	1987
Reggie Miller	8	1986
Lew Alcindor	7	1969
Don MacLean	6	1991
Bill Walton	6	1972
Gail Goodrich	5	1965
Marques Johnson	4	1977

Career Blocked Shots

Jelani McCoy	188
Charles O'Bannon	118
Rodney Zimmerman	97
Ed O'Bannon	95
Tracy Murray	91
Charles Rochelin	88
Keith Owens	87
David Greenwood	76
Brad Wright	74
Mike Sanders	68
J.R. Henderson	68

Career Double-Figure Scoring

Don MacLean (68 straight)	123
Charles O'Bannon	102
J.R. Henderson	95
Toby Bailey	94
Kenny Fields	92
Ed O'Bannon	90
Trevor Wilson	90
Reggie Miller	89
David Greenwood	89
Lew Alcindor (69 straight)	87
Tracy Murray	87
Tyus Edney	87
Shon Tarver	83
Marques Johnson	83
Keith Wilkes	83
Pooh Richardson	80
Bill Walton	78
Walt Hazzard	78

Single-Season Double-Figure Scoring

Ed O'Bannon	33	1995
Tracy Murray	32	1992
Tracy Murray	32	1991
Don MacLean	32	1990
Trevor Wilson	32	1990
Toby Bailey	31	1998
J.R. Henderson	31	1998
Charles O'Bannon	31	1997
Shon Tarver	31	1993
Don MacLean	31	1992
Don MacLean	31	1991
Tyus Edney	30	1993
Richard Washington	30	1976
David Meyers	30	1975
Lew Alcindor	30	1967
Gail Goodrich	30	1965
Gail Goodrich	30	1964

Career Double-Figure Rebounds

Lew Alcindor	78
Bill Walton	75
David Greenwood	52
Sidney Wicks	49
Trevor Wilson	42
Willie Naulls	42

Career Double-Doubles

Lew Alcindor	78
Bill Walton	72
David Greenwood	49
Sidney Wicks	46
Willie Naulls	42
Don MacLean	37
Trevor Wilson	36

Career 20-Rebounds

Lew Alcindor	25
Bill Walton	19

Single-Game Triple-Doubles

Jelani McCoy
15 pts., 10 rebs.,
11 blocks vs. Maryland,
12/9/95

Toby Bailey
23 pts., 10 rebs.,
10 assists vs. S.F. Austin,
12/18/95

Single-Season Double Rebounds

Bill Walton	29	1973
Lew Alcindor	28	1967
Lew Alcindor	27	1968
Willie Naulls	26	1956
Bill Walton	25	1972
Sidney Wicks	23	1971
Lew Alcindor	23	1968
Sidney Wicks	22	1970
Bill Walton	21	1974

Season Double-Doubles

Lew Alcindor	28	1967
Lew Alcindor	27	1968
Bill Walton	27	1973
Willie Naulls	26	1956
Bill Walton	24	1972
Sidney Wicks	23	1971
Lew Alcindor	23	1968
Sidney Wicks	22	1970
Bill Walton	21	1974

Season 20-Rebounds

Lew Alcindor	9	1967
Lew Alcindor	9	1969
Bill Walton	8	1973
Lew Alcindor	7	1968
Bill Walton	7	1972
Bill Walton	4	1974

Single-Game Rebounds

28	Willie Naulls Arizona State, 1/28/56
27	Bill Walton Maryland, 12/1/73; Loyola (Chi), 1/25/73
24	Bill Walton Providence, 1/20/73; Washington, 2/12/72; Texas, 12/29/71
24	Lew Alcindor Washington St., 2/25/67, Georgia Tech, 12/29/66
23	David Greenwood Washington, 1/6/78; Tulsa, 12/18/76
23	Lew Alcindor New Mexico St., 3/15/68; Oregon State, 2/18/67; UCSB, 1/21/67
22	Bill Walton California, 3/1/74; USF, 1/19/73; UCSB, 12/16/72
22	Sidney Wicks California, 3/5/71
22	Lew Alcindor St. John's, 12/30/68; California, 3/2/68; Oregon, 2/10/68; Holy Cross, 1/26/68; Duke, 12/10/66

UCLA's NCAA Results

The Bruins have played in 34 NCAA Tournaments and have compiled a record of 79-27 (.745). They hold the records for most championships (11) and rank second in victories (79).

1950 (0-2)
West Regionals
59 Bradley   73
62 Brigham Young   83
1952 (0-2)
West Regionals
59 Santa Clara   68
53 Oklahoma City   55
1956 (1-1)
West Regionals
61 USF   72
94 Seattle   70
1962 (2-2)
West Regionals
73 Utah State   62
88 Oregon State   69
Championships
70 Cincinnati   72
80 Wake Forest   82
1963 (0-2)
West Regionals
79 Arizona State   93
75 USF   76
1964 (4-0)
West Regionals
95 Seattle   90
76 USF   72
Championships
90 Kansas State   84
98 Duke   83
1965 (4-0)
West Regionals
100 Brigham Young   76
101 USF   93
Championships
108 Wichita   89
91 Michigan   80
1967 (4-0)
West Regionals
109 Wyoming   60
80 Pacific   64
Championships
73 Houston   58
79 Dayton   64

1968 (4-0)
West Regionals
58 New Mexico State   49
87 Santa Clara   66
Championships
101 Houston   69
78 North Carolina   55
1969 (4-0)
West Regionals
53 New Mexico State   38
90 Santa Clara   52
Championships
85 Drake   82
92 Purdue   72
1970 (4-0)
West Regionals
88 Long Beach State   65
101 Utah State   79
Championships
93 New Mexico State   77
80 Jacksonville   69
1971 (4-0)
West Regionals
91 Brigham Young   73
57 Long Beach State   55
Championships
68 Kansas   60
68 Villanova   62
1972 (4-0)
West Regionals
90 Weber State   58
73 Long Beach State   57
Championships
96 Louisville   77
81 Florida State   76
1973 (4-0)
West Regionals
98 Arizona State   81
54 USF   39
Championships
70 Indiana   59
87 Memphis State   66

1974 (3-1)
West Regionals
111 Dayton   100 (3 OT)
83 USF   60
Championships
77 No. Carolina St. 80 (2 OT)
78 Kansas   61
1975 (5-0)
First Round
103 Michigan   91 (OT)
West Regionals
67 Montana   64
89 Arizona State   75
Championships
75 Louisville   74 (OT)
92 Kentucky   85
1976 (4-1)
First Round
74 San Diego State   64
West Regionals
70 Pepperdine   61
82 Arizona   66
Championships
51 Indiana   65
106 Rutgers   92
1977 (1-1)
First Round
87 Louisville   79
West Regionals
75 Idaho State   76
1978 (1-1)
First Round
83 Kansas   76
West Regionals
70 Arkansas   74
1979 (2-1)
Second Round
76 Pepperdine   71
West Regionals
99 USF   81
91 DePaul   95
1980 (5-1)
First Round
87 Old Dominion   74

Second Round
77 DePaul   71
West Regionals
72 Ohio State   68
85 Clemson   74
Championships
67 Purdue   62
54 Louisville   59
1981 (0-1)
Second Round East Regional
55 Brigham Young   78
1983 (0-1)
Second Round West Regional
61 Utah   67
1987 (1-1)
First Round West Regional
92 Central Michigan   73
Second Round
68 Wyoming   78
1989 (1-1)
First Round Southeast Regional
84 Iowa State   74
Second Round
81 North Carolina   88
1990 (2-1)
First Round East Regional
68 UAB   56
Second Round
71 Kansas   70
East Regionals
81 Duke   90
1991 (0-1)
First Round East Regional
69 Penn State   74
1992 (3-1)
First Round West Regional
73 Robert Morris   53
Second Round
85 Louisville   69

West Regionals
85 New Mexico State   78
79 Indiana   106
1993 (1-1)
First Round West Regional
81 Iowa State   70
Second Round
84 Michigan   86 (OT)
1994 (0-1)
First Round Midwest Regional
102 Tulsa   112
1995 (6-0)
First Round West Regional
92 Florida International 56
Second Round
75 Missouri   74
West Regionals
86 Mississippi State   67
102 Connecticut   96
Championships
74 Oklahoma State   61
89 Arkansas   78
1996 (0-1)
First Round Southeast Regional
41 Princeton   43
1997 (3-1)
First Round Midwest Regional
109 Charleston Southern 75
Second Round
96 Xavier   83
Midwest Regionals
74 Iowa State   73 (OT)
72 Minnesota   80
1998 (2-1)
First Round South Regional
65 Miami   62
Second Round
85 Michigan   82
South Regionals
68 Kentucky   94

Stats   **177**

1950

Mar. 24, 1950: NCAA West Regional first game at Kansas City, MO; Bradley 73, UCLA 59. Bradley – Mann 7, Preece 3, Chianakas 4, Melchiorre 19, Schlictman 1, Unruh 13, Behnke 10, Kelly 0, Grover 16. UCLA – Norman 0, Joeckel 13, Matulich 0, Sawyer 14, Saunders 0, Kraushaar 5, Alba 0, Sheldrake 11, Seidel 2, Johnson 0, Stanich 14, Alper 0. Haltime – Bradley 33, UCLA 33.

Mar. 25, 1950: NCAA West Regional consolation game at Kansas City, MO; Brigham Young 83, UCLA 62. Brigham Young – Minson 13, Nelson 30, Hutchins 21, Beem 10, Craig 2, Jones 1, Romney 2, Whipple 4. UCLA – Joeckel 3, Norman 0, Saunders 6, Sawyer 16, Matulich 0, Kraushaar 6, Alba 0, Johnson 2, Sheldrake 21, Stanich 5, Alper 3. Halftime – UCLA 41, Brigham Young 37.

1952

Mar. 21, 1952: NCAA West Regional first game at Corvallis, OR; Santa Clara 68, UCLA 59. Santa Clara – Sears 9, Young 15, Garibaldi 9, Soares 2, Shoenstein 18, Peters 7, Brock 5, Benedetti 2. UCLA – Moore 6, Norman 4, Bragg 7, Pounds 0, Evans 0, Hibler 8, Bane 13, Johnson 5, Livingston 14, Porter 0, Davidson 0, Costello 2. Halftime – UCLA 35, Santa Clara 31.

Mar. 22, 1952: NCAA West Regional consolation game at Corvallis, OR; Oklahoma City 55, UCLA 53. Oklahoma City – Likens 10, Thompson 8, Bullard 0, Penwell 11, Mayfield 2, Dalton 0, Rose 2, Short 22, Couts 0, Rich 0. UCLA – Moore 15, Norman 9, Bane 3, Bragg 1, Pounds 0, Costello 0, Evans 2, Hibler 4, Johnson 1, Livingston 13, Porter 3, Davidson 2. Halftime – Oklahoma City 35, UCLA 29.

1956

Mar. 16, 1956: NCAA West Regional first game at Corvallis, OR; USF 72, UCLA 61. USF – Boldt 0, Farmer 15, Russell 21, Perry 10, Brown 23, Preaseau 3, Baxter 0. UCLA – Herring 7, Burke 2, Naulls 16, Taft 16, Banton 13, Halsten 6, Adams 0, Arnold 0, Hutchins 0, Johnson 1. Halftime – USF 39, UCLA 21.

Mar. 17, 1956: NCAA West Regional consolation game at Corvallis, OR; UCLA 94, Seattle 70. UCLA – Herring 0, Burke 5, Naulls 33, Taft 20, Banton 6, Johnson 12, Halsten 16, Adams 0, Hutchins 0, Eblen 0, Arnold 2, Harrison 0. Seattle – Frizzell 21, Sanford 5, Fuhrer 13, Markey 8, Harney 7, Godes 6, Bauer 10, Stricklin 0, Rajcich 0. Halftime – UCLA 40, Seattle 34.

1962

Mar. 16, 1962: NCAA West Regional first game at Provo, UT; UCLA 73, Utah State 62. UCLA – Cunningham 21, Blackman 8, Slaughter 10, Hazzard 13, Green 11, Stewart 8, Hicks 2, Waxman 0, Rosvall 0. Utah State – Green 26, Johnson 10, Haney 12, Hasen 10, Goldsberry 2, Nate 0, Holman 2. Halftime – UCLA 43, Utah State 30.

Mar. 17, 1962: NCAA West Regional championship at Provo, UT; UCLA 88, Oregon State 69. UCLA – Cunningham 12, Blackman 7, Slaughter 7, Hazzard 17, Green 23, Waxman 12, Hicks 4, Stewart 2, Rosvall 2, Gower 2, Milhorn 0, Huggins 0. Oregon State – Carty 9, Jacobson 5, Counts 24, Baker 6, Pauly 10, Rossi 2, Benner 0, Hayward 6, Campbell 0, Bastor 3, Torgerson 4. Halftime – UCLA 44, Oregon State 30.

Mar. 23, 1962: NCAA Championship semifinals at Louisville, KY; Cincinnati 72, UCLA 70. Cincinnati – Bonham 19, Wilson 3, Hogue 36, Thacker 2, Yates 10, Sizer 2. UCLA – Blackman 4, Cunningham 19, Slaughter 2, Green 27, Hazzard 12, Waxman 6, Stewart 0. Halftime – UCLA 37, Cincinnati 37.

Mar. 24, 1962: NCAA Championship consolation game at Louisville, KY; Wake Forest 82, UCLA 80. Wake Forest – Chappell 26, Christie 2, Wollard 9, Packer 22, Wiedeman 18, McCoy 3, Hull 0, Brooks 0, Hassell 2. UCLA–Cunningham 17, Blackman 11, Slaughter 17, Green 7, Hazzard 15, Waxman 7, Hicks 4, Stewart 2, Milhorn 0. Halftime–Wake Forest 38, UCLA 36.

1963

Mar. 15, 1963: NCAA West Regional first game at Provo, UT; Arizona State 93, UCLA 79. Arizona State – Caldwell 22, Cerkvenik 18, Becker 23, Senitza 13, Dairman 13, Howard 2, Disarufino 0, Orr 0, Jones 2, Owens 0, Sturgeon 0. UCLA – Hirsch 19, Goss 8, Slaughter 14, Hazzard 13, Goodrich 3, Erickson 2, Waxman 5, Stewart 13, Milhorn 2. Halftime – Arizona State 62, UCLA 31.

Mar. 16, 1963: NCAA West Regional consolation game at Provo, UT; USF 76, UCLA 75. USF – E. Thomas 15, Lee 5, Johnson 20, Moffatt 11, Brovelli 13, Brainard 4, H. Thomas 8. UCLA – Waxman 13, Hirsch 6, Slaughter 4, Hazzard 13, Milhorn 6, Stewart 2, Erickson 2, Goodrich 17, Goss 10, Huggins 2. Halftime – UCLA 35, USF 30.

1964

Mar. 13, 1964: NCAA West Regional first game at Corvallis, OR; UCLA 95, Seattle 90. UCLA – Erickson 7, Hirsch 21, Slaughter 13, Goodrich 19, Hazzard 26, McIntosh 2, Stewart 0, Washington 7, Huggins 0, Hoffman 0, Darrow 0. Seattle – Tresvant 20, Vermillion 15, Wheeler 20, Williams 12, Heyward 9, Phillips 6, Turney 8, Tebbs 0. Halftime – UCLA 49, Seattle 39.

Mar. 14, 1964: NCAA West Regional championship at Corvallis, OR; UCLA 76, USF 72. UCLA – Erickson 7, Hirsch 14, Slaughter 9, Goodrich 15, Hazzard 23, McIntosh 3, Washington 5. USF – Lee 6, Mueller 15, Johnson 20, Brovelli 11, Ellis 11, Thomas 0, Brainard 5, Gumina 2. Halftime – USF 36, UCLA 28.

Mar. 20, 1964: NCAA Championship semifinals at Kansas City, MO; UCLA 90, Kansas State 84. UCLA – Goodrich 14, Slaughter 4, Hazzard 19, Hirsch 4, Erickson 28, McIntosh 8, Washington 13. Kansas State – Moss 7, Robinson 4, Simons 24, Suttner 6, Murrell 29, Paradis 10, Williams 4, Nelson 0, Gottfrid 0, Barnard 0. Halftime – UCLA 43, Kansas State 41.

Mar. 21, 1964: NCAA Championship finals at Kansas City, MO; UCLA 98, Duke 83. UCLA – Goodrich 27, Slaughter 0, Hazzard 11, Hirsch 13, Erickson 8, McIntosh 8, Washington 26, Darrow 3, Stewart 0, Huggins 0, Hoffman 2, Levin 0. Duke – Ferguson 4, Buckley 18, Tison 7, Harrison 2, Mullins 22, Marin 16, Vacendak 7, Herbster 2, Kitching 2, Mann 3, Herscher 0, Cox 0. Halftime – UCLA 50, Duke 38.

1965

Mar. 12, 1965: NCAA West Regional first game at Provo, UT; UCLA 100, Brigham Young 76. UCLA – Lacey 15, Erickson 28, McIntosh 2, Goodrich 40, Goss 4, Washington 1, Lynn 8, Hoffman 0, Chambers 0, Lyons 2, Levin 0. Brigham Young – Kramer 10, Roberts 7, Fairchild 23, Gardner 14, Nemelka 5, Hill 4, Quinney 4, Congdon 4, Stanley 4, Raymond 1, Jimas 0, James 0. Halftime – UCLA 51, Brigham Young 40.

Mar. 13, 1965: NCAA West Regional championship at Provo, UT; UCLA 101, USF 93. UCLA – Lacey 15, Erickson 29, McIntosh 5, Goss 13, Goodrich 30, Lynn 7, Washington 2. USF – Gumina 16, Mueller 12, Johnson 37, Ellis 16, Thomas 8, James 2, Blum 2, Esters 0. Halftime – UCLA 51, USF 46.

Mar. 19, 1965: NCAA Championship semifinals at Portland, OR; UCLA 108, Wichita 89. UCLA – Lacey 24, Erickson 24, McIntosh 11, Goodrich 28, Goss 19, Washington 10, Lynn 10, Chambers 0, Lyons 4, Levin 0, Galbraith 0, Hoffman 0. Wichita – Smith 8, Thompson 36, Leach 12, Pete 17, Criss 8, Reed 5, Davis 2, Trope 0, Nosich 1, Reimond 0. Halftime – UCLA 65, Wichita 38.

Mar. 20, 1965: NCAA Championship finals at Portland, OR; UCLA 91, Michigan 80. UCLA – Erickson 3, Lacey 11, McIntosh 3, Goodrich 42, Goss 8, Washington 17, Lynn 5, Hoffman 2, Lyons 0, Galbraith 0, Chambers 0. Michigan – Darden 17, Poemy 4, Buntin 14, Russell 28, Tregoning 5, Myers 0, Ludwig 0, Clawson 6, Dill 4. Halftime – UCLA 47, Michigan 34.

1967

Mar. 17, 1967: NCAA West Regional first game at Corvallis, OR; UCLA 109, Wyoming 60. UCLA – Heitz 6, Shackelford 10, Alcindor 29, Allen 10, Chrisman 6, Nelson 8, Saner 4, Sweek 8, Lynn 0, Sutherland 5, Saffer 8. Wyoming – Hall 19, Asbury 20, Von Krosigk 4, Wilson 5, Eberle 12, Nelson 0. Halftime – UCLA 55, Wyoming 18.

Mar. 18, 1967: NCAA West Regional championship at Corvallis, OR; UCLA 80, Pacific 64. UCLA – Heitz 9, Shackelford 6, Alcindor 38, Allen 13, Warren 12, Sweek 2, Saffer 0. Pacific – Krulish 12, Jones 0, Swagerty 11, Parsons 7, Fox 17, DeWitt 6, Foley 9, Ferguson 2. Halftime – UCLA 37, Pacific 27.

Mar. 24, 1967: NCAA Championship semifinals at Louisville, KY; UCLA 73, Houston 58. UCLA – Heitz 1, Shackelford 22, Alcindor 19, Allen 17, Warren 14, Nielsen 0, Sweek 0, Saffer 0. Houston – Hayes 25, Bell 10, Kruse 5, Chaney 6, Grider

4, Lentz 2, Spain 2, Lee 4, Lewis 0. Halftime – UCLA 39, Houston 28.

Mar. 25, 1967: NCAA Championship finals at Louisville, KY; UCLA 79, Dayton 64. UCLA – Heitz 4, Shackelford 10, Alcindor 20, Warren 17, Allen 19, Saffer 4, Nielsen 0, Saner 2, Sutherland 0, Sweek 2, Lynn 0, Chrisman 1. Dayton – Sadlier 5, May 21, Obrovac 0, Torain 6, Hooper 6, Klaus 8, Waterman 10, Wannemacher 0, Inderrieden 0, Samanich 0, Heckman 0, Sharpenter 8. Halftime – UCLA 38, Dayton 20.

1968

Mar. 15, 1968: NCAA West Regional first game at Albuquerque, NM; UCLA 58, New Mexico State 49. UCLA – Lynn 4, Shackelford 7, Alcindor 28, Warren 10, Allen 6, Heitz 3, Nielsen 0. New Mexico State – Burgess 4, R. Collins 5, Lacey 6, J. Collins 16, Evans 14, Murphy 0, Landis 4, Morehead 0, Las 0. Halftime – UCLA 28, New Mexico State 28.

Mar. 16, 1968: NCAA West Regional championship at Albuquerque, NM; UCLA 87, Santa Clara 66. UCLA – Lynn 10, Shackelford 4, Alcindor 22, Allen 21, Warren 15, Heitz 7, Sutherland 0, Saner 2, Nielsen 4, Sweek 2. Santa Clara – Heaney 4, B. Ogden 13, Awtrey 17, O'Brien 7, Diffley 2, Eagleson 2, Stuckey 5, Donahue 0, Paulson 0, Dempsey 1, R. Ogden 11, Thomas 4. Halftime – UCLA 51, Santa Clara 34.

Mar. 22, 1968: NCAA Championship semifinals at Los Angeles Sports Arena; UCLA 101, Houston 69. UCLA – Shackelford 17, Lynn 19, Alcindor 19, Warren 14, Allen 19, Nielsen 4, Heitz 7, Sweek 2, Sutherland 0, Saner 0. Houston – Lee 4, Hayes 10, Spain 15, Chaney 15, Lewis 6, Hamood 10, Gribben 0, Bell 9, Taylor 0, Cooper 0. Halftime – UCLA 53, Houston 31.

Mar. 23, 1968: NCAA Championship finals at Los Angeles Sports Arena; UCLA 78, North Carolina 55. UCLA – Shackelford 6, Lynn 7, Alcindor 34, Warren 7, Allen 11, Nielsen 2, Heitz 7, Sutherland 2, Sweek 0, Saner 2. North Carolina – Miller 14, Bunting 3, Clark 9, Scott 12, Grubar 5, Fogler 4, Brown 6, Tuttle 0, Frye 2, Whitehead 0, Delaney 0, Fletcher 0. Halftime – UCLA 32, North Carolina 22.

1969

Mar. 13, 1969: NCAA West Regional first game at Pauley Pavilion, Los Angeles, CA; UCLA 53, New Mexico State 38. UCLA – Rowe 8, Shackelford 8, Alcindor 16, Heitz 9, Vallely 10, Wicks 0, Sweek 2, Patterson 0, Schofield 0. New Mexico State – Smith 7, Reyes 5, Lacey 11, Collins 11, Burgess 0, Murphy 2, Bowen 2. Halftime – UCLA 24, New Mexico State 17.

Mar. 14, 1969: NCAA West Regional championship at Pauley Pavilion, Los Angeles, CA; UCLA 90, Santa Clara 52. UCLA – Shackelford 6, Rowe 7, Alcindor 17, Vallely 11, Heitz 6, Sweek 12, Wicks 11, Patterson 9, Schofield 2, Ecker 5, Seibert 2, Farmer 2. Santa Clara – R. Ogden 4, B. Ogden 9, Awtrey 14, Eagleson 0, O'Brien 0, Diffley 2, Paulson 0, Dempsey 5, Tobin 2, Scherer 4, Graves 3, Champ 4. Halftime – UCLA 46, Santa Clara 25.

Mar. 20, 1969: NCAA Championship semifinals at Louisville, KY; UCLA 85, Drake 82. UCLA – Shackelford 6, Rowe 14, Alcindor 25, Heitz 7, Vallely 29, Wicks 0, Sweek 0, Patterson 2, Schofield 0. Drake – Pulliam 12, Williams 0, Wise 13, McCarter 24, Draper 12, Odom 0, Wanamaker 9, Zeller 12, Gwin 0. Halftime – UCLA 41, Drake 39.

Mar. 21, 1969: NCAA Championship finals at Louisville, KY; UCLA 92, Purdue 72. UCLA – Shackelford 11, Rowe 12, Alcindor 37, Heitz 0, Vallely 15, Sweek 6, Wicks 3, Schofield 2, Patterson 4, Seibert 0, Farmer 0, Ecker 2. Purdue – Gilliam 7, Faerber 2, Johnson 11, Mount 28, Keller 11, Kaufman 2, Bedford 7, Weatherford 4, Reasoner 0, Taylor 0. Halftime – UCLA 42, Purdue 31.

1970

Mar. 12, 1970: NCAA West Regional first game at Seattle, WA; UCLA 88, Cal State Long Beach 65. UCLA – Wicks 20, Rowe 15, Patterson 13, Vallely 14, Bibby 20, Booker 0, Ecker 2, Schofield 2, Siebert 0, Chapman 2. CSLB – Robinson 18, Jankans 5, Trapp 20, Gritton 0, Johnson 13, McLucas 0, Taylor 3, Montgomery 6, Williams 0. Halftime – UCLA 42, Cal State Long Beach 29.

Mar. 14, 1970: NCAA West Regional finals at Seattle, WA; UCLA 101, Utah State 79. UCLA – Wicks 26, Rowe 26, Patterson 9, Bibby 15, Vallely 14, Booker 4, Ecker 1, Schofield 0, Chapman 0, Seibert 4, Betchley 2, Hill 0. Utah State – Williams 14, Roberts 33, Tollestrup 6, Jeppesen 12, Epps 12, Hatch 2, Ericksen 0, Wakefield 0,

Wade 0, Bean 0. Halftime – UCLA 51, Utah State 44.

Mar. 19, 1970: NCAA Championship semifinals at College Park, MD; UCLA 93, New Mexico State 77. UCLA – Rowe 15, Patterson 12, Wicks 22, Vallely 23, Bibby 19, Booker 0, Betchley 0, Schofield 0, Ecker 0, Seibert 0, Hill 0, Chapman 2. New Mexico State – Criss 19, Collins 28, Burgess 2, Smith 10, Lacey 8, Reyes 2, Neal 4, Horne 2, Moore 2, Lefeure 0, Franco 0, McCarthy 0. Halftime – UCLA 48, New Mexico State 41.

Mar. 21, 1970: NCAA Championship finals at College Park, MD; UCLA 80, Jacksonville 69. UCLA – Rowe 19, Patterson 17, Wicks 17, Vallely 15, Bibby 8, Booker 2, Seibert 0, Ecker 2, Betchley 0, Chapman 0, Hill 0, Schofield 0. Jacksonville – Wedeking 12, Blevins 3, Morgan 10, Burrows 12, Gilmore 19, Nelson 8, Dublin 2, Baldwin 0, McIntyre 2, Hawkins 1, Selke 0. Halftime – UCLA 41, Jacksonville 36.

1971

Mar. 18, 1971: NCAA West Regional first game at Salt Lake City, UT; UCLA 91, Brigham Young 73. UCLA – Rowe 13, Wicks 14, Patterson 13, Bibby 15, Booker 4, Schofield 12, Farmer 11, Ecker 2, Betchley 7. Brigham Young – Tollestrup 1, Kelly 24, Cosic 18, Fryer 18, Miller 10, Bunker 2, Jorgensen 0, Sarkalahti 0, Bailey 0. Halftime – UCLA 41, Brigham Young 32.

Mar. 20, 1971: NCAA West Regional finals at Salt Lake City, UT; UCLA 57, Cal State Long Beach 55. UCLA – Rowe 12, Wicks 18, Patterson 5, Bibby 11, Booker 0, Schofield 6, Farmer 1, Betchley 4, Ecker 0. Cal State Long Beach – Trapp 15, Terry 11, Lynn 7, Williams 2, Ratleff 18, McWilliams 0, Taylor 2. Halftime – Cal State Long Beach 31, UCLA 27.

Mar. 25, 1971: NCAA Championship semifinals at Houston, TX; UCLA 68, Kansas 60. UCLA – Rowe 16, Wicks 21, Patterson 6, Bibby 18, Booker 3, Schofield 2, Farmer 0, Betchley 0, Ecker 2, Hill 0, Chapman 0. Kansas – Robisch 17, Russell 12, Brown 7, Stallworth 12, Nash 7, Kiuisto 3, Canfield 0, Williams 2, Mathews 0, Douglas 0. Halftime – UCLA 32, Kansas 25.

Mar. 27, 1971: NCAA Championship finals at Houston, TX; UCLA 68, Villanova 62. UCLA – Rowe 8, Wicks 7, Patterson 29, Bibby 17, Booker 0, Schofield 6, Betchley 1. Villanova – Smith 9, Porter 25, Siemiontkowski 19, Inglesby 7, Ford 2, McDowell 0. Halftime – UCLA 45, Villanova 37.

1972

Mar. 16, 1972: NCAA West Regional first game at Provo, UT; UCLA 90, Weber State 58. UCLA – Farmer 15, Wilkes 10, Walton 4, Lee 6, Bibby 16, Curtis 7, Hollyfield 4, Nater 12, Carson 0, Chapman 2, Hill 10, Franklin 4. Weber State – Davis 16, Van Dyke 4, Cooper 8, Small 4, Knoble 9, Wimberly 14, Gubler 2, Soter 1, McGarry 0. Halftime – UCLA 42, Weber State 25.

Mar. 18, 1972: NCAA West Regional finals at Provo, UT; UCLA 73, Cal State Long Beach 57. UCLA – Wilkes 14, Farmer 5, Walton 19, Lee 6, Bibby 23, Hollyfield 0, Nater 5, Curtis 0, Carson 0, Chapman 0, Hill 1, Franklin 0. Cal State Long Beach – Terry 6, Gray 7, McWilliams 7, McDonald 8, Ratleff 17, Lynn 6, Stephens 2, King 4. Halftime – UCLA 34, Cal State Long Beach 23.

Mar. 23, 1972: NCAA Championship semifinals at Los Angeles Sports Arena; UCLA 96, Louisville 77. UCLA – Wilkes 12, Farmer 15, Walton 33, Lee 10, Bibby 2, Curtis 8, Hollyfield 6, Carson 2, Nater 2, Hill 6, Chapman 0, Franklin 0. Louisville – Lawhon 1, Thomas 4, Vilcheck 6, Price 30, Bacon 15, Carter 8, Bunton 3, Bradley 2, Stallings 2, Cooper 2, Pry 4, Meiman 0. Halftime – UCLA 39, Louisville 31.

Mar. 25, 1972: NCAA Championship finals at Los Angeles Sports Arena; UCLA 81, Florida State 76. UCLA – Wilkes 23, Farmer 4, Walton 24, Lee 0, Bibby 18, Curtis 8, Hollyfield 2, Nater 2. Florida State – Garrett 3, King 27, Royals 15, McCray 8, Samuel 6, Harris 16, Petty 1, Cole 0. Halftime – UCLA 50, Florida State 39.

1973

Mar. 15, 1973: NCAA West Regional first game at Pauley Pavilion, Los Angeles, CA; UCLA 98, Arizona State 81. UCLA – Wilkes 12, Farmer 10, Walton 28, Hollyfield 20, Lee 3, Curtis 7, Meyers 6, Nater 4, Carson 0, Franklin 2, Trgovich 2, Webb 0, Corliss 2, Drollinger 0. Arizona State – Gray 4, Wasley 6, Kennedy 9, Contreras 18, Owens 22, White 6, Jackson 10, Brown 7, Schrader 0, Moon 0. Halftime – UCLA 51, Arizona State 37.

Mar. 17, 1973: NCAA West Regional finals at Pauley Pavilion, Los Angeles, CA; UCLA 54, USF 39. UCLA – Wilkes 12, Farmer 13, Walton 9, Hollyfield 0, Lee 2, Meyers 2, Curtis 12, Nater 0, Franklin 2, Carson 0, Webb 0, Trgovich 2. USF – Restani 8, Smith 17, Fernsten 4, Quick 8, Boro 2. Halftime – UCLA 23, USF 22.
Mar. 24, 1973: NCAA Championship semifinals at St. Louis, MO; UCLA 70, Indiana 59. UCLA – Wilkes 13, Farmer 7, Walton 14, Lee 0, Hollyfield 10, Curtis 22, Meyers 4, Nater 0. Indiana – Buckner 6, Crews 8, Downing 26, Green 2, Ritter 13, Laskowski 2, Aber-nethy 0, Smock 0, Noort 0, Wilson 0, Morris 0, Ahlfield 0, Allen 2, Memering 0. Halftime – UCLA 40, Indiana 22.
Mar. 26, 1973: NCAA Championship finals at St. Louis, MO; UCLA 87, Memphis State 66. UCLA – Wilkes 16, Farmer 2, Walton 44, Lee 5, Hollyfield 8, Curtis 4, Meyers 4, Nater 2, Franklin 2, Carson 0, Webb 0. Memphis State – Buford 7, Kenon 20, Robinson 6, Laurie 0, Finch 29, Westfall 0, Cook 4, McKinney 0, Jones 0, Telzlaff 0, Liss 0, Andrews 0. Halftime – UCLA 39, Memphis State 39.

1974
Mar. 14, 1974: NCAA West Regional first game at Tucson, AZ; UCLA 111, Dayton 100 (3 OT). UCLA – Meyers 28, Wilkes 14, Walton 27, Lee 12, Curtis 0, McCarter 10, Washington 0, Trgovich 4, Johnson 14, Franklin 2. Dayton – Sylvester 36, Elijah 2, Von Lehman 2, Smith 26, Davis 17, Fisher 15, Testerman 2. Halftime – UCLA 48, Dayton 36. End of regulation – UCLA 80, Dayton 80.
Mar. 16, 1974: NCAA West Regional finals at Tucson, AZ; UCLA 83, USF 60. UCLA – Wilkes 27, Meyers 12, Walton 17, Curtis 6, Lee 8, McCarter 2, Johnson 5, Trgovich 0, Drollinger 0, Webb 0, Washington 4, Franklin 2. USF – Randell 2, Restani 20, Fernsten 3, P. Smith 18, H. Smith 9, Boro 0, Coleman 0, Quanstrom 6, Redmond 2, Styles 0. Halftime – UCLA 35, USF 23.
Mar. 23, 1974: NCAA Championship semifinals at Greensboro, North Carolina; North Carolina State 80, UCLA 77 (2 OT). North Carolina State – Stoddard 9, Thompson 28, Burleson 20, Rivers 7, Towe 12, Spence 4, Hawkins 0. UCLA – Meyers 12, Wilkes 15, Walton 29, Curtis 11, Lee 8, Johnson 0, McCarter 2. Halftime – North Carolina State 35, UCLA 35. End of regulation – North Carolina State 65, UCLA 65.
Mar. 25, 1974: NCAA Championship consolation game at Greensboro, North Carolina; UCLA 78, Kansas 61. UCLA – Meyers 8, Wilkes 12, Walton 6, Curtis 0, Lee 0, Trgovich 14, McCarter 4, Franklin 2, Johnson 4, Drollinger 7, Washington 8, Webb 10, Spillane 1, Olinde 2. Kansas – Cook 9, Morningstar 3, Knight 12, Greenlee 17, Kivisto 8, Smith 6, Suttle 4, Von Moore 0, Taynor 2. Halftime – Kansas 38, UCLA 31.

1975
Mar. 15, 1975: NCAA First Round game at Pullman, WA; UCLA 103, Michigan 91 (OT). UCLA – Washington 22, Meyers 26, Spillane 4, McCarter 4, Olinde 0, Townsend 0, Trgovich 17, Drollinger 8, Corliss 0, Johnson 22. Michigan – Johnson 11, Baxter 0, Grote 14, Britt 8, White 6, Kupec 28, Robinson 24. Halftime – Michigan 50, UCLA 46. End of regulation – UCLA 87, Michigan 87.
Mar. 20, 1975: NCAA West Regional first game at Portland, OR; UCLA 67, Montana 64. UCLA – Meyers 12, Johnson 7, Washington 16, Trgovich 16, McCarter 6, Townsend 2, Drollinger 8, Corliss 0, Spillane 0, Smith 0. Montana – Hayes 32, Smedley 10, McKenzie 20, Mike R. Richardson 2, Peck 0, DeMers 0, Stambaugh 0, Blaine 0. Haltime – UCLA 34, Montana 33.
Mar. 22, 1975: NCAA West Regional finals at Portland, OR; UCLA 89, Arizona State 75. UCLA – Meyers 11, Johnson 35, Washington 16, Trgovich 8, McCarter 9, Vroman 0, Drollinger 9, Olinde 1. Arizona State – White 15, Schrader 9, Lloyd 20, Moon 4, Hollins 16, Holliman 3, Wright 4, White 0, Jackson 4. Halftime – UCLA 46, Arizona State 36.
Mar. 29, 1975: NCAA Championship semifinals at San Diego, CA; UCLA 75, Louisville 74 (OT). UCLA – Meyers 16, Johnson 10, Washington 26, Trgovich 12, McCarter 6, Drollinger 3, Olinde 0, Spillane 2. Louisville – Murphy 33, Cox 14, Bunton 2, Bridgeman 12, Bond 6, Whitfield 0, Gallon 0, Brown 2, Wilson 0, Howard 0. Halftime – Louisville 37, UCLA 33. End of regulation – UCLA 65, Louisville 65.
Mar. 31, 1975: NCAA Championship finals at San Diego, CA; UCLA 92, Kentucky 85. UCLA – Meyers 24, Johnson 6, Washington 28, Trgovich 16, McCarter 8, Drollinger 10. Kentucky – Grevey 34, Guyette 16, Robey 2, Conner 9, Flynn 10, Givens 8, Johnson 0, Phillips 4, Hall 2, Lee 0. Halftime – UCLA 43, Kentucky 40.

1976
Mar. 13, 1976: NCAA First Round game at Eugene, OR; UCLA 74, San Diego State 64. UCLA – Washington 25, Johnson 19, Greenwood 4, Townsend 6, McCarter 10, Vroman 0. Drollinger 0, Spillane 2, Olinde 0, Smith 4. San Diego State – Leary 6, Earle 0, Delsman 4, Brown 0, Copp 20, Dodd 0, Kovach 11, Connelly 11, Kramer 2, Bunting 10. Halftime – UCLA 35, San Diego State 32.
Mar. 18, 1976: NCAA West Regional first game at Pauley Pavilion, Los Angeles, CA; UCLA 70, Pepperdine 61. UCLA – Washington 16, Johnson 18, Greenwood 10, McCarter 4, Townsend 8, Drollinger 8, Smith 6, Spillane 0, Vroman 0. Pepperdine – Matson 10, Skophammer 8, Leite 16, Williams 10, Johnson 16, Dallmar 0, Ellis 1, Goorjian 0. Halftime – UCLA 40, Pepperdine 35.
Mar. 20, 1976: NCAA West Regional finals at Pauley Pavilion, Los Angeles, CA; UCLA 82, Arizona 66. UCLA – Washington 22, Johnson 14, Greenwood 10, Townsend 16, McCarter 9, Smith 2, Drollinger 3, Spillane 2, Vroman 0, Holland 4, Hamilton 0, Olinde 0. Arizona – Taylor 14, Fleming 14, Elliott 10, Rappis 4, Harris 18, Gladney 2, Gordy 0, Myles 0, Harrison 0, Maxey 2, Jung 0, Marshall 0, Demic 2, Aleska 0. Halftime – UCLA 38, Arizona 35.
Mar. 27, 1976: NCAA Championship semifinals at Philadelphia, PA; Indiana 65, UCLA 51. Indiana – Abernethy 14, May 14, Benson 16, Wilkerson 5, Buckner 12, Crews 4. UCLA – Washington 15, Johnson 12, Greenwood 5, Townsend 4, McCarter 4, Drollinger 2, Holland 0, Spillane 0, Smith 6, Hamilton 1, Vroman 0, Lippert 2, Olinde 0. Halftime – Indiana 34, UCLA 26.
Mar. 29, 1976: NCAA Championship consolation game at Philadelphia, PA; UCLA 106, Rutgers 92. UCLA – Washington 11, Greenwood 5, Drollinger 12, McCarter 26, Johnson 30. Townsend 8, Vroman 0, Smith 8, Spillane 4, Olinde 2. Rutgers – Sellers 23, Copeland 18, Bailey 7, Jordan 8, Dabney 21, Anderson 13, Conlin 0, Hefele 2. Halftime – UCLA 57, Rutgers 49.

1977
Mar. 12, 1977: NCAA First Round game at Pocatello, ID; UCLA 87, Louisville 79. UCLA – Johnson 17, Greenwood 8, Sims 4, Hamilton 11, Spillane 16, Holland 16, Townsend 2, Vroman 9, Olinde 0, Vandeweghe 4. Louisville – Cox 23, Williams 14, Gallon 4, Wilson 6, Bond 10, Brown 0, Branch 0, Turner 8, Harmon 0, Griffith 14. Halftime – UCLA 39, Louisville 36.
Mar. 17, 1977: NCAA West Regional first round game at Provo, UT; Idaho State 76, UCLA 75. Idaho State – Griffin 12, Cook 8, Hayes 27, Thompson 14, Goold 2, Wheeler 4, Robinson 8, Wilson 1. UCLA – Greenwood 20, Johnson 21, Sims 0, Spillane 4, Hamilton 11, Vroman 2, Holland 9, Vandeweghe 6, Townsend 2, Olinde 0, Wilkes 0. Halftime – UCLA 38, Idaho State 32.

1978
Mar. 11, 1978: NCAA First Round game at Eugene, OR; UCLA 83, Kansas 76. UCLA – Hamilton 23, Townsend 22, Greenwood 14, Vandeweghe 11, Allums 6, Wilkes 5, Sims 2. Kansas – Mokeski 18, Johnson 15, Douglas 14, Valentine 11, Von Moore 8, Koenig 8, Anderson 0, Folwier 0, Gipson 0. Halftime – Kansas 45, UCLA 42.
Mar. 16, 1978: NCAA West Regional first round game at Albuquerque, NM; Arkansas 74, UCLA 70. Arkansas – Delph 23, Moncrief 21, Brewer 18, Schall 8, Counce 2, Zahn 2, Reed 0. UCLA – Hamilton 19, Greenwood 17, Allums 12, Holland 8, Wilkes 6, Vandeweghe 4, Townsend 2, Thomas 2, Sims 0. Halftime – Arkansas 42, UCLA 29.

1979
Mar. 11, 1979: NCAA Second Round game at Pauley Pavilion, Los Angeles, CA; UCLA 76, Pepperdine 71. UCLA – Greenwood 18, Vandeweghe 8, Sims 8, Holland 14, Hamilton 14, Allums 4, Wilkes 8, Naulls 2. Pepperdine – Matson 14, Ramsey 2, Ellis 10, Brown 27, Fuller 10, Graebe 2, Scott 6. Halftime – Pepperdine 38, UCLA 36.
Mar. 15, 1979: NCAA West Regional first game at Provo, UT; UCLA 99, USF 81. UCLA – Greenwood 18, Vandeweghe 11, Sims 0, Holland 22, Hamilton 36, Allums 0, Wilkes 8, Sanders 0, Thomas 0, Kelly 0, Naulls 3. USF – Jemison 4, Bowers 4, Cartwright 34, Williams 12, Reid 13, Bryant 10, Cornelious 0, DeLoatch 0, McAlister 2, Gilberg 2. Halftime – USF 43, UCLA 41.

The Bruin 100

Mar. 17, 1979: NCAA West Regional finals at Provo, UT; DePaul 95, UCLA 91. DePaul – Aguirre 20, Watkins 24, Mitchem 14, Garland 24, Bradshaw 13, Nikitas 0, Madey 0. UCLA – Greenwood 37, Vandeweghe 17, Sims 0, Holland 19, Hamilton 16, Wilkes 2, Naulls 0, Allums 0, Sanders 0, Thomas 0. Halftime – DePaul 51, UCLA 34.

1980
Mar. 7, 1980: NCAA First Round game at Tempe, AZ; UCLA 87, Old Dominion 74. UCLA – Vandeweghe 34, Wilkes 15, Sanders 11, Foster 11, Holton 12, Daye 4, Pruitt 0, Anderson 0. Old Dominion – McAdoo 25, Valentine 14, West 0, Mann 6, Robinson 0, Vaughn 15, Branch 8, Southerland 0, Haithcock 2, Griekspoor 0, Kragtwijk 4. Halftime – UCLA 36, Old Dominion 26.
Mar. 9, 1980: NCAA Second Round game at Tempe, AZ; UCLA 77, DePaul 71. UCLA – Wilkes 10, Vandeweghe 13, Sanders 15, Foster 18, Holton 8, Daye 0, Allums 3, Pruitt 10. DePaul – Aguirre 19, Mitchem 0, Cummings 23, Bradshaw 13, Dillard 14, Grubbs 2. Halftime – UCLA 34, DePaul 31.
Mar. 13, 1980: NCAA West Regional first game at Tucson, AZ; UCLA 72, Ohio State 68. UCLA – Wilkes 8, Vandeweghe 12, Sanders 19, Foster 19, Holton 0, Allums 0, Daye 10, Pruitt 4. Ohio State – Smith 2, Kellogg 12, Williams 10, Ransey 29, Scott 6, Hall 2, Ellinghausen 4, Huggins 1, Penn 2, Miller 0. Halftime – UCLA 35, Ohio State 31.
Mar. 15, 1980: NCAA West Regional finals at Tucson, AZ; UCLA 85, Clemson 74. UCLA – Wilkes 2, Vandeweghe 22, Sanders 22, Foster 12, Holton 6, Daye 7, Allums 6, Pruitt 6, Arrillaga 2. Clemson – Nance 13, Wyatt 4, Campbell 5, Conrad 9, Williams 18, Gilliam 13, Wiggins 4, Dodds 8, Ross 0. Halftime – UCLA 46, Clemson 35.
Mar. 22, 1980: NCAA Championship semifinals at Indianapolis, IN; UCLA 67, Purdue 62. UCLA – Wilkes 4, Vandeweghe 24, Sanders 12, Foster 9, Holton 4, Allums 0, Daye 6, Sims 0, Pruitt 8. Purdue – Morris 12, Hallman 12, Carroll 17, Edmonson 23, B. Walker 6, Stallings 0, Scearce 0, Barnes 2, S. Walker 0. Halftime – UCLA 33, Purdue 25.
Mar. 24, 1980: NCAA Championship finals at Indianapolis, IN; Louisville 59, UCLA 54. Louisville – Brown 8, Smith 9, McCray 7, Eaves 8, Griffith 23, Burkman 0, Wright 4, Branch 0. UCLA – Wilkes 2, Vandeweghe 14, Sanders 10, Foster 16, Holton 4, Pruitt 6, Daye 2, Allums 0, Anderson 0. Halftime – UCLA 28, Louisville 26.

1981
Mar. 14, 1981: NCAA Second Round game at Providence, RI; Brigham Young 78, UCLA 55. Brigham Young – Roberts 17, Trumbo 4, Kite 12, Ainge 37, Craig 8, Webb 0, Christiansen 0, Ballif 0, Bartholomew 0, Saarelaingn 0, Furniss 0, McGuire 0. UCLA – Sanders 14, Daye 12, Pruitt 8, Jackson 2, Holton 10, Foster 2, Sears 2, Anderson 1, Fields 4. Halftime – Brigham Young 31, UCLA 22.

1983
Mar. 19, 1983: NCAA Second Round game at Boise, ID; Utah 67, UCLA 61. Utah – Williams 18, Mannion 18, Winas 6, Hendrix 6, Robinson 18, Furgis 0, McLaughlin 0, Cecil 0. UCLA – Daye 9, Fields 18, Wright 2, Jackson 4, Foster 14, Holton 4, Miguel 6, Gray 4. Halftime – UCLA 34, Utah 32.

1987
Mar. 12, 1987: NCAA First Round game at Salt Lake City, UT; UCLA 92, Central Michigan 73. CMU – Murray 13, Leavy 14, Johnson 18, Miller 2, Majerie 17, Richmond 3, Scott 2, Wilcox 0, McGuire 4. UCLA – Haley 3, Richardson 13, Immel 11, Miller 32, Rochelin 9, Wilson 8, Hatcher 8, Foster 6, Walker 0, Jackson 2. Halftime – UCLA 53, Central Michigan 21.
Mar. 14, 1987: NCAA Second Round game at Salt Lake City, UT; Wyoming 78, UCLA 68. Wyoming – Dent 2, Fox 1, Leckner 20, Dembo 41, Sommers 6, Boyd 6, Jones 2, Hunt 0, Lodgins 0. UCLA – Richardson 8, Immel 10, Haley 5, Miller 24, Rochelin 5, Wilson 2, Hatcher 10, Palmer 0, Foster 0, Jackson 4. Halftime – UCLA 44, Wyoming 38.

1989
Mar. 17, 1989: NCAA First Round game at Atlanta, GA; UCLA 84, Iowa State 74. Iowa State – Urquhart 2, Baugh 16, Alexander 22, Woods 9, Born 6, Mack 8, Moore 9, Goodman 0, Suffren 0. UCLA – Wilson 14, MacLean 23, Walker 2, Martin 8, Richardson 19, Rochelin 16, Owens 2. Halftime – UCLA 39, Iowa State 35.
Mar. 19, 1989: NCAA Second Round game at Atlanta, GA; North Carolina 88, UCLA 81. UCLA – Wilson 21, MacLean 16, Walker 17, Martin 4, Richardson 14, Rochelin 7, Owens 2. North Carolina – Bucknall 19, Fox 18, Williams 14, Lebo 12, Rice 3, Madden 22, Chilcutt 0, Davis 0, Denny 0. Halftime – UCLA 52, North Carolina 44.

1990
Mar. 16, 1990: NCAA First Round game at Atlanta, GA; UCLA 68, Alabama-Birmingham 56. UAB – Kennedy 9, Rembert 6, Ogg 8, Bearden 8, Kramer 10, Rogers 11, Wilkerson 0, Devaughn 3, Jackson 0. UCLA – Wilson 23, MacLean 10, Murray 14, Madkins 7, Martin 8, Butler 4, Walker 2. Halftime – UCLA 30, UAB 27.
Mar. 18, 1990: NCAA Second Round game at Atlanta, GA; UCLA 71, Kansas 70. UCLA – Wilson 18, MacLean 10, Murray 12, Madkins 3, Martin 18, Butler 8, Walker 2, Owens 0. Kansas – Calloway 14, Randall 4, Markkanen 0, Pritchard 15, Gueldner7, Maddox 10, Brown 15, Jordan 0, West 5, Jamison 0. Halftime – Kansas 36, UCLA 35.
Mar. 22, 1990: NCAA East Regional first game at East Rutherford, NJ; Duke 90, UCLA 81. UCLA – Wilson 16, MacLean 21, Murray 15, Madkins 17, Martin 4, Butler 6, Owens 0, Mason 0, Walker 2. Duke – Brickey 7, Laettner 24, Abdelnaby 14, Henderson 28, Hurley 12, McCaffrey 3, Koubek 0, Davis 2, Hill 0, Palmer 0. Halftime – Duke 47, UCLA 38.

1991
Mar. 18, 1991: NCAA East Regional first round game at Syracuse, NY; Penn State 74, UCLA 69. Penn State – Barnes 19, Hayes 16, Degitz 10, Barnes 4, Brown 10, Jennings 10, Johnson 3, Joyner 0, Carter 2, Dietz 0. UCLA – Murray 17, MacLean 15, Madkins 13, Owens10, Butler 9, Martin 3, Tarver 2. Halftime – UCLA 36, Penn State 32

1992
Mar. 20, 1992: NCAA West Regional first round game at Tempe, AZ; UCLA 73, Robert Morris 53. UCLA – Murray 20, MacLean 17, Butler 0, Edney 0, Madkins 16, Martin 4, Tarver 10, O'Bannon 4, Zimmerman 0, Elkind 0, Zidek 2. Robert Morris – Carney 2, Falletta 2, Cannon 9, Timmerson 12, Walker 15, Bilall 7, Jones 0, Donnelly 6, Williams 0. Halftime – UCLA 26, Robert Morris 22.
Mar. 22, 1992: NCAA West Regional second round game at Tempe, AZ; UCLA 85, Louisville 69. UCLA – Murray 26, MacLean 23, Butler 9, Edney 5, Madkins 16, Tarver 4, O'Bannon 0, Martin 2, Zidek 0, Elkind 0. Louisville – Minor 11, Morton 4, Holden 10, LaGree 5, Sullivan 11, Smith 7, Hopgood 2, Brewer 13, Wingfield 0, Webb 2, Stone 4, McLendon 0. Halftime – UCLA 32, Louisville 25.
Mar. 26, 1992: NCAA West Regional first game at Albuquerque, NM; UCLA 85, New Mexico St. 78. NMS – Traylor 13, Reed 14, Hickman 9, Crawford 16, Benjamin 11, Sittler 0, Leak 3, Coleman 4, Bartleson 0, Thompson 8, Putzi 0. UCLA – MacLean 19, Murray 20, Butler 4, Madkins 15, Edney 1, Zimmerman 0, Martin 13, Tarver 5, O'Bannon 7. Halftime – UCLA 47, New Mexico St. 31.
Mar. 28, 1992: NCAA West Regional finals at Albuquerque, NM; Indiana 106, UCLA 79. IND – Cheaney 23, Henderson 10, Nover 16, Reynolds 8, Bailey 22, Graham 3, Meeks 5, Leary 0, Anderson 17, Lindeman 2. UCLA – Murray 15, MacLean 12, Butler 0, Edney 12, Madkins 18, Zimmerman 0, Martin 2, Tarver 20, Elkind 0, Zidek 0, O'Bannon 7. Halftime – Indiana 44, UCLA 29.

1993
Mar. 19, 1993: NCAA First Round game at McKale Center, Tucson, AZ: UCLA 81, Iowa State 70. Iowa State – Hoiberg 11, Eaton 6, Meyer 6, Bayless 19, Thigpen 20, Michalik 2, Wheat 6, Beechum 0, Bivens 0, Brown 0. UCLA – Butler 14, O'Bannon 20, Petruska 14, Tarver 11, Edney 19, Dempsey 3, Zimmerman 0. Halftime –UCLA 37, Iowa State 30.
Mar. 21, 1993: NCAA Second Round game at McKale Center, Tucson, AZ: Michigan 86, UCLA 84 ot. Michigan – Webber 27, Jackson 19, Howard 14, Rose 12, King 11, Riley 3, Pelinka 0, Talley 0, Voskuil 0. UCLA – Butler 14, O'Bannon 19, Petruska 7, Tarver 24, Edney 10, Zimmerman 1, Dempsey 9, Zidek 0, Boyle 0. Halftime –UCLA 52, Michigan 39. Regulation: 77-77.

1994

Mar. 18, 1994: NCAA First Round game at The Myriad, Oklahoma City, OK; Tulsa 112, UCLA 102. UCLA – Charles O'Bannon 15, Ed O'Bannon 30, Zidek 8, Edney 10, Tarver 11, Dollar 3, Zimmerman 0, Burns 11, Dempsey 14. Tulsa – Collier 34, Seals 20, Rollo 5, Dawkins 14, Williamson 20, Hernadi 0, Johnson 12, Maldonado 3, Bonner 4, Grawer 0. Halftime – Tulsa 63, UCLA 38.

1995

Mar. 17, 1995: NCAA First Round game at Boise, ID; UCLA 92, Florida International 56. UCLA – Charles O'Bannon 14, Ed O'Bannon 10, Zidek 8, Edney 8, Bailey 7, Dollar 5, Myers 4, Dempsey 2, Nwankwo 6, Givens 2, Henderson 16, Johnson 10. Florida International – Mazyck 21, Forbes 6, Eason 4, Tchir 5, Dozier 8, Davis 7, L. Johnson 2, J. Johnson 1, Allen 2, Johnston 0, Eathorne 0, Nicolls 0, Pimburton 0. Halftime – UCLA 43, Florida International 23.

Mar. 19, 1995: NCAA Second Round game at Boise, ID; UCLA 75, Missouri 74. UCLA – Charles O'Bannon 6, Ed O'Bannon 24, Zidek 10, Edney 15, Bailey 9, Dollar 0, Henderson 11. Missouri – Winfield 8, Grimm 13, Sa. Haley 3, O'Liney 23, Sutherland 15, Moore 10, Sim. Haley 2, Walther 0, Combs 0. Halftime – Missouri 42, UCLA 34.

Mar. 23, 1995: NCAA West Regional Semifinal at Oakland, CA; UCLA 86, Mississippi State 67. UCLA – Charles O'Bannon 9, Ed O'Bannon 21, Zidek 11, Edney 10, Bailey 12, Dollar 2, Myers 0, Dempsey 0, Nwankwo 4, Givens 4, Henderson 8, Johnson 5. Mississippi State – Grant 2, Bullard 10, D. Wilson 22, Dampier 11, Honore 6, Price 4, Walters 10, B. Wilson 0, Hughes 0, Young 0. Halftime – UCLA 40, Mississippi State 19.

Mar. 25, 1995: NCAA West Regional Final at Oakland, CA; UCLA 102, Connecticut 96. UCLA – Charles O'Bannon 10, Ed O'Bannon 15, Zidek 8, Edney 22, Bailey 26, Henderson 18, Dollar 3. Connecticut – Marshall 15, Allen 36, Knight 12, Sheffer 24, Ollie 2, Hayward 2, Fair 3, King 2, Johnson 0, Willingham 0. Halftime – UCLA 48, Connecticut 41.

Apr. 1, 1995: NCAA Championship Semifinal at Seattle, WA; UCLA 74, Oklahoma State 61. UCLA – Charles O'Bannon 19, Ed O'Bannon 15, Zidek 6, Edney 21, Bailey 2, Henderson 2, Dollar 9, Dempsey 0, Nwankwo 0, Givens 0, Johnson 0, Myers 0. Oklahoma State – Pierce 2, Collins 6, Reeves 25, Rutherford 15, Owens 3, Roberts 10, Skaer 0, Alexander 0, Baum 0, Nelson 0, Miles 0. Halftime – UCLA 37, Oklahoma State 37.

Apr. 3, 1995: NCAA Championship Final at Seattle, WA; UCLA 89, Arkansas 78. UCLA – Charles O'Bannon 11, Ed O'Bannon 30, Zidek 14, Edney 0, Bailey 26, Henderson 2, Dollar 6. Arkansas – Thurman 5, Williamson 12, Martin 3, McDaniel 16, Beck 11, Stewart 12, Dillard 6, Robinson 4, Rimac 2, Wilson 7, Williams 0, Garrett 0. Halftime – UCLA 40, Arkansas 39.

1996

Mar. 14, 1996: NCAA First Round game at The RCA Dome, Indianapolis, IN; Princeton 43, UCLA 41. UCLA – O'Bannon 8, Henderson 2, McCoy 2, Bailey 13, Dollar 0, Johnson 10, Loyd 6, Myers 0, Dempsey 0. Princeton – Doyal 3, Lewullis 10, Goodrich 8, Johnson 11, Henderson 8, Earl 3, Mastaglio 0. Halftime – UCLA 19, Princeton 18.

1997

Mar. 13, 1997: NCAA First Round game at Auburn Hills, MI; UCLA 109, Charleston Southern 75. UCLA – O'Bannon 14, Henderson 21, McCoy 21, Dollar 15, Bailey 14, Sylvester 0, Loyd 3, Harbour 2, McGautha 0, Myers 4, Farnham 6, Parker 0, Johnson 9. Charleston Southern – Hourruitiner 14, Daniels 0, Roper 0, B. Larrick 32, A. Larrick 8, Elam 2, McPherson 1, Gordon 0, Bradley 1, Amaya 10, Sales 2, Parker 5. Halftime – UCLA 53, Charleston Southern 38.

Mar. 15, 1997: NCAA Second Round game at Auburn Hills, MI; UCLA 96, Xavier 83. UCLA – O'Bannon 28, Henderson 22, McCoy 10, Dollar 9, Bailey 10, Sylvester 0, Loyd 7, Harbour 0, McGautha 0, Myers 0, Farnham 0, Parker 0, Johnson 10. Xavier – Johnson 7, Williams 16, Braggs 15, Brown 15, Lumpkin 5, Kelsey 0, Turner 1, Anderson 5, Harvey 2, Murray 0, Payne 3, Kromer 0, Posey 14. Halftime – UCLA 45, Xavier 40.

Mar. 20, 1997: NCAA Midwest Regional Semifinal at San Antonio, TX; UCLA 74, Iowa State 73 (OT). UCLA – O'Bannon 16, J.R. Henderson 12, McCoy 6, Dollar 20, Bailey 13, Loyd 3, Johnson 4. Iowa State – Bankhead 6, Pratt 14, Cato 10, Holloway 7, Willoughby 34, Johnson 0, Edwards 2, Ranpton 0. Halftime – Iowa State 37, UCLA 25. End of regulation – UCLA 64, Iowa State 64.

Mar. 22, 1997: NCAA Midwest Regional Final at San Antonio, TX; Minnesota 80, UCLA 72. UCLA – O'Bannon 22, Henderson 9, McCoy 0, Dollar 7, Bailey 21, Loyd 3, Myers 0, Johnson 10. Minnesota – James 12, Jacobson 14, Thomas 7, Jackson 18, Harris 0, Archambault 0, Stauber 0, Lewis 15, Thomas 14, Tarver 0, Winter 0. Halftime – UCLA 33, Minnesota 28.

1998

Mar. 13, 1998: NCAA First Round game at Atlanta, GA; UCLA 65, Miami (FL) 62. UCLA – Henderson 26, Johnson 3, Davis 13, Bailey 21, Watson 2, Reed 0, Hines 0, Loyd 0. Miami – James 12, Bland 18, Norris 14, Frazier 0, Jennings 1, Hemsley 13, Tyler 4, Wimbley 0, Byars-Dawson 0, Schlie 0, Wiseman 0. Halftime – UCLA 32, Miami 32.

Mar. 15, 1998: NCAA Second Round game at Atlanta, GA; UCLA 85, Michigan 82. UCLA – Henderson 13, Johnson 25, Davis 7, Bailey 19, Watson 10, Hines 0, Reed 11. Michigan – Ward 16, Traylor 19, Reid 18, Bullock 16, Conlan 2, Baston 11, Asselin 0. Halftime – UCLA 45, Michigan 34.

Mar. 20, 1998: NCAA South Regional Semifinal at St. Petersburg, FL; Kentucky 94, UCLA 68. UCLA – Reed 7, Johnson 18, Henderson 10, Bailey 16, Watson 6, Knight 3, Daley 4, Ramasar 0, Harbour 0, Loyd 0, Hines 4, McGautha 0, Farnham 0. Kentucky – Edwards 10, Padgett 19, Mohammed 15, Turner 8, Sheppard 16, Masiello 0, Smith 0, Evans 10, Mills 0, Hogan 6, Anthony 5, Bradley 2, Magliore 3. Halftime – Kentucky 40, UCLA 23.

NIT Games
1985

Mar. 13, 1985: NIT First Round game at Pauley Pavilion, Los Angeles, CA; UCLA 78, Montana 47. UCLA – Maloncon 9, Miller 21, Wright 12, Hatcher 10, Miguel 14, Gaines 2, Butler 0, Immel 8, Haley 2, Morris 0, Dunlap 0. Montana – Krystkowiak 14, Boyd 6, McBride 2, Wnek 0, Washington 5, Jones 0, Burns 4, Zanon 2, Vanek 2, Bates 0, Powell 12. Halftime – UCLA 34, Montana 21.

Mar. 19, 1985: NIT Second Round game at Pauley Pavilion, Los Angeles, CA; UCLA 82, Nebraska 63. UCLA – Maloncon 10, Miller 29, Wright 4, Hatcher 18, Miguel 14, Butler 2, Gaines 1, Immel 0, Haley 2, Jones 2, Dunlap 0, Morris 0. Nebraska – Moore 8, Jackman 8, Hoppen 23, Carr 4, Marshall 8, Smith 2, Matzke 2, Buchanan 6, Martz 0, Sealer 2, White 0. Halftime – UCLA 41, Nebraska 31.

Mar. 23, 1985: NIT Third Round game at Pauley Pavilion, Los Angeles, CA; UCLA 53, Fresno State 43. UCLA – Maloncon 8, Miller 8, Wright 16, Hatcher 6, Miguel 12, Butler 0, Gaines 0, Jackson 3, Haley 0, Morris 0. Fresno State – Barnes 16, Kuipers 8, Emerson 6, Strain 0, Arnold 2, Salone 7, Carter 0, Gustin 0, Trice 0, Means 2, Cook 2. Halftime – UCLA 27, Fresno State 18.

Mar. 27, 1985: NIT Championship semifinals at New York, NY; UCLA 75, Louisville 66. UCLA – Maloncon 0, Miller 16, Wright 23, Hatcher 12, Miguel 20, Butler 0, Gaines 2, Jackson 2. Louisville – Thompson 16, Forrest 13, Sumpter 10, Abram 2, Hall 8, McSwain 11, Crook 2, Jeter 2, West 2. Halftime – UCLA 36, Louisville 33.

Mar. 29, 1985: NIT Championship finals at New York, NY; UCLA 65, Indiana 62. UCLA – Maloncon 8, Miller 18, Wright 5, Hatcher 15, Miguel 18, Butler 0, Gaines 0, Jackson 1. Indiana – Eyl 8, Meier 2, Blab 11, Alford 16, Robinson 8, Smith 10, Thomas 1, Brooks 4, Hillman 0, Dakich 2. Halftime – UCLA 29, Indiana 29.

1986

Mar. 13, 1986: NIT First Round game at Pauley Pavilion, Los Angeles, CA; UC Irvine 80, UCLA 74. UC Irvine – Rogers 29, Engelstad 2, Murphy 20, Brooks 5, Buchanan 5, Carmon 9, Hess 10, Ciaccio 0. UCLA – Miller 16, Jackson 2, Haley 9, Hatcher 24, Richardson 7, Gaines 2, Jones 8, Butler 0, Rochelin 6, Palmer 0. Halftime – UC Irvine 39, UCLA 31.

Team Records

Wins
1.	32	1995
2.	30	1973
	30	1972
	30	1967
	30	1964
6.	29	1971
	29	1969
	29	1968
9.	28	1992
	28	1976
	28	1975
	28	1970

Games Played
1.	33	1998
	33	1995
	33	1993
	33	1992
	33	1990
	33	1985
7.	32	1997
	32	1991
	32	1987
	32	1980
	32	1976
	32	1952

Field Goals Scored
1.	1161	1968
2.	1140	1972
3.	1112	1976
4.	1083	1970
5.	1082	1967
6.	1079	1995
7.	1078	1991
8.	1063	1975
9.	1054	1973
10.	1053	1979

Field Goal Attempts
1.	2335	1950
2.	2321	1968
3.	2262	1972
4.	2256	1964
5.	2217	1975
6.	2216	1976
7.	2197	1971
8.	2184	1970
9.	2172	1965
10.	2158	1952

Field Goal Percentage
1.	.555	1979
2.	.530	1983
	.530	1980
4.	.528	1996
5.	.524	1981
6.	.520	1997
	.520	1978
8.	.519	1973
	.519	1967
10.	.517	1991

Free Throws Scored
1.	642	1991
	642	1956
3.	639	1992
4.	620	1964
5.	618	1980
6.	613	1995
7.	604	1998
8.	593	1970
9.	590	1957
10.	589	1965

Free Throw Attempts
1.	963	1964
2.	942	1956
3.	909	1998
4.	892	1965
5.	869	1991
6.	865	1995
7.	864	1980
8.	862	1952
9.	859	1992
10.	852	1970

Free Throw Percentage
1.	.756	1979
2.	.744	1992
3.	.739	1991
4.	.727	1986
5.	.722	1962
6.	.720	1978
	.720	1982
8.	.719	1976
9.	.717	1977
10.	.715	1980
	.715	1957

Rebounds
1.	1670	1964
2.	1647	1972
3.	1603	1968
4.	1574	1971
5.	1559	1965
6.	1519	1970
7.	1513	1969
8.	1501	1963
9.	1495	1967
10.	1493	1956

Rebound Average
1.	55.7	1964
2.	55.6	1959
3.	54.9	1972
4.	53.4	1968
5.	53.3	1956
6.	52.5	1971
7.	51.9	1965
8.	51.8	1963
9.	50.6	1970
10.	50.5	1961

Assists
1.	673	1974
2.	660	1980
3.	653	1995
4.	634	1991
5.	613	1976
6.	605	1992
7.	597	1975
8.	584	1990
9.	565	1979
10.	552	1989

Steals
1.	312	1995
2.	284	1998
3.	266	1993
4.	259	1997
5.	258	1992
6.	253	1998
7.	250	1991
8.	231	1988
9.	222	1980
10.	220	1990

Blocked Shots
1.	180	1993
2.	164	1991
3.	162	1996
4.	143	1979
5.	139	1995
6.	123	1997
7.	119	1994
8.	110	1987
9.	109	1998
10.	106	1980

Points Scored
1.	2954	1991
2.	2889	1995
3.	2838	1972
4.	2802	1968
5.	2786	1992
6.	2759	1970
7.	2743	1998
8.	2687	1967
9.	2666	1964
10.	2656	1990

Scoring Average
1.	94.6	1972
2.	93.4	1968
3.	92.3	1991
4.	91.9	1970
5.	89.6	1967
6.	88.9	1964
7.	87.5	1995
8.	86.3	1965
9.	86.1	1994
10.	85.6	1979

Defensive Rebounds
1.	897	1995
2.	825	1990
3.	821	1997
4.	792	1991
5.	780	1996
6.	778	1992

Offensive Rebounds
1.	472	1994
2.	460	1990
3.	437	1995
4.	435	1998
5.	431	1991

Three-Point Field Goals
1.	173	1992
2.	169	1998
3.	156	1991
4.	152	1998
5.	142	1987

3-Point Field Goal Attempts
1.	490	1998
2.	452	1991
3.	438	1998
4.	434	1992
5.	374	1990

3-Point Field Goal Percentage
1.	.426	1989
2.	.421	1987
3.	.399	1992
4.	.376	1996
5.	.362	1988

UCLA's Basketball Record in Pauley Pavilion

Year	Record
1965-66	11-0
1966-67	17-0
1967-68	12-0
1968-69	13-1
1969-70	15-1
1970-71	15-0
1971-72	17-0
1972-73	17-0
1973-74	16-0
1974-75	16-0
1975-76	19-1
1976-77	16-2
1977-78	17-1
1978-79	17-1
1979-80	12-4
1980-81	12-2
1981-82	14-1
1982-83	13-2
1983-84	13-4
1984-85	15-3
1985-86	13-4
1986-87	17-2
1987-88	11-6
1988-89	12-2
1989-90	13-2
1990-91	15-2
1991-92	14-2
1992-93	14-3
1993-94	14-1
1994-95	15-0
1995-96	12-1
1996-97	13-3
1997-98	13-2
33 Years	473-53

Pauley Pavilion Attendance

Year	Games	Total	Avg
1966	11	132,775	12,070
1967	17	212,567	12,504
1968	12	147,203	12,267
1969	14	174,992	12,499
1970	16	196,694	12,293
1971	15	187,473	12,498
1972	17	211,357	12,433
1973	17	212,750	12,515
1974	16	198,200	12,388
1975	16	198,142	12,384
1976	20	244,934	12,247
1977	18	201,180	11,177
1978	18	204,010	11,339
1979	18	212,042	11,780
1980	16	179,481	11,216
1981	14	162,017	11,573
1982	15	164,418	10,961
1983	15	162,760	10,850
1984	17	150,236	8,834
1985	18	152,934	8,496
1986	17	134,763	7,927
1987	*16	169,353	10,584
1988	17	133,534	7,855
1989	14	119,858	8,561
1990	15	143,010	9,534
1991	17	170,384	10,023
1992	16	177,003	11,063
1993	17	132,771	7,810
1994	15	163,531	10,902
1995	15	170,994	11,400
1996	13	154,331	11,872
1997	16	163,840	10,240
1998	15	161,089	10,739
Total	523	5,700,626	10,900

*Does not include three home games in the Pacific-10 Conference Post-Season Tournament.

Stats

UCLA's All-Time Top Crowds

52,693 – 1/20/68 vs. Houston at the Astrodome, Houston, Texas

40,589 – 3/20/98 vs. Kentucky at the St. Petersburg Tropicana Dome in the NCAA South regional semifinal

38,540 – 4/3/95 vs. Arkansas at the Seattle Kingdome in the NCAA Championship finals

38,540 – 4/1/95 vs. Oklahoma State at the Seattle Kingdome in the NCAA Championship semifinals

31,930 – 3/22/97 vs. Minnesota at the Alamodome, San Antonio in the NCAA Midwest regional final

31,765 – 3/27/71 vs.Villanova at the Astrodome, Houston in NCAA championship finals

31,569 – 3/14/96 vs. Princeton at the RCA Dome, Indianapolis in the NCAA first round

31,428 – 3/25/71 vs.Kansas at the Astrodome, Houston in NCAA championship semifinals

29,231 – 3/20/97 vs. Iowa State at the Alamodome, San Antonio in the NCAA Midwest regional semifinals

28,885 – 12/19/92 vs. Georgia at the Georgia Dome in Atlanta,GA

28,880 – 12/23/81 vs. LSU at the Superdome, New Orleans, Louisiana

23,023 – 11/26/82 vs. Brigham Young at Provo, UT

21,639 – 3/17/77 vs.Idaho State at Provo, Utah in NCAA West regional semifinals

21,020 – 3/15/97 vs. Xavier at the Palace of Auburn Hills in the NCAA Midwest second round

21,020 – 3/13/97 vs. Charleston Southern at the Palace of Auburn Hills in the NCAA Midwest first round

20,712 – 12/17/88 vs. North Carolina at Chapel Hill, North Carolina

20,303 – 12/ 3/88 vs.Brigham Young at Provo, UT

20,043 – 1/25/97 vs. Louisville in Freedom Hall

19,872 – 3/5/95 vs Louisville in Freedom Hall

19,500 – 12/30/68 vs. St. John's in Madison Square Garden, New York, in Holiday Festival

19,466 – 2/2/92 vs. Louisville in Freedom Hall

19,455 – 1/7/90 vs. Louisville in Freedom Hall

19,423 – 3/15/98 vs. Michigan at the Georgia Dome, Atlanta in NCAA second round South Regional

19,384 – 2/1/86 vs. Louisville in Freedom Hall

19,301 – 3/26/73 vs. Memphis State at the Arena, St. Louis in NCAA championship finals

19,253 – 1/16/88 vs. Louisville in Freedom Hall

19,115 – 11/29/75 vs. Indiana at the Arena, St. Louis

19,029 – 3/24/73 vs.Indiana at the Arena, St. Louis in NCAA championship semifinals

18,892 – 3/25/67 vs.Dayton in Louisville in NCAA championship finals

18,889 – 4/24/67 vs.Houston in Louisville in NCAA championship semifinals

18,669 – 3/22/69 vs.Purdue in Louisville in NCAA championship finals

18,667 – 1/25/69 vs.Loyola in Chicago Stadium

18,641 – 12/15/73 vs. North Carolina State at the Arena, St. Louis

18,499 – 1/27/68 vs.Boston College in Madison Square Garden, New York

18,496 – 12/27/49 vs. CCNY in Madison Square Garden, New York

18,496 – 12/28/55 vs. Duquesne in Madison Square Garden, New York

18,477 – 12/30/46 vs. NYU in Madison Square Garden, New York

18,476 – 12/28/68 vs.Princeton in Madison Square Garden, New York, in Holiday Festival

18,469 – 3/24/62 vs.Wake Forest in Louisville in NCAA consolation game

18,435 – 3/20/69 vs.Drake in Louisville in NCAA championship semifinals

18,350 – 12/29/47 vs. Long Island Univ. in Madison Square Garden, New York

UCLA's Top Pauley Pavilion Crowds

13,478 – 2/23/97 vs. Duke

13,382 – 2/19/97 vs. USC

13,079 – 2/12/98 vs. Stanford

13,037 – 3/11/95 vs. Oregon

13,023 – 3/1/92 vs. Duke

13,014 – 2/15/96 vs. Arizona

12,961 – 12/23/69 vs. Louisiana State

12,912 – 2/20/71 vs. Oregon

12,903 – 3/ 8/69 vs. USC

12,898 – 3/12/92 vs. Arizona

12,897 – 1/18/69 vs. Houston

12,893 – 2/13/71 vs. Washington State

12,884 – 2/ 1/75 vs. USC

12,883 – 2/10/67 vs. Oregon State

12,883 – 3/ 1/75 vs. Stanford

12,881 – 1/13/96 vs. California

12,875 – 3/13/71 vs. USC

12,874 – 1/26/74 vs. Notre Dame

12,857 – 2/26/95 vs. Duke

12,853 – 12/ 1/73 vs. Maryland

12,853 – 2/19/71 vs. Oregon State

12,842 – 1/29/92 vs. USC

12,834 – 3/ 5/71 vs. California

12,832 – 1/20/94 vs. Arizona

12,829 – 12/11/76 vs. Notre Dame

12,823 – 2/10/91 vs. Arizona

12,820 – 12/30/71 vs. Ohio State (Bruin Classic)

12,817 – 3/13/69 vs. New Mexico State (NCAA Western Regionals)

12,815 – 3/ 4/66 vs. USC

12,812 – 3/15/69 vs. Santa Clara (NCAA Western Regionals)

12,805 – 1/14/72 vs. Stanford

12,802 – 1/19/73 vs. USF

12,802 – 11/30/68 vs. Purdue

12,801 – 12/30/66 vs. USC (Los Angeles Classic)

UCLA and the Hall of Fame

Seven members of the basketball Hall of Fame in Springfield, Mass., have UCLA ties:

• Kareem Abdul-Jabbar, inducted 1995. Played at UCLA 1967-69. Three-time Player of The Year in college and the all-time leading scorer in the pros.

• Denny Crum, inducted 1994. Played at UCLA 1958-59. Starting guard as a senior and later an assistant coach on John Wooden's staff from 1968-71. Made his real mark in coaching career at Louisville, winning two national championships.

• Denise Curry, inducted 1997. Played at UCLA 1978-81. Set 14 school records and a collegiate mark by scoring in double figures in each of her 130 games. Two-time Olympian, with the 1980 team that boycotted the Moscow Games and in 1984.

• Gail Goodrich, inducted 1996. Played at UCLA 1963-65. All-American guard as a senior, when he set a then-NCAA record of 42 points in the title game, and five-time NBA all-star who played 14 years in the pros.

• Ann Meyers, inducted 1993. Played at UCLA 1975-78. The first four-time All-American in women's basketball. Player of The Year in 1978 and member of the 1976 Olympic team.

Bill Walton.

• Bill Walton, inducted 1993. Played at UCLA 1972-74. Leader of the Walton Gang that won a pair of NCAA championships and Player of The Year three years in a row. Won two more titles in the NBA, despite a career frequently hampered by injury.

• John Wooden, inducted 1960 as a player and 1972 as a coach. Coached at UCLA 1948-75. Guided Bruins to a 620-147 record and an unparalleled 10 national crowns and 19 conference championships. Three-time All-American (1930-32) as a player at Purdue.

Olympians

It is difficult, if not impossible, to decipher where the picture was taken. Perhaps on board the ship that ferried the Olympic basketball team, and maybe competitors from other sports, from the United States to Europe for the 1936 Berlin Games. But we can be safe in assuming the snapshot—two rows, players in uniforms, coaches in jacket, tie and sweater vest, AAU official looking like a commodore—did not come from Westwood.

That would have been the fitting spot, of course, this practically being as much UCLA team picture as Olympic team picture. The first U.S. basketball team to take part in the Games included five current or former Bruins, which came, strangely, while the school endured a string of six losing seasons in the eight previous years, but also came as the first of several representations.

Frank Lubin was captain of the squad that won gold. He was joined by Sam Balter, Carl Knowles, Don Piper and Carl Shy. A few guys who didn't attend UCLA apparently were also allowed to play.

The next Bruin was historic in his own way—Don Barksdale went to London in 1948 as the first African-American U.S. Olympian in basketball. He also earned a gold medal.

Walt Hazzard was a member of the 1964 squad that won in Tokyo. So was North Carolina guard Larry Brown. Both would one day become UCLA coaches, and Brown would even take his 1980-81 team back to Yoyogi Sports Center for a nonconference game against Temple that marked the first NCAA basketball competition outside the United States.

It was not until 1996 that the Bruins again participated—sort of. Reggie Miller had been in the pros and a member of the Indiana Pacers for nine years by the time he went to Atlanta with the Dream Team.

UCLA's Olympic basketball representation also includes the women's side. Ann Meyers played on the 1976 team in Montreal that Bruins Coach Billie Moore guided to a silver medal. Four years later, Denise Curry was a member of the 1980 squad that boycotted the Moscow Games, and four years after that she won gold in Los Angeles. At the Forum, to be exact. Just down the freeway from Westwood.

Reggie Miller went on to play in the Olympics on the Dream Team.

Pauley Pavilion

It's inconspicuous as shrines go, rising out of the ground only a couple stories, bookended by an intramural field and the football practice field and separated by about 30 feet of walkway from the newer Morgan Center that is the home of the athletic department. There is nothing overly impressive or imposing about Pauley Pavilion from the outside.

Inside, all that changes. Opposing teams have been known to look to the rafters, see all the championship banners and get psyched out, before even considering the current UCLA team they'll face. The Bruins themselves have the constant reminder of the tradition they have to uphold, impossible to forget since the banners surround the court from above, staring down at the players at every turn.

There are 11 from the basketball team alone, one for each of the NCAA championships, the first two of which, from 1964 and 1965, were earned before Pauley opened. The one commemorating the 1985 NIT title used to hang with its big brothers, but has since been removed. Flags to signify the ultimate success of other sports—volleyball, gymnastics, etc.—remain.

The Bruins of the early years played at several spots around Southern California, from suburban Long Beach to the downtown Shrine Auditorium that today is best known for being the host of major entertainment awards to the Pan-Pacific Auditorium and area high schools and junior colleges. The early 1960s brought some sense of permanence with the construction of the Sports Arena, a building they shared with USC and the recently arrived Lakers.

In 1964, the drive began for a $5-million on-campus arena. California taxpayers took care of $2 million, the student body another $1 million, and an alumni contribution of $1 million was matched by the head of the state board of regents—Edwin W. Pauley. When the building opened for commencement in June of 1965, it did so with his name attached in recognition of his generosity.

There were three courts, important to the basketball program then because it allowed the freshman team to practice at the same time as the varsity. The inclusion of fold-out bleachers allowed fans to sit behind the baskets for games. Just not too close.

"I didn't want the fans close enough to grab the hair on the legs of my players, as I had happen in other arenas," John Wooden said in the book *Pauley Pavilion: College Basketball's Showplace*. "I wanted the seating far enough back so that players would not run into the crowd on a layup, too."

The Bruins went 149-2 there under Wooden, and his retirement dinner was held there in 1975, either because it was only fitting or because few other places could accommodate the more than 600 people who attended. Eventually, the home of greatness became the setting for other interests. It was the site of the October 13, 1988, presidential debate between George Bush and Michael Dukakis, a women's Final Four, numerous championships in men's and women's volleyball and gymnastics. On September 9, 1992, MTV even held its annual video awards show there.

Pauley contains 10,337 permanent upholstered seats and has another 2,482 spots available on retractable bleachers, making what should be a basketball capacity of 12,819. But the single-game attendance record, set when Duke came in on February 23, 1997, is 13,478.

Pauley Pavilion

The Bruin 100

John Wooden

A major reason UCLA developed into a basketball dynasty and the University of Minnesota did not:

One hour.

Legend has it that John Wooden, though also considering a proposal from the Bruins, was actually waiting for a Minnesota official to phone with a job offer to lure him from Indiana State in 1948. The Golden Gophers didn't call when they said they would, so Wooden accepted the deal to go to the West Coast. When the Minnesota representative called about an hour later, Wooden said he had already given his word to UCLA.

To this day, it says as much about the coach as the school's good fortune. He had given his word. That simple. Life had structure, and honesty was one of them.

Just like preparation—so one former player, Keith Erickson, once told a reporter of the man who won 80.8% of his games at UCLA that "Wooden beats you Monday through Thursday with his practices."

Just like patience—so it took 14 years to complete the renowned Pyramid of Success, a diagram for life that was started with English students at South Bend (Ind.) Central High in mind, not any basketball player.

John Wooden, ever the teacher, in the mid-1960s.

Just like discipline no matter the stature—so Bill Walton, an All-American back for his senior season, was thrown out of practice the first day because his hair was too long.

Just like teams looking like a team—so Wooden would give incoming players lessons on how socks were supposed to be pulled up and worn.

Even in his moments of frustration and disappointment, it was impossible to forget he strived to be a gentleman, which is mostly the way he comes across now, more than 20 years after retirement, as his standing in the sport and at the school could best be described as a treasure.

He coached superstars—Walton, Hazzard, Wilkes, Alcindor, Wicks—but always coached a team game. Give him a well-executed two-hand chest pass over a 360 dunk any day.

The Wizard of Westwood, along with Lenny Wilkens the only person inducted in the basketball Hall of Fame as a player and coach, spent 27 years at UCLA, went 620-147 and won 10 national championships. In a 40-season career that also included two campaigns at Dayton High in Kentucky, nine at Central High and two at Indiana State, John Robert Wooden was 885-203, a winning percentage of .813.

Ralph Bunche

Winner of the Nobel Prize. Diplomat. Guard on the UCLA basketball team.

Before he became a world figure, Ralph Bunche played for the Bruins in the backcourt from 1925-27. How crazy that they didn't make him a team captain.

In the years that followed, nations looked to him. After earning an undergraduate degree at UCLA and a Ph.D. at Harvard, Bunche's diplomatic career began in 1944, when he joined the Department of State, and progressed to where he helped with the groundwork for the United Nations, became an undersecretary and a delegate or advisor to nine international conferences.

In 1949, as a member of the U.N. Palestinian Commission, he arranged an armistice in the Arab-Israeli dispute. Bunche was awarded the Nobel Peace Prize the next year, the first African-American so honored.

Born in Detroit in 1904, he died in 1971.

Photo Credits:

All photos courtesy of ACUCLA Photo except the following:

Page 66 - provided by the University of Notre Dame